MONEY SMARTS

MONEYSMARTS is more thorough than Adam Smith's **PAPER MONEY**, more complete than William Donoghue's **COMPLETE MONEY MARKET GUIDE** and more practical than **CRISIS INVESTING**. It is the *only* money book you will need for investing during the inflationary 1980s.

From **HOW TO DIVERSIFY YOUR DOLLARS** to **HOW TO BARTER AND BARGAIN**, from **BUILDING A MAGIC PORTFOLIO** to **DEVELOPING INFLATION-BEATING HOBBIES**, from **UPPING YOUR SALARY** to **INFLATION-PROOFING FOR RETIREMENT**,
MONEYSMARTS
IS THIS DECADE'S KEY TO
A WINNING LIFE-STYLE.

MONEY SMARTS

MICHAEL ASSAEL

PLAYBOY
PAPERBACKS

This publication is designed to provide the author's opinion of the subject matter covered. This book is sold with the understanding that neither the author nor the publisher is engaged in rendering investment services. The information contained in this book has been taken from reports the author believes accurate, but neither the author nor the publisher guarantees the accuracy of such reports. The author and publisher specifically disclaim any liability, loss or risk incurred as a result of the use and application, either directly or indirectly, of any advice or information presented in this book.

MONEYSMARTS

Copyright © 1982 by Michael Assael

Cover illustration copyright © 1982 by PEI Books, Inc.

All rights reserved. No part of this book may be reproduced, stored in a retrieval system or transmitted in any form by an electronic, mechanical, photocopying, recording means or otherwise without prior written permission of the author.

"Forever Young" by Bob Dylan, copyright © 1973, 1974 Ram's Horn Music. Used by permission. All rights reserved.

Published simultaneously in the United States and Canada by Playboy Paperbacks, New York, New York. Printed in the United States of America. Library of Congress Catalog Card Number: 81-83255. First edition.

Books are available at quantity discounts for promotional and industrial use. For further information, write to Premium Sales, Playboy Paperbacks, 1633 Broadway, New York, New York 10019.

ISBN: 0-867-21009-5 (U.S.)
      0-867-21026-5 (Canada)

First printing March 1982.

*For my most Magic Assets
Helen and Albert,
who made this book possible*

CONTENTS

Introduction ... 13

Part One / LET'S GET RICH

1. Dollar Diversification ... 21
2. Gold Rush ... 25
3. Sleeping Beauties ... 38
4. Art and Antiques and Auctions ... 49
5. Every Investor's Best Friend ... 67
6. Colored Gemstones ... 85
7. Silver ... 95
8. The Strategics ... 108
9. Investor's Delight? ... 119
10. Magic Portfolios ... 124

Part Two / THE WINNING LIFESTYLE

11. Bartering, Bargaining, and Borrowing ... 137
12. Outsmarting OPEC ... 145
13. Inflation-Beating Hobbies ... 160
14. The Robey Affair ... 170
15. Right on the Money ... 179
16. Futures ... 190
17. Self-reliance ... 196
18. Upping Your Salary ... 199
19. You Are the Best Cash Captain ... 206
20. Gimme Shelter ... 213
21. Bringing It All Back Home ... 223
22. Inflation-Proofing for Retirement ... 240
23. The Money Sages ... 252
24. Moneysmarts Boosters ... 259
    Index ... 277

May your hands always be busy
May your feet always be swift
May you have a strong foundation
When the winds of changes shift
May your heart always be joyful
May your song always be sung
And may you stay forever young
                          Bob Dylan

ACKNOWLEDGMENTS

Moneysmarts owes special thanks to my long-time friend and colleague—a communications buff—who most influenced its style: Dale Weinberg.

Edith, Gene, and Jon Tannen contributed a wealth of expertise in the fields of art, real estate, and stamps. Jon Tannen is the photographer who shot my picture for the back cover.

Gordon Pinkham brought practical insights while Marion Dreyfus and Sarah Uman supplied the snap and crackle.

The translation of the manuscript from pen and ink into type was done primarily by Debbie Leonard with substantial assistance from Pat Gunn and additional aid from Beverlie Largie.

The book also owes to the wisdom of Martin Bruce, Robert Assael, Shelley Blatt, Monroe Meyerson, Marie Hill, Mark Tannen, Bart Reiss, Steffie Maslin, Susan Jubelier, Robert Dunn, and Harry Jonas.

Finally, two important friends deserve mention: Seth Kelsey, who graciously accommodated me at his home during my writing excursions to the West Coast; and Eiko Sato, my liaison to the Japanese business community, who consistently pinch hit for me while the work was in progress.

While *Moneysmarts* has grown from the seeds of its contributors, all of the book's shortcomings are my own.

INTRODUCTION

America is dealing economic death to its own people. So say our ablest financial experts from San Francisco to Scarsdale. This realization now transcends the business world: talk to a retired schoolteacher living on Social Security in Boston, an executive secretary supporting her family in New York City, a housewife in Beverly Hills, an aspiring cable news reporter in Washington, D.C. We still think of ourselves as an incredibly rich people—better educated, better housed, and in better health than any other people in the world—but we are haunted by a feeling that something unwelcome is happening economically. As inflation spreads through our marketplaces like brushfire, everything—from medical bills to Maseratis, from mortgage rates to margin requirements—recedes from our ability to pay for it. The inflation rate is kindling a silent and invisible socioeconomic heat wave that is burning up our money.

Because *money* is so central to the American way of living, our well-being, our property, even our social institutions are now endangered. It would help if we at least could put our money jitters in perspective. What is the nature of the present American money crisis? Most of us see it as a collection of phenomena:

1. *Money rapidly losing buying power.* As prices in America rocket to alarming levels, the value of the dollar drops. Each greenback we earn decreases in purchasing power as it waits in our wallets to be spent. Every time we shop at the supermarket, fill up on gas, pay the doctor or last month's utility bill, we feel this loss of buying power immediately.

Skyrocketing prices take ever larger bites out of personal

and family budgets, leaving less and less for those "extras" we always believed we could afford. Suddenly we can afford nothing beyond necessities. And today even necessities are becoming hard to pay for.

2. *Savings and investments dwindling before our eyes.* Tens of billions of dollars' worth of savings, stocks, bonds, pensions, and insurance have been erased since the Bicentennial. As inflation pumps the prices of tangibles up, it forces the value of nontangible traditional forms of American paper dollar wealth down. Automatically. Our concept of "money in the bank" has undergone a great change of meaning. The renaissance of tangibles has begun. Today, heirlooms of gold, silver, gemstones, and art and antiques invoke greater feelings of security than paper money. Traditional investments have lost much of their vitality.

3. *Energy squeeze.* In recent years, no facet of the economic scene has generated more consistent scare headlines than widespread fuel shortages. After several seasons of skyrocketing fuel prices, we don't need the front pages to tell us about short-falls. The petrosqueeze, whether brought to us care of the Organization of Petroleum Exporting Countries (OPEC) or our own giant multinational oil companies, reaches promiscuously into everyone's home and life. The energy crisis, by squeezing American workers of thousands of dollars from petrochemical derivatives, has had hidden and uncalculated impact on us.

We look for alternative sources of supply only to find that the perpetual energy crisis includes the threat of faulty nuclear reactors, which headlines show are capable of transforming whole cities into lingering radioactive nightmares. Witness, as we did, the 1979 near meltdown of the Three Mile Island nuclear reactor in Harrisburg, Pennsylvania, one example of what sloppily harnessed nuclear technology has in store for future generations.

The petrosqueeze is the one aspect of the economic enigma that undermines the American lifestyle and the American dream more than any other. Most predictions maintain that the energy squeeze has only *begun* to make its impact felt.

4. *Costly government bureaucracy gobbling tax dollars quicker than we earn them.* Once upon a time, our forebears designed the U.S. government to serve the people. Not the other way around. Today, government mismanage-

ment gobbles up taxpayer dollars at an insatiable rate. Political candidates and editorialists talk of the absurdity of working *five months* out of twelve for the government. As citizens, we are given fewer "bangs" in return for more and more bucks. The sixties and seventies were a time when we conditioned ourselves to believe that throwing money at a problem—from defense to social services—solves it, so we continue to pitch dollars at Washington as if it were a great pleasure. But, as it's turning out, we still see no major improvements. The more money we spend on defense the more we *need* to spend on defense. The same goes for hundreds of types of social services. This is true, in fact, in every area of government bureaucracy. We've learned only one lesson well: that U.S. bureaucracy is by far the most inefficient middleman and the greatest taxpayer burden we have ever endured in the two hundred years of our history.

5. *Personal economic impotence*. Of all the forms of economic crisis seen or felt in America, the departure of individual confidence is perhaps the most profoundly defeating. As individuals, we are gripped by a mood of pessimism and anxiety about our economic futures. We have never experienced such a long term of self-doubt. This lack of verve cuts deeper than falling purchasing power and shrinking savings. It cuts deeper than sinking stocks and bonds, the petrocrash, or wasteful government mismanagement. As back-up evidence—if we need any—public opinion polls say fear of our monetary future is the greatest single source of discontent in the country today. Individually, we feel a loss of personal financial drive. On a larger scale, we feel a chunk being taken out of our national soul.

The money crisis is a trust buster. The nature of modern inflationary transactions is so complicated that its exact impact on our lives and on our country is difficult to ascertain: we will not completely pin down the effects of the money plague for years to come. This inability to count our chips in life, to know what they will be worth tomorrow or the next day, is the most important determinant of American life today. We can only be certain that we are collectively losing billions in potential prosperity through today's inflationary money game.

How did we get into this economic quagmire? Where will the economic enigma lead? How do we travel as individuals safely from today into the future? Respected Harvard economist John Kenneth Galbraith once quipped that no one ever respects a man "who understands the economy well enough to explain it to the average person." Behind the joke lies the implication that we have a deep-rooted fear of finding out the economic truth, as if we could not possibly bear to hear the extent of the economic realities molding our lives.

Following up on Galbraith's observation, whenever any attempt is made to confront our economic ills, a profound lack of understanding, almost fear, greets the attempt. This lack of understanding is not limited to the median-income man or woman alone, but extends to those in all social and economic areas. Most of us have a picture of America—its economy and how it is governed—that is fantastically out of keeping with 1980s bottom-line reality. The discrepancy between the American economy and our beliefs about it cannot be overstressed.

As every historian knows, what we do not understand, we cannot hope to control. And when we cannot comprehend the major economic pulses that pervade our existence, they must inevitably come to dominate us. This is where we stand today. *We are out of touch with economic reality.* This has led to an economy on the trot; in turn, the economic system has taken over. It will take an unprecedented toll from each of us. If we don't get smart.

I have written this book in the hope that we as individuals can wrest back personal economic control and outdistance inflation before it is too late. The book is a game plan for beating inflation. While *Moneysmarts* may not make you a millionaire, it should help you to become more financially secure and grow significantly richer during times of inflation.

The book is based on the premise that inflation has been built into the American economy, so much so that the United States will experience inflation well into and even beyond the 1980s. These chapters will show you that you can predict the effects of inflation on your own life and that if you understand how inflation diminishes your wealth and affects your well-being, you can easily prosper through it.

Several books have been written on the current American money crisis. Most are for sophisticated investors. These pages, by contrast, are specifically designed for the ordinary

INTRODUCTION 17

citizen with little or no inflation-beating experience. They concern themselves with common, everyday matters: the money you earn and spend, the products you buy and use, the institutions you support and inhabit, the people who pass through your lives. Leisure activities are explored. Social behavior is analyzed. Most important, you'll find here inflation-beating strategies and techniques you can adapt to your own lifestyle.

The first part of *Moneysmarts* sets forth a safe and effective approach to individual as well as family survival and profit. I call this technique Dollar Diversification. Its whole purpose is to help you personally protect and increase the value of your savings and investments. It explains and examines the most profitable ways to use the inflationary cycle itself to take advantage of gold, stocks, bonds, gemstones, art, antiques, silver, and other strategic materials to multiply your wealth. To this end, Dollar Diversification puts forward a broad new theory of economic adaptation.

Don't worry if your present net worth is limited. Remember, this is *not* a book strictly for upper-income investors; you can start your own personalized inflation-beating program with as little as $500. I've provided guidelines together with sixteen sample inflation-beating portfolios—each suited to different investment levels from $500 to $500,000. Even if you're living on a fixed income or require constant cash inflow, these portfolios can accommodate you.

The second part of *Moneysmarts* places a unique collection of fun-to-use inflation-beating tools and techniques at your disposal. In general, these *non*-investment-type inflation fighters will serve one of two functions: 1) to maximize your wealth by making your net worth swell with inflation, or 2) to get you more bang for the bucks you spend. Here, we'll explore everything from inflation-beating hobbies to the art of bargaining. You'll even experience how easy it is to get what you want *without* money. This is the part of the book you can rely on to develop an inflation-beating *lifestyle*.

Throughout the book you will find detailed guidance on how to obtain more information on any topic you would like to know more about. I have included references to books, publications, and various helpful services. I have also listed these aids in Chapter 24, "Moneysmarts Boosters," giving addresses and phone numbers where appropriate.

Everything I am suggesting to you I have done myself within the limits of my own financial and personal situation. I plan to grow wealthier in the days ahead and have already begun charting the most profitable course I can through inflation. In the pages that follow, I have explained my strategies. Hopefully, they will arouse the economic selves in all who travel through them by demonstrating the vast opportunity for personal gain. For those who are about to set inflation-beating sail for the first time, I hope the book will prove profitable. For those already on course, I hope the book will add new and enriching dimensions to life. Most of all, first-timers or not, I hope you will enjoy it.

PART ONE

LET'S GET RICH

1. DOLLAR DIVERSIFICATION

It's 9:15 A.M. and Carole Consumer is prowling down her local supermarket aisles hunting for the week's best buys. Her eyes scan the shelves of food with the thought of saving. She sees that while her favorite cookies are speeding up faster than ever, over in the fruit bin Grannie apple prices have tumbled. It looks like she and her sweet-toothed boyfriend are out of luck again. Carole then notes that both white wine and cheese price tags have done some climbing, so she opts for mineral water, French bread, and raspberry jam. Carole knows that although *all* prices are not moving up, *most* prices are soaring.

Carole knows all about inflation because inflation is extremely easy to recognize. It's a time when her money—her fives and tens as well as her checks and credit cards—buys less and less every time she stops at the checkout counter, whether at her local supermarket, sporting goods store, or chic boutique. Carole doesn't need a Ph.D. in economics to tell her about the effects this situation has on her lifestyle. She *feels* it.

Carole is all of us, of course. We may feel the inflation *rate* accelerate from 8 percent to 10 percent to 12 percent or decelerate back from 12 percent to 10 percent to 8 percent, but as far as anyone today can see, inflation will be with us for years to come. In fact, leading economists tell us it will take at least until 1990, perhaps much longer, or an economic horror similar to the Great Depression of 1929, for the government to freeze inflation from our checkout counters. (President Reagan, now in his most challenging role, currently faces the task of eliminating the most stubborn inflation in American history: the inflation we are living through today has *already* outlived President Nixon's price freezes and controls, President Ford's Whip Inflation Now [WIN] campaign, and a whole set of President Carter's Inflation Plans. It has also outlived the highest interest rates in our history and three major recessions, one of which was the largest since the Great Depression.)

I don't mean to scare you, but at the time of this writing our money is losing purchasing power at the rate of about 50 percent *every* seven years. But money isn't everything. Like money, most other forms of our paper money wealth are becoming impotent too—at the same rate. This includes all the various types of bank accounts that we see advertised claiming high interest yields and runs the gamut from pension funds and retirement plans to 98 percent of all insurance policies. This weakening is also true of bonds and most likely of your stocks.

Despite the run-fast mentality of most investors, however, now is *not* the time to fear the future. On the contrary, now is the time to sharpen your awareness of the current situation and assume a position to take fullest advantage of it.

The most elemental natural force we have in our favor is faith—faith that in any given set of circumstances of which we are a part there is an optimum way to proceed. Reassessing current events, then, we have to view the inflationary situation as a self-contained set of circumstances for opportunity and profit. As an individual, you must now focus and concentrate these opportunities around you.

Economically speaking, this means you must begin to weave your present resources, savings, and investments—no matter how small or large—into security and profit blankets that will increase your comfort level through inflation. Bank savings, retirement funds, insurance policies, and stocks and bonds were unquestionably the wealth multipliers during our preinflationary days. But the longer inflation continues, the less satisfying these investments become. Consequently, we have to find their counterparts for today, the new Xeroxes and IBMs. Once you do this, you can relax and enjoy the pleasures of life to the fullest.

Our key to taking advantage of the current economic state of affairs is to realize that paper money and paper forms of wealth are really not necessarily the best investment media available today. Paper forms of money were invented to pay for the things we want to buy and own such as food, a home, clothing, transportation, and entertainment. Paper money's only function is to make buying these things easier by serving as a storehouse of value until we actually exchange it for what we want and need in life. In truth, dollars and dollar-backed paper assets are worthless in and of themselves. They are only pieces of paper, and have only as much value as the way of life we can trade them in for, which today is not too much.

Today, then, more than ever, a tightly woven security and comfort blanket will include alternatives to dollar-backed savings and investments, and a truly secure plan to offset inflation's effects will include a wide diversity of alternative storehouses of wealth.

The best alternatives are *tangible* investments. Silver is a tangible. So are gems. Tangibles have *intrinsic, self-contained value*. Because of this they will *increase* in value *with* inflation rather than *lose* purchasing power *to* inflation. They gain value automatically. Tangibles will save you from inflation because inflation will actually force their values up. By owning tangibles, instead of paper, your net worth will automatically be forced higher. (But we'll profit from some nontangibles too—stocks and bonds. However, as a general rule, we'll want to own them when the inflation rate decelerates.)

The key behind our Dollar Diversification technique, then, is to exchange dollars for forms of wealth whose prices are buoyed up most by inflation, then convert these forms back to cash when you need the money. It's that simple. I like to call these stronger-than-dollar storehouses of wealth the Magic Assets, because like Aladdin's lamp and flying carpets, they have magic qualities.

Possessing intrinsic, self-contained value, the Magic Assets will serve not only as wealth storehouses but also as wealth multipliers. The most highly prized tangibles on earth, the Magic Assets have found favor in nearly all societies and cultures, in all historical periods. They are, today, still accepted and acknowledged for their value throughout the world. While paper currencies have come and gone, the Magic Assets and the concepts of survival, security, trade wealth, status, and power they represent whirl like a financial time machine into the twenty-first century. Let's get started.

2. GOLD RUSH

Put the Magic Asset gold high on your list if you want to keep ahead of inflation in the eighties. Gold can fluctuate wildly and tumble especially hard when it falls, but its track record of generally accelerating inflation over the past decade clearly speaks for itself. According to a study team at Wall Street's Salomon Brothers, gold has been an outstanding performer, appreciating at a compound rate of over 20 percent per year—more than three times the rate of inflation during the last decade.

Foresighted investors, who sensed the inflation explosion and took their money out of stocks, bonds, and banks to invest in gold even as recently as 1978, saw gold's price leap from $166 that January to more than $240 by October. Then they rode gold up in 1979 as inflation caused the precious metal to burst into the $300 to $400 range. And as the inflation rate continued to accelerate into the first quarter of 1980—when the inflation hit an unprecedented 18 percent—they pulled their seat belts tighter for a trip through the $500, $600, $700, and $800 barriers. As they sensed Jimmy Carter losing his grip on the presidency and a new economically conservative American mood ready to whip inflation, at least temporarily, they sold out and took incredible profits. But, with continued inflation, you should not be surprised to find gold ultimately work its way back up into the starry $1,000 to $2,000 realm during the eighties.

The problem with gold is you have to know when to own it. You should own gold when inflation is *accelerating*, that is, when the inflation *rate* is moving upward, say from 8 percent to 12 percent to 16 percent. You should *not* own too much of it when inflation is *decelerating,* that is, when the inflation rate is moving downward, say from 16 percent back down to 8 percent. Nor should you own gold when you *expect* the inflation rate to decelerate. We'll see how to actually use this buy-sell technique for gold later in Chapter 10, "Magic Portfolios."

But first, to understand why gold is a high performance vehicle—why its price rises with accelerating inflation and falls with decelerating inflation—you have to see the world through the eyes of people who want to own gold—our nation's international trading partners, who hold U.S. dollars abroad. During accelerating inflation, that is, when inflation is pulsing ahead at progressively rapid speeds, Arab, German, and Japanese exporters, bankers, and foreign government treasuries which hold U.S. dollars as part of their net worth sell the anemic U.S. money. They buy gold for fear of losing their purchasing power at faster and faster rates. Gold serves as a guaranteed cash crop. Smart money would rather hold gold as a storehouse of value than constantly cheapening American paper. U.S. paper dollars no longer preserve their wealth as well. It's as simple as that.

Put yourself in OPEC's shoes. The Organization of Petroleum Exporting Countries is disgruntled when it receives unsteady dollars in return for its prized oil. What it does is immediately convert these flaccid dollars into— *voilà*—gold. *It sells dollars; it buys gold.* Having graduated from American business schools, the members of OPEC know that this is the best way to preserve their purchasing power.

So the theory is: as U.S. dollars lose purchasing power at an accelerating rate, smart money flows into gold and pushes the gleaming metal's value higher. Dollars go down in value; gold goes up. As long as the dollar keeps losing more and more purchasing power at faster rates, foreigners who receive dollars will sell them and buy gold. Smart American money now does the same.

WHY GOLD SHINES

Why should you convert your savings to gold instead of mink, oil, or a Mercedes when the inflation rate accelerates? The reason is that gold has attributes that mink or a

Mercedes lack, which makes it a safer inflation beater. Because of its *permanence, utility,* and *scarcity* gold has always been the world's most sought after preserver of wealth when the economic going gets tough. It remains today the ultimate storehouse of value during inflation.

Gold is a great inflation hedge because it is virtually indestructible. It does not deteriorate or depreciate. It will not rust, break, or rot because it is unaffected by wind, air, rain, or heat. The gold on King Tut's tomb is timeless, gleaming as brightly today as it did over three thousand years ago. Governments and wealthy individuals who use gold as their storehouse of value can store gold for eternity and it won't lose a sou of beauty or worth. (Name one tangible that can claim that distinction. Neither mink nor a Mercedes can. Give up? Diamonds.)

Gold is a great inflation hedge also because it has *utility*. Not only has it been used as money for thousands of years, it also possesses unique properties which give it new uses in industry each year. It is more malleable and ductile than almost any other metal. One ounce of gold can be hammered into a sheet covering one hundred square feet or drawn into a wire thirty-five miles long without breaking, so it has always been an ideal metal for industry and jewelry.

Lastly, gold is a great inflation hedge because it is extraordinarily *scarce*. Gold cannot be created in excessive quantities as paper money can. It's been estimated that all the gold produced in the entire history of the world could fit comfortably into a very large barn. If you drained a barrel of oil and filled it with gold, the amount of the precious resource inside would be worth over $25 million. Because it packs a lot of value into a tight space and always has been accepted worldwide as a medium of exchange, it has been the greatest wealth preserver the world has ever known.

From early civilization gold has been man's ultimate standard of wealth. The pharaohs of ancient Egypt enslaved tens of thousands of people to labor in their gold mines. (Visit the Museum of Cairo.) Medieval alchemists expended their lives in the attempt to synthesize gold from base metals and arsenic. The Spanish conquistadores killed untold thousands of Indians for the gold in their artifacts and religious ikons. No surprise that even today men and women continue to risk their all exploring the ocean's depths for gold left in sunken galleons.

For most of the world's history, the story of gold has been the story of money and the standard-bearer of value. Every megastate—meaning those such as Egypt, Babylonia, Assyria, Persia, Greece, and Rome—traded heavily in gold. Now again, the most powerful cartel history has ever produced—OPEC—converts dollars to gold to prevent lost purchasing power. Even the recent United States-Iran hostage agreement was transacted in gold. While countless paper currencies the world over have become inflated and then failed, gold has never lost its value.

Gold has proved itself to be a Magic Asset, the all-potent preserver of purchasing power; the protector against economic, political, and social uncertainty; and the ultimate means of exchange. It remains so today, rising as the consumer price index (CPI) accelerates. Once the demand is seen as something beyond a passing fad, you can begin to weigh the use of gold to insulate your life from inflation.

WHEN GOLD SHINES

The key to preserving and multiplying your wealth with gold is knowing *when* to own it. To repeat, gold moves up in value as the inflation rate accelerates. That is when you should own it. Accelerating inflation simply means the inflation *rate* is on its way up, say from 8 percent in the first quarter of the year, 10 percent in the second quarter to, say, 12 percent in the third quarter.

Gold's price fluctuations over the short term will seem erratic. There will be weeks at a time, even months, when gold will move contrary to its generally upward inflationary trend. Fluctuations occur simply because there are short-term speculators who buy out of fear that the economy is flying out of control, then sell out of fear that the president will submit a string of balanced budgets to Congress and stop the Treasury's printing presses from printing inflationary money.

So don't buy gold merely out of fear. Wait until some time after you have digested this book to allocate your savings and investment dollars. Don't rush to buy gold in the midst of a national or world crisis. Investors who buy in panic pay top dollar. They usually sell in panic a few days later when situations calm down, then wonder why they have not realized a profit.

Buy gold as part of your *overall* Dollar Diversification program. Buy it when markets are calm and *after* you consider how you will diversify with regard to the other Magic Assets. The following chapters, especially Chapter 10, "Magic Portfolios," will help with your diversification decisions.

Once you decide how much gold you want to own, there are many ways to do it. You can buy coins, bars, certificates, or stocks. You can even go prospecting. However you own gold, rest assured that you can usually convert it into dollars within minutes. In other words, the gold market is very *liquid*, which in money talk means there are many buyers to whom you can sell your personal holdings.

THE KRUGERRAND

The most popular way of investing in gold is putting cash into gold coins. The *Krugerrand*, a South African coin of exactly one ounce of gold, is the current favorite. The reason: you can buy one for the price of an ounce of gold (about $500 at the time of this writing) to protect your purchasing power and then convert it back to cash on a moment's notice. Instant money.

Krugerrands are ideal investments for protecting small amounts of money because they are affordable. You can buy a Krugerrand for just about the price of an ounce of gold. In fact, by the time you read this, Krugerrands will be available in three smaller versions containing exactly a *half ounce,* a *quarter ounce,* and a *tenth ounce* of gold. The price is pegged directly to the official London gold price, with the coins selling at a 5- to 8-percent premium— or "commission"—over the official London gold price. Because the London price is quoted in dollars per ounce in newspapers and on radio and television news broadcasts, you can easily figure out what your Krugerrands are worth daily.

If you can afford to buy ten or more of the one-ounce coins (about a $5,000 investment), you usually pay only about a 5 percent premium over the price of a single ounce of gold. If you buy one or two Krugerrands you will pay about 8 percent commission.

Here are four important rules for buying Krugerrands:

1. *Shop around for the best price.* Coin dealers, banks, brokerage firms, and jewelers all sell Krugerrands and other forms of gold. They differ as to prices for which they sell the coins and in the prices they offer to buy them back —the "spread." Each person makes his or her own market, and you should make at least three phone calls to gold sources before choosing. For example, on March 27, 1980, Deak-Perera, the large coin and currency dealer in New York, was selling Krugerrands at $500 each. New York's Republic National Bank, on the other hand, was offering them at $503.

2. *Check the market in your area before you buy to see what kind of price you can get if you decide to sell.* Many small towns and rural areas have only one place to buy Krugerrands. These are usually jewelry shops, some of which tell you they are "doing you a favor" by buying them back. They do offer to repurchase the coins, but give you less than you could get at one of the large city dealers. Although the difference is not usually worth worrying about, it is important to check your seller's policy *before* you buy.

3. *Note the size of the sales tax, if any.* A buyer of Krugerrands must pay a sales tax on the coins in many states, even though the coins are legal tender in South Africa. In New York City the tax is 8 percent, which means that a Krugerrand selling at $500 has to rise to $540 before you begin to profit.

One method to beat the tax is to take delivery outside the states having high sales taxes. Or, have your precious coins shipped to a friend across the state border.

4. *Deal with a reputable dealer.* You can always call upon Deak-Perera, New York; Monex, Newport Beach; Republic National Bank of New York; and Manfra, Tordella & Brookes, New York (see Chapter 24). These are among the many reputable dealers who sell and buy Krugerrands and give daily gold quotes. Many commercial banks, brokerage houses, coin and jewelry dealers sell Krugerrands now, too.

GLEAMERS

Years ago, U.S. citizens could not legally own bars of gold. But the laws have changed so that most of the same dealers who sell Krugerrands now can sell you gold bullion as well.

If you want to own large quantities of gold, bullion is the most convenient way to hold the metal directly. You can buy these gleaming bars ranging in size from one hundred grams costing you about $2,000 to one thousand grams (one kilogram) costing about $20,000. (One kilogram equals 32.15 ounces).

Since gold is so compact your bars can be stored easily in your safe deposit box or concealed in a private vault. If you move cross country, or even around the world, you can easily carry your wealth with you.

You are generally charged a small commission of 3 percent to 5 percent when buying bars of gold, and often there is a nominal assay charge. But these are regular bullion dealer charges which should not influence your decision to own gold. Remember, you pay commission on stocks and that's never stopped you.

If you would like to own bullion but hesitate because you don't want to store it, you can simply have a commercial bank buy and store it for you. This, in fact, is a way to avoid the assay charge.

The European banks have been in the sales and storage business the longest, and with their recent move into many U.S. cities, you can now call on them directly. The "Big Three" Swiss banks—the Swiss Bank Corporation, Union Bank of Switzerland, and Credit Suisse—are among the biggest and most prestigious dealers in the international gold markets. The huge German Dresner Bank and its U.S. subsidiary, ABD Securities, can also help you, as well as the Belgian Bruxelles Lambert Bank, through its link with the American Drexel Burnham Lambert.

You can also manage to have a U.S. bank buy and store bullion for you, since many American banks now participate in this aspect of the gold market. So check with your local commercial bank first. By "buying American," you'll be helping the U.S. economy as well.

PAPER GOLD

One alternative to buying gold bars is to buy gold certificates. Although not as shiny, certificates are easier to store. Gold certificates are nontransferable statements of gold ownership in warehouses generally located in states or countries that do not levy sales taxes. They enable you to purchase gold in modest quantities without taking physical possession.

The "initial order" (minimum investment) is usually $2,500, but additions of only $100 are permitted afterward. You can buy a gold certificate through major brokerage firms and through large commercial banks.

Commissions are usually 2 percent to buy and 2 percent to sell and the normal warehouse storage cost where the gold represented by your certificate is kept is about fifteen cents an ounce per year.

GOLD STOCKS

The most familiar and potentially profitable way for you to cash in on rising gold prices is to buy gold stocks—that is, shares of stock in gold mining companies. As gold shot up and doubled from about $200 to about $500 in 1979 and then doubled again to around $800 in 1980, some gold *stocks* went up in price by a much greater percentage than did gold. In other words when the price of gold doubles, the price of many gold stocks will *more* than double.

The reason why you can more than double your money when the price of gold doubles is that gold stocks give you *leverage*. If it cost a gold mine $190 to find and retrieve an ounce of gold worth $200, the mine's profit is $10 per ounce. But with gold selling at, say, $400 per ounce, that same mine will have a profit of $210 per ounce. That's a profit of twenty-one times the gold mine's original $10 profit. Presumably this increase in profits will be reflected in the gold mine's stock price. This is leverage, and a good reason to buy gold stocks.

Another major advantage of owning gold stocks is that some of these gold mining companies will pay you high dividends. You don't get dividends on Krugerrands or bullion but you can if you own gold shares. In fact, many gold stocks pay out higher annual dividends than banks, bonds, or other financial instruments. Many South African gold stocks pay dividends of 15 percent, some yield 20 percent and more. And when the price of gold rises, the prospect exists for the boards of directors of these companies to increase payouts to their shareholders to even higher levels. Keep in mind that gold is a leveraged situation not only from your viewpoint but from the gold mining companies' perspective as well. So, if you're seeking high yields, gold stocks are probably the best financial vehicle you can get into in times of accelerating inflation.

But besides earning you high dividends, gold stocks are also a good way to get in on a gold boom after it has begun. The full significance of a higher bullion price is usually not added to the stock price until some time after gold lifts off its launching pad, after investors realize how much the mining company will profit from the new gold price. This can take months. Thus gold stocks present you with the opportunity to take advantage of a gold boom after it is well under way.

Sometimes, the full significance of higher bullion prices is not reflected in a gold stock until the mining company itself has officially predicted it will have higher earnings. If you run into a situation where the stock has risen on predictions of higher earnings as you're about to invest, it may pay to wait a week or two to see if the stock's price comes down from its brief high just after the prediction and settles at a little lower plateau. After this happens and if the stock does not retrace but stays where it is, you have lost nothing.

As gold stocks often follow the trend of their sister, gold bullion, by several weeks or months, the opportunities for appreciation in gold stocks are very good. But just because gold bullion lifts off the launching pad when there are rumors of economic turmoil, it doesn't necessarily mean that *every* gold stock will do the same, because when you buy a gold stock you are counting on more than bullion movement.

Special Risks. When you buy a gold stock, you are also betting that the gold mining company you buy will not be adversely affected by labor or management problems, natural disasters, changing governmental policies, or political turmoil. For example, the best, most profitable gold mines in the world are in South Africa, an area which often experiences severe political turbulence. This casts some doubt upon the uninterrupted profitability of South African mines. In addition, the same leverage that can make a gold stock's profits soar when gold is rising can devastate that stock when its profits subside.

To guard against profitability uncertainties, you will do best to deal through a stockbroker who keeps abreast of the fortunes of the gold companies. Try to deal through a broker and a firm that closely examines gold companies' earnings potential. Perhaps the greatest mistake you can make with gold stocks is to talk to an *average* stockbroker —especially if he or she works for a firm whose research department does not have a precious metals specialist. You would do well to use a brokerage house that employs research analysts specializing in precious metals. Even better, if possible, find a specialized gold firm with a good track record. Search for a knowledgeable broker backed by specialized research with as much care as you would a marriage partner. Dealing with a firm that keeps abreast and can keep *you* abreast of the market will maximize your earnings potential while minimizing the uncertainties.

Which Gold Stocks to Buy. There are many large, relatively stable U.S. and Canadian gold mining corporations you and your broker can choose from. These companies, listed on the major stock exchanges, will provide you with full, detailed reports of their operations.

While the U.S. and Canadian stocks are attracting increased attention, it is the "kaffirs"—the stocks of the South African gold mines—that attract the most action. You can buy stocks of South African gold companies which are traded on the American Stock Exchange and Over-the-Counter Securities Markets on the basis of what are called American Depository Receipts—otherwise known as ADRs. These are simply receipts for shares kept in South Africa. Buying ADRs amounts to the same thing as buying the shares.

Some of the South African stocks are not strictly stocks in gold mines but rather gold mining *houses* that finance gold mining operations and own interests in the mines. Buying shares in a gold mining house is like buying into a mutual fund of gold stocks and a good way to diversify your gold holdings.

You can also buy shares in *individual* South African gold mines. As some of the mining investment houses may have other less certain interests besides gold, one school of gold-investment thought holds that buying the shares of the individual gold mines is the better approach. This, of course, has to be balanced by the problem of putting all of your golden eggs in one basket.

If you're looking for high current yield and constant income, concentrate on the more conservative mines. They have a proven high profitability record. Since many yield more than 15 percent in annual dividends, some occasionally as much as 20 percent to 25 percent, these should be seriously considered to do the job bonds once did—yielding constant cash flow.

PENNY GOLD STOCKS

Besides the larger, relatively stable U.S., Canadian, and South African companies, many investors will want to speculate by buying shares of small mines that are traded on the Toronto and Vancouver stock exchanges in Canada, hoping that these small mines will strike it rich. Although every once in a while they do, buying into these speculative situations is more like shooting craps than investing in gold and it is not a very safe way to beat inflation.

If you have the funds to gamble, and *must* do it, however, penny gold stocks (and silver stocks) *are* uniquely positioned. During each of the several precious metal booms throughout the sixties and seventies, a few of these stocks moved upward over one hundred times in price. Since they sell for pennies apiece and have extremely few shares outstanding, only a small amount of buying can drive their prices up fifty or one hundred times. It's not likely to happen, but sometimes it does. If you want to speculate, don't put all your eggs in one basket. Buy a few different penny stocks and pray that one flies.

STRIKE IT RICH!

At the turn of the century, when gold mining was in its heyday, Cripple Creek, Colorado, was considered the richest twenty-four square miles on earth. Once the center of a colorful mining district boasting 50,000 residents, fifteen newspapers, dozens of millionaires, its own stock exchange, and one of the West's choicest brothels, today there are only 950 inhabitants. The brothel is a museum, the stock exchange is gone, and until just recently, about the only gold miners around were down at petered-out shafts giving guided tours for $4 a head plus tips.

But all that has changed now. Suddenly gold mining fever has sprung up anew. Not only in Cripple Creek, Colorado, but in California and Oregon as well, certain enterprising individuals have been making rather tidy fortunes not leading guided tours but prospecting for gold. With the price of gold hovering around $500, compared with around $200 four years ago, some of the more creative prospectors are hiring helicopters to hop to relatively remote and inaccessible areas in hope of spotting the gold that their prospecting forebears abandoned as too much trouble a century ago.

It's not a terrific idea to give up everything in life to search for gold. But why not make your next *vacation* one to remember? One gold digger recently stumbled across a twenty-eight-ounce gold nugget worth more than $15,000. Another prospector was reported to have dredged up from the bottom of a stream twelve ounces of gold worth more than $6,000. These are just two of the tales I have read about in the newspapers over the past several months.

Experts say there is plenty of gold left to find. The United States Geological Survey has published a report, number 610, called *Principal Gold-Producing Districts of the U.S.* (write to the Government Printing Office, Washington, D.C.), which lists the 508 most important districts where gold has been found. Most states with known gold deposits have also cannily published detailed brochures with maps showing known gold localities. Many of these brochures also describe the techniques for panning or sluicing gold.

After doing your homework with the maps and brochures (check Chapter 24 for some recommended reading), your next step will be making your reservations early, then hitting the road. When you find a stream that looks good—slow current, mossy rock formations, shallow water, gravel or sand banks—then you can begin panning.

The basic tools are a shovel and a gold pan. A gold pan is a shallow pan with a reinforced lip that you use to separate the heavier gold by washing away the lighter gravel and sand. All you do is scoop up a pan of gravel, stick it in the water, and slosh the goop around. You continue this process until only the heavier metals, hopefully gold, remain.

The panning technique is something of an art, and if possible, it's a good idea to learn from an old hand. Once you get a feel for it you may want to become more sophisticated by employing a simple dredge—a suction pump for sucking out gravel and sand from deep crevices between boulders.

While gold panning is wholesome and potentially profitable exercise, be careful not to keep your hands and other extremities in the cold stream water for too long. You may catch cold getting rich. Happy prospecting.

CONCLUSION

When the inflation rate is rising some portion of your savings and investments should be in gold. You can own modest amounts of gold directly by buying Krugerrands and larger amounts by buying bullion. If you don't feel you want to store the metal yourself, your bank will store it for you; or you can simply buy gold certificates. If high current income or leveraged capital gains are what you're after, it pays to buy gold stocks. Some of the South African gold stocks pay particularly high dividends. These are ideal for using gold as a hedge against inflation, but always check with a knowledgeable broker before buying *any* gold stock because the individual fortunes of these companies can and do change.

3. SLEEPING BEAUTIES

Imagine December 1929, at the auction gallery of Adrian H. Moller and Son, a few blocks from Wall Street. The market has been free-falling since Black Tuesday—some weeks earlier. On the auction block: beautifully engraved paper—corporate stock certificates representing ownership of dead and dying companies such as the Magazine Repeating Razor Company, the Goldstream Golf Club Corporation, and the Floridale Townsite Corporation. The colorful certificates were being sold for what they were worth: practically nothing.

"One dollar for this entire lot!" called auctioneer Henry Leake, holding up as many securities as he could bunch together in his two hands. "Do I hear one dollar?"

Thousands of Wall Street skydivers had dug the worthless paper out of their safe deposit boxes for the Moller auction house to sell for them. No longer the oneway blue sky tickets to cloud nine, the securities were being offered to settle estates and qualify for tax losses before the end of the best and the worst year in stock market history.

From a record high of 381 for the Dow Jones industrial average on September 3, 1929, to the year's low of 199, on November 31, 1929, the market lost 47 percent of its total value. The common stock of AT & T plummeted from a 1929 peak of 310 to end the year at 199; G.E. fell from 396 to a low of 168; and RCA—then the IBM of the stock market—from 114 down to 44. This was the kickoff of the bottomless recession, later to be known as the Great Depression. By the depths of 1932 the value of the majority of stocks, as well as the savings of most American families, was to be slashed in half again.

"I was just twenty, starting a family," recalls a "twenty-niner," "and what happened that year taught me an important lesson. I learned that stocks move in cycles. Stocks are great wealth multipliers only in certain seasons. There are times to buy, and times to sell."

Stocks have a life of their own and move in cycles. We talk of "bull" markets as the phase of the cycle when stocks are rising; we speak of "bear" markets as the phase of the cycle when stocks are falling.

But when do charging bulls turn bear? When do retreating bears turn bull? When do you get into the market? When do you get out?

THE NATURE OF STOCKS

Our answers on buying and selling can be found in *Security Analysis*, a book written two years after the bottom of the Great Crash, by Benjamin Graham and David Dodd, two professors at the Columbia University Business School. The book has become the security analysts' bible.

Very simply, we deduce three rules which make stocks go up or down:

1. *Corporate Profits*
   When profits *increase*, stocks go *up*.
   When profits *decrease*, stocks go *down*.
2. *Interest Rates*
   When interest rates *increase*, stocks go *down*.
   When interest rates *decrease*, stocks go *up*.
3. *Economic Uncertainty*
   When economic uncertainty *increases*, stocks go *down*.
   When economic uncertainty *decreases*, stocks go *up*.

The obviously critical question for the moneysmart investor becomes: What's happening to corporate profits, interest rates, and economic uncertainty? Which are increasing? Which are decreasing? When we know this, we know when to own stocks and when not to own them.

Curiously, *inflation* helps to provide our answers. The direction of the inflation rate will generally tell us when to buy and when to sell.

40 MONEYSMARTS

RULE: An Accelerating Inflation Rate Overvalues Profits. Stock Prices Fall. Sell Stocks and Buy Gold.

Accelerating inflation (for example, when the inflation rate goes from 8 percent to 10 percent to 12 percent) spells trouble for corporate profits. Profit figures are artificially puffed up. Reports to stockholders show exaggerated income due to the effects of inflation. That is, profits are actually *lower* than companies report. Recent data from the Commerce Department suggest that in any year corporate profits may be overstated by an astounding $50 billion or more—a gap of almost 40 percent between the amounts companies report and their adjusted earnings. So avoid stocks during accelerating inflation. Stick with gold, as outlined in Chapter 2.

The reason to steer clear of stocks when inflation is accelerating is quite simple. *You don't get full value for your money.* Inflation always has caused corporate profits to be artificially overstated. This happens in two ways:

1. Inventories such as shoes, handbags, or cars, produced by manufacturers or purchased by merchants at lower prices, are sold to customers at higher, inflated prices, boosting profits on the income statement. But these profits are illusory since companies must also *replace* these inventories at much higher prices to remain in business. Profits coming from inflation are therefore inventory windfalls and are no basis on which to build stock market dreams.

We can understand this concept better if we think of John Consumer making a profit on the sale of his fur coat. Because of rising fur values, John feels richer when he sells because he gets more than what he paid for it. Yet obviously the gain on his raccoon coat is a misnomer—unreal because chances are good he will end up buying another fur that has also escalated unreasonably in price. He's not *really* any richer.

2. The second reason that we do not get full value for our money if we buy stocks during a period of accelerating inflation is somewhat more difficult to understand. Profits are artificially overstated during accelerating inflation because companies "depreciate," or deduct from their income for tax purposes, on the basis of *original cost*. But in reality they have to replace this equipment at inflation's *higher cost*. This procedure results in companies not setting aside enough money to replace old equipment. When the time

comes to replace their production equipment, corporations are short on cash and can't afford new technology. They end up having to use worn-out equipment. Their financial statements to the public usually don't reflect this fact and this is why, in a sense, their profits and competitive position vis-à-vis the foreign competition are overstated.

RULE: When Interest Rates Go Up, Stocks Go Down. Sell Stocks. Get into Gold.

Stock prices fall when accelerating inflation boosts interest rates on bonds and other financial instruments. In this case inflation renders bonds' and other financial instruments' solid yields highly attractive to pension and mutual fund managers. So financial asset managers sell stock and buy these higher yielding financial instruments. Stocks then fall as they are sold.

In 1973–74, for example, when interest rates rose dramatically, money managers sold stocks and bought bonds. Stock prices meanwhile hit the skids. While the Dow Jones "corrected" from 1067 to 570, the vast cross section of the market experienced huge losses averaging 70 percent, as measured by broad, unweighted market indexes. No wonder. Inflation and interest rates hit their highest levels in postwar history. More recently, the same phenomenon happened as inflation and interest rates climbed to an even higher plateau through 1979 and into the first quarter of 1980. Stocks plunged.

So your rule is: *don't own stocks when inflation and interest rates are busy skyrocketing. As discussed in Chapter 2, this is the time to own gold.*

RULE: Inflation Up, Uncertainty Up. Stocks Sink. Sell Stocks. Stick with Gold.

Inflation raises uncertainty and increases doubts about the prosperity of the individual and the profitability of American industry. Stocks sink. Reality impinges: people have more legitimate reasons to worry than when prices are stable.

One explanation is that inflation brings with it the unwelcome fear of recession. When rampant price increases become politically intolerable, government raises interest rates which in turn leads to recession. Recession invades corporate profits and multiplies business failures.

Severe inflation, then, carries a calling card of financial collapse. The sky-high interest rates generated by inflation force financial asset prices downward, because it costs more in terms of interest expense to own them. This spells trouble for financial institutions like banks, and even ordinary manufacturing and service companies who must pay higher and higher interest rates to stay in business.

Inflation is a world traveler with a carte blanche visa for severe recession. In an era when countries are more interdependent than ever before, a liquidity crisis or supply shortage in one country can and does spill over to other countries. New international financial markets such as the Eurodollar (dollars held by Europeans) and petrodollar (dollars held by oil-rich countries) markets have just been spawned. Linked with the system of floating exchange rates, these markets intensify the inherent risk in financial dealings, particularly for banks and similar institutions. As double-digit inflation here cuts the purchasing power of the dollar, holders of dollars in the international markets—notably the Arab oil interests—relinquish dollars in favor of gold. A weak dollar on the international money market nearly always sends the stock market down.

WHEN TO BUY STOCKS

From these stock market axioms, we can deduce a simple two-part strategy for profiting in the stock market: 1) *Shun stocks during inflationary surges*, and 2) *Buy stocks when the inflation rate is decelerating*.

When inflation is slowing or about to do so, *sell your gold holdings* (as outlined in Chapter 2) and *buy stocks*. Stocks are ideal vehicles when the inflation cycle is in the declining stage.

The richest stock market rewards occur just as the inflation rate begins to point down. So the best time to buy stocks is just before the CPI (consumer price index) decline occurs. At this time precisely, and for a fleeting moment, stocks will shine with the glow that lit them in the starry 1950s and 1960s.

The Dollar Diversified strategist will have advance warning of the impending downturn in the consumer price index. The CPI historically decelerates during recession periods. The gold price will already have weakened, and short-term interest rates will have started to head downward but still be above long-term interest rates. People will

CHART 3-1

THE STANDARD & POOR'S STOCK MARKET AVERAGE

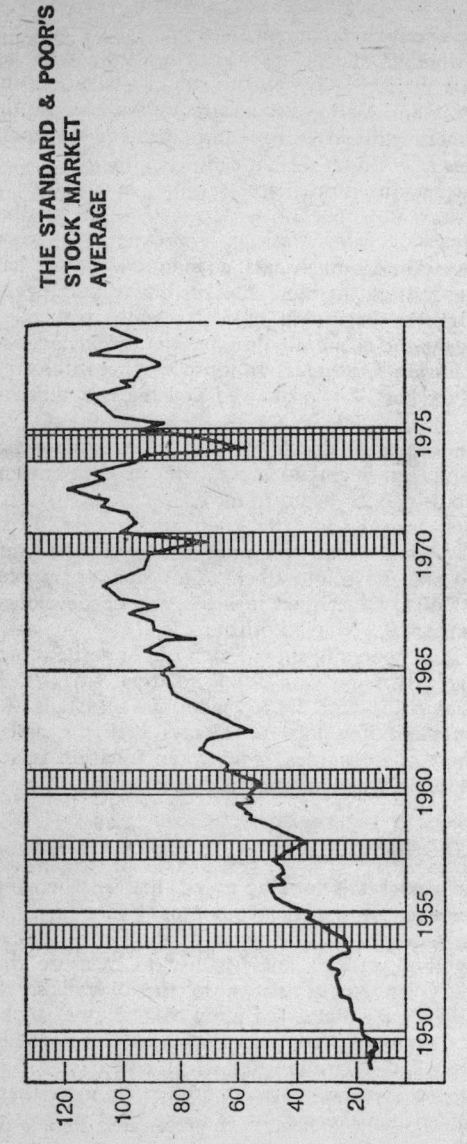

The National Bureau of Economic Research has concluded that there have been six recessions since the end of World War II through 1978. The stock market usually begins to decline before the beginning of a recession (the recessions are shown in black) and begins to recover well before the recession has ended. The chart shows the market's recovery from a recession low has invariably exceeded the prerecession decline. So your stock market buying rule is—buy during the depths of recession.

be pessimistic about the economy. They will have reservations about whether stocks are a worthwhile investment vehicle. This is the ideal time to buy stocks—when no one seems to want them. You get some great buys because the only place stocks will go is back up. Remember, stocks move in cycles.

During a recession, stocks are "sleepy" and afford an unusually attractive opportunity. Chart 3-1 shows that recessionary periods have consistently proved to be good times to buy stocks. Although each economic cycle has had its own characteristics, the stock market has usually begun to drop before the beginning of a recession, reached a major low during the economic decline, *and awakened well before the recession has ended.* In most instances, the subsequent recovery has been prolonged and the rise substantial.

As inflation begins to decelerate during recession—that is, when the inflation begins to move from its then-current level, downward—stocks begin to move higher, and it isn't long before gold moves down. So when stocks begin to rise during the recession, what you want to do is take your profits in gold and move into stocks. This standard procedure for the Dollar Diversified investor will be developed further in Chapter 10, "Magic Portfolios."

Stocks and gold generally show a trend in opposite directions. When gold is rising with rising inflation, stocks fall; when stocks are rising with falling inflation, gold falls. As a Dollar Diversified investor you always seek the assets offering the best opportunities: gold when inflation is accelerating and stocks when inflation is decelerating.

WHICH STOCKS TO BUY: THE BETA OF OZ

When the stock market is looking good, that is, when the inflation rate is decelerating, put your money into the high "beta" stocks. Beta (the second letter of the Greek alphabet) is the symbol security analysts use to measure the volatility of a given stock relative to the overall stock market. The higher the beta, the more volatile the stock.

Suppose, for example, that a security analyst calculates the beta for the Oz Corporation to be 1.5. This means that the price of Oz, on average, increases 50 percent more than stocks in general when the market is rising, and decreases

50 percent more when stocks are falling. In short, we say that Oz is a high beta stock because it is more volatile than stocks in general. A stock with a beta of 1.0 would on average give you precisely the same price volatility as the stock market in general. Stocks with a beta of less than 1.0 would on average give you less volatility than the stock market in general.

When you expect the stock market to go up and you are willing to live with the extra high beta volatility, you can outperform the stock market in general by buying stocks with betas significantly greater than 1.0. Chart 3-2 shows the betas for twenty-five well-known stocks.

Don't buy just any high beta stock. Check with your broker to ensure that the specific high beta stocks you buy are healthy companies with favorable earnings prospects.

Many readers naturally want clues as to which specific

CHART 3-2

BETTING ON BETA
BETAS FOR 25 POPULAR STOCKS

Company	Beta	Company	Beta
Abbott Labs	1.15	IBM	1.00
American Hospital Supply	1.10	Johnson & Johnson	0.95
		Kmart	1.00
AT & T	0.65	Eli Lilly	1.10
BankAmerica	0.95	3M	0.95
Burroughs	1.05	Mobil	1.10
Citicorp	1.10	Olin	1.20
Dow Chemical	1.25	Pepsico	0.95
Eastman Kodak	1.05	Procter & Gamble	0.80
Exxon	0.90	Schlumberger Ltd.	1.10
General Electric	1.00	SmithKline	0.95
General Motors	0.85	Upjohn	1.15
Hewlett-Packard	1.20	Xerox	1.20

Source: *Value Line* 5

stocks to invest in. But there are no clues. Fortunes change. Stocks in favor one year may be out of favor the next. The best advice that I can give here is to stick with stocks in growing industries (energy, health, high technology) that have both good management and favorable earnings prospects.

NO-LOAD MUTUAL FUNDS CAN HELP YOU DO IT

A simple way to accomplish the objectives we are talking about is to buy a "no-load" mutual fund whose beta is significantly greater than 1.0. On most mutual funds, particularly those sold by brokers, you must pay a sales commission of up to 8½ percent. This means every $100.00 invested brings $91.50 of investment when you start. With a no-load mutual fund, there is no sales charge, so for every $100.00 you put in, you get $100.00 worth of investment. The no-load fund's portfolio doesn't have to rise by 8½ percent before you profit. Moreover, the preponderance of evidence indicates that no-load funds perform just as well when the market is rising and no worse when the market is falling than funds that charge sales commissions. Chart 3-3 shows the approximate betas for twenty no-load funds. (Mutual fund betas are *approximate* because there are no generally accepted beta figures for them.)

INTEREST SENSITIVITY

Besides buying high beta stocks, you can seek opportunities in interest-rate sensitive stocks. You'll get this opportunity when inflation begins to decelerate.

Recall that the stock market moves *opposite to interest rates* and *opposite to inflation*. When inflation and interest rates rise, stocks tend to fall. When inflation and interest rates fall, stocks rise. This presents a special buying opportunity.

Historically, certain types of banking and financial company stocks will have exaggerated movements when interest rates change direction. The banking and financial company stocks respond particularly to changes in short-term interest rates such as the prime rate and rates on Treasury bills. Among these stock groups most sensitive to

CHART 3-3

APPROXIMATE BETAS FOR 20 NO-LOAD FUNDS

Fund	Objective	Beta 3/27/80 to 1/6/81
Afuture Fund	Maximum capital gains	1.30
American Investors Fund	Maximum capital gains	2.28
Babson Investment	Long-term growth	0.89
Beacon Hill Mutual Fund	Long-term growth	0.97
Colonial Growth Shares	Long-term growth	1.30
Columbia Growth Fund	Maximum capital gains	1.49
Dodge & Cox Stock Fund	Growth and current income	1.02
Drexel Burnham Fund	Long-term growth	0.98
Energy Fund	Long-term growth	1.02
Growth Industry Shares	Long-term growth	1.23
Mathers Fund	Maximum capital gains	1.38
National Investors Corp.	Long-term growth	1.07
Nicholas Fund	Maximum capital gains	1.35
Northeast Investors Trust	Income	0.04
One William Street Fund	Growth and current income	0.79
T. Rowe Price Growth Stock	Long-term growth	1.09
T. Rowe Price New Era Fund	Long-term growth	1.69
T. Rowe Price New Horizons	Maximum capital gains	1.91
Scudder Development Fund	Maximum capital gains	1.68
Selected American Shares	Growth and current income	0.72

Source: *Wiesenberger Financial Services 1981 Report.*

interest rates are those of finance companies, real estate investment trusts, and savings and loan associations. Companies in these stock groups rise as interest rates fall and fall when interest rates rise.

WHEN TO GET OUT OF THE STOCK MARKET

When inflation is accelerating or about to accelerate, you should not own stocks—sell them, and invest in gold. Chapter 10 will demonstrate just how to tell which way the inflation rate is headed and explain more about when to sell.

4. ART AND ANTIQUES AND AUCTIONS

A few years ago, an appraiser from a New York auction gallery was called to a convent in Yonkers, New York, to assess its modest collection of paintings for possible sale. His careful inspection, however, revealed that although the works of art had been lovingly retouched by the sisters, their own careful brushstrokes had rendered the canvases worthless.

With regret, the appraiser informed the nuns of his unfortunate finding, and in appreciation for his time and expertise, the sisters invited him to share their hospitality. During the course of an unusually pleasurable meal, the man's glance fell on what appeared to be an antique Oriental sugar bowl. On closer inspection, the curious appraiser found that the sisters' bowl bore the letter *F*. This was quite strange since F is hardly an Oriental marking.

The appraiser's intuition told him something was up, that he must somehow persuade his gallery's porcelain expert to examine the sisters' piece personally. It was no easy task since the expert insisted that nothing of value would ever come out of a convent in Yonkers. But he did eventually agree to make the examination.

As it turned out, the F stood for *Firenze*—Italian for "Florence." The sugar bowl had been commissioned in the sixteenth century by the Medici family to emulate chinoiserie, the Eastern mode. Part of a short-lived pottery venture, the bowl was one of only fifty-four surviving pieces. The sisters were thrilled by the appraiser's findings and sold their unrecognized Magic Asset on the auction block shortly thereafter. They got almost $200,000!

THE COLLECTIBLES BOOM

Similar stories are making the Wall Street rounds as eager bidding from monied investors now sends the prices of art and antiques to fantastic levels. Wall Street itself, in fact, is now diversifying through "soft" dollar investments—banks, stocks, and bonds—and into a wide variety of fine *investment* tangibles. These collectibles—art and antiques of bygone eras—have at last come into their own as prime inflation beaters.

The increases in the prices of most investment-quality art and antiques are astounding and are expected to continue. In the last twenty years, for example, Chinese porcelain has multiplied its value by a factor of ten. A retired Pompano Beach couple recently found $1,200 they never knew they had when they came across a porcelain plate they had received as a retirement gift a few years previously. They were planning to sell the plate at a garage sale for about $10 until the wife checked with her local antique dealer. He sold it for them for $1,200.

Similarly, the prices of some antique American silver have more than quintupled in value in the past five years alone. But investment areas aren't limited—they run the gamut from simple English and American Victorian furniture (many pieces still undervalued in the $200 to $6,000 range) to antique and not-so-antique toys and dolls selling for $100 to $10,000.

Antiques, by the way, also include everything from old photographs to old books, all of which, nontechnically speaking, can be far "newer" than one hundred years old. Regional auctioneers, in fact, single out lower-priced Oriental rugs at $500 to $5,000; antique clocks at $100 to $1,500; and old guns, circa 1870–90, at $150 to $3,000 as specializations having strong investment potential. But anything is game.

Not that anyone can afford them, but at the higher end of the market the prices of French Impressionist paintings have appreciated quite well parallel with seventeenth-century Italian canvases, British and American eighteenth- and nineteenth-century paintings, and twentieth-century European and American oils. At the more modest end of the art scale, and mere speculations until relatively recently, contemporary lithographs by such living greats as Joan Miró and Salvador Dali have been climbing nicely over the long term.

In short, quality art and antiques of nearly every stripe are moving well and can serve as sure-shot storehouses for your wealth and vehicles for outdistancing inflation in the decade ahead.

What's behind the collectibles boom? The obvious spark is inflation. During inflationary times, tangible, rare, innately valuable objects are favorite investment vehicles for smart money. Growing numbers of Americans are taking a centuries-old cue from their counterparts across the Atlantic who have always put less faith in paper money and more in soon-to-be-rare tangibles. And so, the word *collectibles* has entered the inflation beaters' vocabulary.

And an important word it is. Besides protection from the possible, but unlikely, "coming currency collapse" many doom-and-gloomers speak of, you can also develop the satisfying hobby of collecting aesthetic objects for their own sake while basking in their beauty as you use them. Take advantage of the fact that certain pieces of art are appreciated beyond their heirloom or financial value. Antique furniture is used and enjoyed; art nouveau lamps shed light; early American pewter goblets hold liquids; antique jewelry is worn; and Oriental rugs are obviously used to soften and enrich.

ANYONE CAN DO IT

First, rid yourself of the notion that the inflationary benefits and enjoyment of art, antiques, and rare exotica remain the exclusive preserve of the wealthy. Not true! Of the almost $150 million worth of goods sold in a recent year at New York's Sotheby Parke Bernet Galleries, four out of every five lots went for under $1,000, and a very significant portion went for $100 to $200. This shows that anyone can take advantage of inflation simply by owning art, antiques, or a whole array of collectibles that rise faster and higher than the general price level. And if the unlikely currency collapse does come suddenly, you'll be protected from that, too.

Difficult as it is to predict how much capital appreciation an individual artistic collection or antique investment might realize, anyone guided by experienced investment advice or a personal, *assured* sense of taste can reasonably expect an annual value increase of several percentage points more than the inflation rate over the long term.

But walk, don't run to your nearest gallery or auction house. Remember that good lots favor a *prepared* buyer. Investing in *fine* art and antiques is no mere fling. It's a long-term commitment, not a mere dalliance.

You have to be patient in choosing what to buy and in determining what you want to pay. If you pay too much, you won't realize your expected return. You have to take it easy, because every piece of art, every antique is an original. You have to be willing to appraise these souvenirs of yesteryear, then be willing to wait: at least three to four years, probably as long as ten to fifteen, before trying to cash in. This is not a real problem, however. Because the higher the inflation rate, the faster your art and antiques will appreciate. As long as there is 5-, 10-, or 20-percent inflation, art and antiques will be a safe money haven. And you'll enjoy them to the hilt in the meantime, secure in the knowledge that after inflation increases their value they'll fetch a handsome return when you sell.

KNOWLEDGE IS POWER

To be sure, you do need some know-how to distinguish, investmentwise, between the great, the near-great, and the so-so in art. If you lack the expertise or feel you don't have time to develop any savoir faire, you might want to hire a well-trained art expert.

You should always buy what you like, of course, but it's the art ace's business to advise you on soup to nuts in art investing. Many art and antique dealers and brokers will gladly perform this function on an hourly or commission basis. Their rates vary depending on their own expertise; and when you buy directly from a dealer's own store, all the expertise you want is free.

In any event, if you are a novice, educate yourself as much as you can. A little knowledge goes a long way in the acquisition of collectibles. Begin by concentrating on a narrow specialty within a given field that you like. You can start off, for example, within the field of early American textiles by collecting flags with some special historical significance. Then you can branch out to a related area—early American quilts, perhaps. Be dogged about sources. Visit galleries and auctions. Subscribe to and collect relevant art and antique magazines. Read books on anything to do with your chosen periods. Now you'll have a clearer idea of what areas you really find rewarding and what's minimally affordable.

Remember, the values in *almost* every but *not every* class, period, and price range of antiques (which are technically defined as older than a century) are rising over the long term. So although you don't have to be an expert yourself, you do have to have *some* expertise to know what's going up and keep on top of the market. But don't worry, the supply of antiques in specialty shops, antique stores, estate sales, and auctions is limited. No one will ever go back to 1877 and make more '77 vintage credenzas. And after decades of benign neglect, now that the investing public has finally discovered art and antiques as an inflation haven, *nearly* everything of investment quality has to go up, no matter how much or how little you know personally. Now let's take a look at some of the livelier investment areas.

VINTAGE TOYS, DOLLS, CLOTHING, AND GIFTS

Some toys and dolls increased in price more than 100 percent from 1975 to 1980 and their rise in value is expected to continue. At Parke Bernet recently, a 1930 six-car Lionel train set was sold at auction for $8,500. A googly-eyed doll by J. D. Kestner went for $2,000—about 20 percent more than it would have merited a year before.

Because old toys and dolls were once thought of as the poor relations in the world of antiques, many are still undervalued. Tin toys, vintage 1900 to 1940, are especially good investments, many of which are still in the $100 to $500 range. Dolls are not expected to appreciate in the coming years as rapidly as toys, but investment prospects are still excellent.

Many doll experts expect more than 15 percent per year appreciation. They advise buying German bisque dolls, or lifelike, closed-mouth character dolls at prices of up to $2,000. The caviar of the doll line, which you can pick up for $10,000 or so, is the French Bru doll—double its 1975 price.

Even on a more modest budget you can sink some savings into old English wax dolls depicting historical figures or typically American cloth and wood dolls from the 1880s and 1890s. You can also get a good return out of early mechanical flipping monkey dolls (you wind their arms) and early American teddy bears (named after Teddy Roosevelt).

If you are a clotheshorse, vintage clothing is another galloping area. Clothes from the turn of the century through the thirties are good investments. Avoid the forties and fifties. (The rule is to be about fifty years removed from the period.) With exhibitions in museums and racks of these articles in thrift shops and resale clothing stores, you don't have to go far to get started.

Prices range from below $100 for fine gabardine shirts into the thousands of dollars for turn-of-the-century coats by Worth. Compared with the price tags of current designer clothing and especially compared with its upward price momentum, vintage clothing is a virtual steal.

For those who have an important occasion on their calendar, antiques also offer interesting gift ideas (if you can bear to part with your purchases). Americana, such as early hand-carved duck decoys, make wonderful graduation presents for young men. New England tinware, utensils of the Civil War period, may be appropriate for the women in your life. Late nineteenth-century art pottery and porcelains are also attractive and useful for many more types of occasions than a gold or silver fountain pen set.

PAINTINGS

Far more money goes into oil paintings as a hedge against inflation than any other art form. As with toys, dolls, and other antiques, the prices of so many paintings have risen so dramatically of late that some of the wealthier investors who buy, sell, and trade regularly now suggest that famous canvases be published weekly in the trade newspapers—just like stock and bond quotations. Imagine seeing "Picasso, *The Musicians* . . . $450,000"; or "Miró, *The Statue* . . .

$180,000" listed on the financial pages alongside Exxon and United Technologies.

Rapid growth areas in the art market abound. At the top of the line, if you can afford them, are fine Old Master paintings and drawings. Because they have been favorites of the well-to-do, worldwide and for centuries, they are surefires, certain to continue rising in value as far into the future as we can see. You can get excellent original Old Master oils from Rembrandt to Rubens for a few million dollars, or their sketches for prices ranging from $10,000 to $50,000 or more. But before you sink this much into just any Old Master, get the advice of a *reputable dealer* on what drawings are available at good prices.

If Old Masters are beyond your pocket, there are other lively painting markets to penetrate. One of the hottest is the Hudson River school—1850 to 1900 oils experiencing steady to sensational appreciation for quite some time. At the top of the market are names such as Thomas Cole, Thomas Doughty, and Asher Durand, who bring prices in the tens of thousands and up. But you can also get some fine oils by John William Casilear, Samuel Colman, and David Johnson for about $2,000 to $10,000. And you can pick up some of their smaller works for as little as $1,000.

The American Barbizon school of the late nineteenth century also offers good appreciation opportunities. These are mostly landscapes, somber and subdued, and range anywhere from $1,500 to $10,000 each work. As the paintings are not particularly well known, prices are still very reasonable. For paintings in the one-hundred-year-old range, their potential is tremendous (especially if the landscape mood ever comes back into vogue).

Marine paintings also present unusual opportunities. Prices for these late 1800s to 1910 artworks run from $1,000 to $25,000. Look for top-of-the-line names such as Antonio Jacobsen, James Buttersworth, Robert Salmon, and William York to rise the fastest. They generally start in the $5,000 range. You can also visit the obscure shops in your area and pick up some minor "marines" in the $1,000 to $5,000 range.

If all this sounds steep just to have some colored oils protect your future comfort level, why not concentrate on the more modern works? You can still pick up fine investment-quality oils for about $500. Look for early twentieth-century styles and artists at your smaller dealers and at auctions.

American and European Postimpressionism, for example, has been coming into its own and is a good place to start. As you should with other paintings, look for specimens of unusual historical, social, or geographical interest, if you have the choice. And, of course, famous names like Picasso, Miró, or Rothko can't hurt.

PRIMITIVES AND CLASSICALS

Primitive art, including authentic African wood carvings, pre-Columbian works such as sculptured figurines and ceramics, and primitive oceanic pieces from the southwestern Pacific Islands can be particularly refreshing investments especially for those moving in today's fast lane. You can expect to pay from as little as $50 up to a few hundred to a few thousand dollars for a piece of our more instinctive past.

Classical antiquities including everything from small bronzes to pottery and sculptures from the Mediterranean also offer relief from a world on a collision course with the future. You can build a fairly respectable collection for a few thousand dollars, as most individual objects in this category cost only $100 or so.

If you choose to build a collection, try to do so in a specific field, small bronzes, for instance. Get the best pieces for your money first, then winnow out the least valuable from time to time. This will give you cash inflow to build your collection.

PHOTOGRAPHICA

During its experimental decades in the nineteenth and early twentieth centuries, photography was taken lightly as an art form but is now one of the hottest and relatively undiscovered art markets that exists. Portraiture was always popular, of course, but it was only a few years ago that photography emerged from the darkroom and into the investment arena.

As recently as 1970, you could buy a signed Ansel Adams, the great West Coast nature photographer, for as little as $100. If you bought then, your $100 investment would have been worth about $200 by 1972, $400 by 1974, $800 by 1976, and more than $1,000 by 1980. Now is not too late to buy. Although Adams's work is now very high and may be susceptible to some temporary softness, no doubt his work will continue to climb in value through the eighties. The artist himself, now in his seventies, says he will limit his activities because of his arthritis.

The lift-off in price of Adams's photographs from mere dollars a decade ago into the thousand-dollar range today is just one example of the unprecedented photographic collectibles explosion. The portraits and scenes of photography's early masters such as Mathew Brady, Julia Margaret Cameron, Lewis Carroll, and John Thomson—bearing the unique qualities of primitive techniques—have also doubled again and again in price over the past few years. Some of them, which sold for mere hundreds of dollars three to five years ago, fetch thousands of dollars today and are recognized as thoroughly covetable investments.

Anything you buy that is very early, particularly photographs developed during the decade or so following the daguerreotype invention in 1839, is practically guaranteed to grow in value over the long term. Daguerreotypes are early photographic images on silver-plated copper sheets, many of which can still be picked up for under $100.

If you prefer more modern images, photographs of the American West, especially those dated before 1930, should rise quite nicely and are reasonably priced. It also pays to seek out works by such twentieth-century master photographers as Edward Steichen and Alfred Stieglitz. The twentieth-century price boom is bound to continue as photography grows out of its investment incubation period.

You can still buy vintage photographs for less than $100 at auction or through photography dealers or galleries in major cities. And there are also bound to be thousands of rare photographs around the country propped up at flea markets or garage sales, since people don't yet realize their value. To help you in this regard, the newest and best in who's who of photography is the 440-page *The Photograph Collectors' Guide*. It lists late and living masters alphabetically. You'll also get current price ranges at all market levels. And to help you identify value in old photographs, the guide describes distinguishing marks and styles.

ART AND ANTIQUE GALLERIES

In general, when buying art, don't be afraid to patronize top galleries and art dealers. Make it a point always to deal with the best—the reasons are obvious. Major galleries are interested in keeping your patronage; if you aren't satisfied with a purchase, they will do their best to resell your purchase so you'll make your original expense back.

In addition, most top dealers will guarantee the authenticity of anything you buy so it's easier for you to resell. These galleries and dealers will also allow you to "trade up": they repurchase or recycle your artwork when you have money to invest in higher-quality pieces. Many of them will offer to let you have a "trial marriage" with your prospective purchase by taking a piece home for a week or two before making your final decision.

Whether you're most comfortable with prize pics or Revolutionary American flags, always remember the inflation-beating rule of art and antiques: buy the best you can possibly afford. *The best rises surest and fastest.*

SPECULATING IN STYLE: A TRIP TO YOUR LOCAL SOHO

Another enticing way to enter the art and antique market to beat inflation is to use the speculative technique. With the speculative technique you buy relatively inexpensive items coupled with the faith that the taste of the collecting community in general will soon rise and rally to your personal choices. It's a risky path to take, but that's why it's called speculative.

Consider those who in the 1890s gambled $1,000 or so for a Renoir canvas. That's worth millions today. Consider the man or woman who paid as little as a few hundred dollars in the early part of the century for original paintings by unknowns Pablo Picasso and Salvador Dali. But because you can't be sure your own choices will turn out quite as rewarding, your rule when speculating is: buy only what you love, what you will enjoy living with, even if your best friend disagrees.

One way to begin your collection is to go to avant-garde galleries and lofts in the SoHo (*So*uth of *Ho*uston Street) or TriBeCa (*Tri*angle *Be*low *Ca*nal Street) sections of New York City. For those who can remember *Mercury 1*'s countdown, lift-off, and splashdown, a walk through the galleries there may not only serve as a fountain of youth but also a real education. If you're not old enough to remember *Mercury 1* personally, you'll at least get a real feel for the up-to-the-minute in speculative art.

Several galleries in SoHo show works by young *photorealist* painters such as Richard Estes, Jack Mendenhall, and John Clarke. These artists make ten-foot-square canvases look like actual photographs. The photorealists, whose art is as new and different as cubism was in 1910, are just being recognized. Much of their art, now valued at $1,500 to $15,000 each work, has been doubling and redoubling in value in recent years.

But it's not only photorealism that is new. So is *material illusionism*. SoHo is also the place where the works of Marilyn Levine, a material illusionist who can make ceramics look like old leather, have likewise increased in value. Her price now for an old "leather" M.D. bag lookalike ranges from $500 to $5,000. Five years ago you'd have paid maybe $150 to $1,500.

You don't have to live in New York City to experience the joys of SoHo and TriBeCa. There are experienced gallery dealers in speculative SoHo-type art districts throughout the country. Gallery owners there can point you toward their own favorite works.

Besides investing in paintings and sculptures by the new realists and illusionists you might also do well both financially and in decorating your home by buying *original prints* by some of these blossoming artists. An original print, as defined by the prestigious Print Council of America, is made from a plate, block, stone, or other medium that the artist himself has used to create an image. In most cases, the slate, block, or stone is used to create several, even hundreds of similar prints, each one usually distinguished by the artist's hand signature. If you cannot afford the prices asked for paintings and sculpture it's a good idea to consider prints because they are very colorful and relatively inexpensive.

The current print revolution in art has recently lifted many prints out of speculative second-class status and into an artistic niche of their own. So besides speculating by buying prints of relative unknowns, you can (if you can afford) pick up prints by Toulouse-Lautrec, Mucha, Picasso, and Miró. Once iffy investments at best, they are now the grandfathers of wise, first-class print investing.

Before you put down a single dollar on a print, however, examine print catalogues you will find at galleries, print exhibitions, and auctions where you shop. Print catalogues will educate you as to the artist's schooling and experience. Most important, they will list his or her works. You'll get descriptions of individual prints, including whether each is signed by the artist, the number of impressions in the entire edition, the print's size and date, and the process or processes used, such as lithography or silk screen.

Buy only original prints, rather than *reproductions* of prints, and buy only from established print dealers. Seek the guidance of these dealers on the quality and authenticity of the prints you are considering. When you make your purchase, ask for whatever descriptive data you need on the invoice or get a certificate of authenticity. Reputable dealers will be happy to oblige. They benefit from the high standards maintained because inadequate information about a print casts a shadow on everything they sell.

Besides paintings, sculptures, and prints, other fruitful areas of speculation abound. Consider *books*. An astute reader with a finger on the pulse of the popular direction might have been able to feel that half a century later a first edition of Graham Greene's *Babbling April*, published in the 1920s, would be worth more than $400 almost solely on the basis of the writer's reputation. That's a return of several hundred times on a very small and smart investment. Even shorter term, early Capotes, Saroyans, Anaïs Nins, Thomas Wolfes, and James T. Farrells which could have been picked up for a few dollars only a decade ago are today worth hundreds of dollars. The investment is small; the potential payoff is great.

You could today, say the expert book collectors, establish a comprehensive library of first edition Vonnegut, Barth, or Brautigan for as little as $300. It is conceivable that your collection would be worth ten to fifteen times that amount by 2001.

One obvious problem with this speculative approach is

that you can't know whether you are buying a future Picasso or Vonnegut or the work of just another bearded wonder who probably should have stayed in his father's hardware store. This is the principal reason that, unless you develop a feel for the market yourself or rely on expert advice, you must buy what you like and what you will enjoy living with.

A COLLECTOR'S PARADISE

A visit to your local auction house—whether it be Parke Bernet on New York's Madison Avenue or otherwise—is a tremendous experience and can vastly enrich your life as well as your portfolio. Auctions offer the opportunity to make new acquaintances and find bargain purchases of everything from toys and dolls to old paintings and photos.

Auctions are exciting. You start by attending gallery presale exhibitions; this will take you a long way toward developing the necessary expertise in your chosen areas of interest. Then by bidding on auction day, believe it or not, you can usually save 25 percent or more against what you would pay in a gallery.

Throughout the United States once listless salesrooms throb with "auctiophiles" in search of a piece of the past. As a result of the new bidding fever, what was once an isolated event or two found exclusively in and around major cities is now available to all inflation-conscious investors across the land, in barns and storefronts as well as grand old estates. In fact, the top firms, such as Sotheby Parke Bernet and Christie's, sometimes hold several simultaneous sales per day, six days a week. Check your newspaper for times and places.

AUCTION SMARTS

But how do you make the most of these auctions? How do you become an astute buyer? What are the secrets of bidding with a cool head? How do you choose an auction in the first place? And above all, how do you avoid mistakes?

A word about mistakes. Everyone makes them and they can happen in lots of interesting ways, not only financial. A New York tax attorney, recently thrilled with his one-time-only bargain purchase of an early American oak

62 MONEYSMARTS

conference table, returned it in embarrassment after discovering that the table wouldn't fit into his conference room. Luckily, he realized a profit the next week when the same gallery sold it for him. Then there was the plastic surgeon in Boston who bid successfully on a luxurious nine-and-a-half-foot sofa, only to find it too large for his building's elevator and impossible to lug up the stairs. The precious piece had to be hoisted from the street and brought into the apartment through his living-room window at a cost of $300. But *you* won't be plagued by these troubles if you remember some simple, often-overlooked buying guidelines.

CHOOSING THE RIGHT AUCTION

First of all, choose your auction carefully. Don't walk in off the street during a weekend stroll and immediately begin bidding. Browse through the leisure or lifestyle section of your local newspaper for several weeks, first to familiarize yourself with the names of dealers as well as the dates and locations of the different auctions. This way you'll know beforehand what's for sale.

It may be fine to spend time at a small, local auction, but the more sophisticated and refined your interest, the harder it will be to find the right investment for you. Large metropolitan houses offer the best opportunities to find rare objects and genuine antiques. Country auctions are not the best places to find inflation beaters unless you know exactly what you are looking for and its approximate value. Very often at these auctions, plenty of junk that will never rise in price is offered alongside the few better pieces. Many experts now warn that with the astounding increases at the top of the auction market, there is real danger that the novice will be tempted to overpay at the obscure country auctions.

THE PRESALE EXHIBITION

In choosing your auction, always try to take advantage of the presale exhibition. This way you'll see exactly what's being offered beforehand and have a good idea of its monetary value. Since all items at auctions are sold "as is," scrutinize the merchandise carefully, and don't hesitate to bring along a tape measure, color swatches, or even a camera for second-thought comparison. Examine each item thoroughly, including inside drawers of furniture, hardware, and linings. Be critical.

The finest and scarcest of what you buy will rise in value the fastest. This is the basic law of supply and demand and applies as much to antiques as to anything else. So look for damages, holes, and distress markings. Make sure that the $600 Victorian couch has four legs and not three. If your heart's desire needs work, keep in mind the additional costs for restoration, reupholstering, or refinishing.

The presale exhibition is also the time to see whether the item you want may need special attention and care. All but one of the pieces in a fine set of Limoges china, for example, had to be brought back to the auction house for resale by its Scarsdale owner when she found that the fragile china wouldn't survive her jet-spray dishwasher.

Your lifestyle is a factor if you intend to use what you buy and not just contemplate it. So always inspect the offerings before the auction begins. Don't hesitate to ask questions—as many of them as you feel are needed. Most reputable exhibitions are staffed by knowledgeable people who are only too happy to show off their expertise. If for some reason you require even more knowledge, you can always invite a friend or advisor who is considered an expert in that area.

At the presale exhibition make sure to pick up the listing or illustrated catalogue of items to be sold. There are few things more exciting to auction buffs than to sift through this literature. But don't judge a catalogue by its cover. A glossy auction catalogue filled with high-contrast pictures, expensive backgrounds, and a lot of white space is unfortunately no guarantee of fine merchandise.

Disregard the catalogue's cosmetic formula, and learn to read beyond the verbiage. If the word "style" is used, as in "Lionel style," it means that the set is a *copy* of the original Lionel model trains. Although it may be of the same vintage, it will probably not be as valuable as the classic Lionel trains would be and certainly has fewer potential buyers. Only consider the actual item up for sale;

don't rely on its description when deciding what you want to pay. Again, examine the offerings at the presale exhibition, and ask questions about the objects you wish to purchase. That's what presale exhibitions are all about.

THE PRESALE ESTIMATE

The tool that will probably help you most in deciding what to pay for an item is the *presale estimate*, contained in the auction catalogue available at the presale exhibition. The presale estimate is the gallery's item-by-item assessment of what it believes each article will fetch on auction day.

Each of these estimates is typically a range. For example, the listing in a particular catalogue you pick up might read: "Queen Anne Carved Cherrywood Flat-top Desk, circa 1740, estimated at $6,000–$8,000." According to a recent study performed by the Massachusetts Institute of Technology ("Evaluating the Accuracy of Art Auction Estimates"), although the estimates are accurate enough at the bottom of the range, galleries often underestimate the top by wide margins. Prices frequently break through the ceiling estimates, making their way to unanticipated heights.

In New York at a Christie's sale of fine English and Continental furniture, a Dutch Baroque clock recently sold for $28,000. Presale estimates had put the range at $8,000 to $10,000. A Regency rosewood sofa and writing table left Christie's at $23,000—almost five times the presale ceiling estimate of $5,000. The weakness in the estimates shows that it's often impossible to evaluate how much hidden interest a particular item will spark. Again, the presale exhibition is the place to go to determine what you think a piece is worth and where you want to set your bidding limit.

HOW MUCH SHOULD YOU PAY?

In deciding what price you want to pay, look to three criteria: the object's *condition, rarity,* and *historical importance*. These criteria hold true with most specimens offered on the market, whether they originally belonged to Pablo Picasso, Ansel Adams, or Louis XIV. Keep in mind that you also pay for *aesthetic* and *intrinsic value*. Works by some artists, Fabergé (whose eggs are legendary), for instance, incorporate precious metals that automatically make them worth more as the prices of precious metals peak. Attention to detail adds to the overall value, too.

When you've decided what appeals to you and what you think an item's worth, write down the number and title so you'll be prepared when it comes up on the auction block. Decide on an upper limit for an item and always stick to it; this will prevent you from getting hurt in too-passionate bidding.

A DAY AT THE AUCTION

On auction day there are several important things to remember. Most important, don't be nervous. The era is past when an unfortunate neophyte could mistakenly buy something because of an ill-timed scratch of the head or wink to an attractive member of the opposite sex. Most auctions now feature bidding by raising a numbered paddle to avoid misunderstandings.

When "your" piece is brought to the block, don't be too eager or start bidding immediately. Be frosty. Overzealous bidding occasionally invites competition from "phantom bidders," who are sometimes employed by those who are interested in increasing the bids, thereby the ultimate sale price. So allow the bidding to get under way before you jump in. Bidding may start considerably lower or higher than your own estimate. Only after a couple of other bids have been made should you throw your own hat into the ring.

Stay cool. Undisciplined, emotional bidding is your worst enemy. An old Civil War gun that's a bargain at $350 may be no treat at $1,000. If others are willing to give in to the heat of bidding, let them. Set your own limit and stop there.

Following a successful bid on your heart's desire—that Victorian sofa or that Alexander Calder lithograph—it's yours for the taking, right then and there. Auction galleries usually do not provide packing or shipping services; so make certain your mode of transportation will accommodate your purchase.

THE BARGAIN-HUNTING MENTALITY

In general, off season is the time you can find more bargains and less competition. The holidays, December and the vacation periods of June, July, and August, abound with bargains; moreover, with many people away during these times bidding is sure to be "softer."

But beware of the bargain-hunting mentality. Hugh Hildesley, a senior vice president of Sotheby Parke Bernet, tells the story of journeying to the gallery one snowy morning, expecting to see no one at the sale but himself. As he fought his way through the blizzard and into the front doors of Parke Bernet, there were scores of dealers prompting him with "You'd better go on with that sale!" He did, for record prices. The moral, he teaches, is that the bargain-hunting mentality offsets the challenge of the natural elements "very handily on every occasion."

Soon after you've assimilated the suggestions we've made in this chapter and once you've been to a few auctions yourself, you'll be an old hand at evaluating art and antiques in your special areas and begin to enjoy the excitement and challenge of bidding. Even more, you'll experience the joy of living with your unique purchases. And best of all, you won't be living with faded yesterdays, you'll be investing in plush tomorrows.

5. EVERY INVESTOR'S BEST FRIEND

Despite the once uncontested supremacy of gold, a great deal of evidence now suggests that *investment* diamonds are on the threshold of rivaling the precious metal as the premier inflation beater. After forty years of steady and respectable rises at the *wholesale* level—which is the *only level at which you should ever buy*—diamond values are rising even higher.

In the last five years, *investment-grade* diamonds, which are defined as *one carat or larger near-flawless stones*, have scored gains averaging about 18 percent appreciation per year. Many of the rarer stones, which the very wealthy have been hoarding for years, have been appreciating at even higher rates.

The past is not a perfect predictor of the future, however. According to most qualified sources, we can expect the price rises to average about twice the inflation rate over the *long term*. As diamond prices have skyrocketed of late, particularly during the late 70s, no doubt there will be individual years, probably during the early 80s, in which their prices will soften. But over the long term, they will probably prove to be the safest and surest inflationary wealth multiplier your money can buy.

For the past decade, owning an investment-grade diamond, like owning gold, has been like owning shares of the glamorous growth stocks of the 1960s. Still, today a restricted market and diminishing supply of investment-quality stones, coupled with a growing worldwide demand to get into the inflation-beating action, assures continued price appreciation for many years. We can begin to understand the value of diamonds as an inflation hedge once we understand how certain special factors combine to generate higher diamond prices.

SPECIAL FACTORS

Scarcity. Diamonds are naturally scarce. This is explained by their formation, a miraculous one-time-only fluke of nature occurring more than a hundred million years ago. Tiny quantities of carbon were somehow crystallized by tremendous amounts of sustained heat and pressure within the molten rock far below the earth's surface. The carbon became transformed into a new substance that had never existed before.

Diamonds are found in various parts of the world, from Africa to Brazil, from Australia to the USSR. Nevertheless, centuries of mining have sharply exhausted the natural, limited supply. According to some estimates, including one by the Smithsonian Institution in Washington, D.C., all known diamond deposits will most likely be depleted within the next half century. With increased scarcity of this natural resource, prices tend to accelerate faster and faster as its supply nears exhaustion.

Restricted supply and controlled market. The diamond supply is restricted, and prices are controlled by the De Beers syndicate, a publicly owned company based in both London, England, and Johannesburg, South Africa. De Beers effectively controls approximately 80 percent of the world's diamond supply. De Beers's fundamental strength is retained by its ownership of the diamond mines.

The De Beers syndicate controls diamond prices by offering parcels of rough diamonds—in London, Lucerne, Switzerland, and Kimberley, South Africa—on a no-bargain, accept-or-reject basis to only a few hundred specially selected diamond dealers throughout the world. De Beers limits this procedure to ten times a year. They set prices to account for worldwide inflation as well as increases in their own production costs. Generally, dealers accept De Beers's diamonds at the asking price for fear that if they reject, De Beers will terminate their distributorships. When recession or depression lowers demand, De Beers curtails diamond supplies to maintain firm market prices. Similarly, if prices seem to be escalating too rapidly, De Beers releases a countervailing inventory into the market. But the diamonds are nearly always allowed to appreciate *faster* than inflation over the long term. Even in the 1950s, when the inflation rate was 1 percent to 2 percent, wholesale diamond prices rose two or three times as fast, at 5 percent to 6 percent annually.

Romantic reputation and special qualities. The unique classic and romantic qualities and properties of diamonds keep their demand and value constantly growing. The great demand for diamonds dates back as early as four centuries before the Christian Era when diamonds were regarded as coveted treasures. First found and traded in India, many of the precious stones soon reached Ceylon (now Sri Lanka) and the Middle East. Others found their way into the Roman Empire, where the jewels were believed to possess medical and magical powers. Arabian and Persian merchants brought by caravan the gleaming, glittering beauties to China, where they served as jade-cutting and pearl-drilling tools in the first few centuries of the Christian Era. Because of their hardness and durability, diamond tools were highly regarded in China and were considered prized gifts.

Because India was the early leading source of diamonds, Indian superstitions about diamonds spread throughout the world. Buddhists believed that a person's soul had to be purified before joining the "universal soul," or *karma;* the steps in this process involved serial incarnations as animals, plants, even minerals and gems—especially diamonds. This fostered the belief that gems had life, a notion that persisted for centuries. Even the Greek philosopher Plato believed in life among gems and rated the diamond as the most noble of all. Such ideas were held well into the Renaissance period and served to guarantee diamond values.

Diamonds were supposed to have numerous other mystical powers. They could repel phantoms and demons and even prevent nightmares. If worn into battle, a diamond could protect the wearer. Courage, virtue, and invincibility were imparted under extraordinary circumstances.

Although the incredible myths about the precious gem have been gradually discredited through the centuries, diamonds are still an extraordinarily concentrated form of wealth and are the most portable storehouse of value in the world. In times of extreme crisis, a million dollars' worth of diamonds can be readily concealed in a space as small as a tiny perfume bottle—to be easily hidden or transported to safety.

DIAMONDS AS INVESTMENTS

The true test of a Magic Asset comes during history's storms not the calms. We know that diamonds outdistance inflation. But in times of uncertainty, too, diamonds tenaciously hold their value better than most other assets. Over the long term, diamonds have provided security and appreciation through inflation, recession, devaluation, war, and depression. As of this writing there hasn't been a significant air pocket in wholesale diamonds' price levels for well over a generation. Certainly air pockets will come, but when they do, they should exist for relatively brief periods. So for long-term price appreciation diamonds are the safest investment you can make. Although they don't pay any interest or dividends, they are much safer than stocks and even safer than gold because they hardly ever go down.

There are several strategies used in diamond investing. Depending on your investment outlook, different approaches may be useful. Here are the most popular diamond investment routes you can take:

Conservative investment strategy. This strategy stresses a long term of survival over all potential circumstances: inflation, recession, depression, political crisis. Investment-grade diamonds provide both high investment appreciation and an easily hidden, highly portable form of wealth. While gold and particularly silver (discussed in Chapter 7) are easier divisible and therefore more spendable in times of economic collapse, diamonds are the better long-term store of wealth. The key here is long term.

Beautiful adornment or gift-giving strategy. Over the ages, diamonds have represented the ultimate tangible gift of love and admiration. Today, as in past generations, investment diamonds are a way to express close feelings to a loved one. In fact, many families never sell their precious stones but rather pass them down from generation to generation.

Pension fund strategy. Diamonds are a great asset to stockpile for retirement since historically they have offered excellent returns and protection from all types of economic circumstances. This type of "golden years" strategy ties in with the fact that the longer a diamond is held, the more profitable it becomes. In Chapter 22, "Inflation-Proofing for Retirement," we'll explain the advantages of using diamonds to fund Keogh plans and Individual Retirement Accounts. Although there is much talk in Congress of repealing the tax benefits with regard to using diamonds in retirement funds, as of this writing the benefits are very real.

Barter strategy. Investment-grade diamonds have always retained excellent barter value. This strategy works well in both prosperous and lean times. The trick is to acquire diamonds at wholesale value (or as close to wholesale as possible) and then barter or trade them for goods at their full retail value. While it is not the easiest task in the world to buy a diamond for $12,000 wholesale, place a realistic $20,000 or $25,000 value on it and it is not entirely impossible to trade it in for a BMW or Mercedes or even use it as a down payment on a house. Most people who are inclined to trade will readily take diamonds. More on barter in Chapter 11.

Tax-dodger strategy. Some people manage to (illegally) skirt gift or estate taxes by passing their diamonds on to their children or relatives without "declaring" them. Diamonds have always had a special allure for persons in the upper tax brackets, as they can serve as an advantageous tax shelter. It is not uncommon for high-income investors to buy diamonds at wholesale prices, get their gems appraised at retail, and then donate them to charitable or educational institutions for a significant tax write-off. I'm not suggesting breaking the law, but rather checking with a qualified tax advisor for the best counsel before you act.

CHOOSING THE CORRECT INVESTMENT DIAMOND

Although many people have always known that a diamond is an excellent inflation beater, some hesitate or are scared off completely because they don't know exactly how or what to buy. First, you should know that there are three types of diamonds: 1) industrial grade, 2) jewelry grade, and 3) investment grade. Of the three types of diamonds, *only the investment-grade diamond has proved itself as a safe and effective inflation beater*. Of all the diamonds mined in the world, only about 2 percent are of high enough quality to qualify as investment grade.

A diamond is rated as investment grade based upon an internationally recognized grading system. In this system, diamonds are ranked and rated by five factors, known in the diamond business as the "five C's": the diamond's *carat weight, color, clarity, cut,* and *certification.*

1. *Carat weight.* The weight of a diamond is given in carats. As a general rule, the larger the stone the faster it will appreciate.

When buying a diamond, you will see that its price does not go up in simple steps along with carat weight. The smallest variation in carat weight will have a striking effect on price. Generally speaking, as carat weight goes up, the price per carat multiplies. In other words, a one-carat stone will cost you far more than twice as much as a one-half-carat stone of the same quality. This is because in diamond mining, about 10 tons of diamond-bearing rocks can be expected to produce several diamonds whose combined weight would add up to about one carat. Approximately 250 tons of rock, however, must be processed to find a rough diamond large enough to produce a single, finished one-carat diamond. Thus, a one-carat diamond can be several times as valuable as a one-half-carat diamond of the same quality.

It is these larger stones—one carat and above—that are considered large and scarce enough to be appropriate for investment purposes. Only these are the ones that have gained the reputation for increasing in value at about twice the inflation rate.

Diamond buying advice: *buy an investment-grade stone which is at least one carat in weight.*

2. *Color.* The factor that will contribute most to your diamond's value as an inflation beater is its color. Color refers to the amount of visible tinting of the stone. In general, the closer your diamond is to absolute colorlessness, called pure white, the more valuable it will be and the faster it will appreciate.

Crystal clear, or absence of any color in the body of the stone, is considered the finest quality. Completely colorless, icy-white diamonds are very rare. More common diamonds have varying tinges of body color, usually a yellowish tint, and they naturally do not command as high a price as those that appear crystal clear in the loupe.

Of course, if a diamond's yellow is very strong and attractive, the gem might be considered a fancy color and its value correspondingly higher than that of the so-called off-color stone. Besides yellow, there are fancy colored-gem diamonds with very definite natural body color in virtually all hues of the spectrum—blue, pink, coffee, orange, green, red. All are valued for their rarity.

To help distinguish diamond color, the Gemological Institute of America (GIA) has developed a diamond color grading system. Chart 5-1 illustrates the GIA system, which uses the alphabet from D to X. The highest quality color grades are D, E, and F, all corresponding to a pure white color—actually colorless—with no tinge of yellow, followed by G and H, which possess a trace of color, not noticeable to the untrained eye.

Diamond buying advice: *purchase a diamond which is grade D through H only*. Further along the scale, corresponding to moving through the alphabet from I through X, graded diamonds have increasingly yellowish tints and are not investment-grade hedges against inflation. (This does not mean that as jewelry I through X colored diamonds will not rise in value, just that they may not outdistance inflation.)

3. *Clarity*. Now let's consider a diamond's clarity, which determines approximately 30 percent of its value. Clarity is the degree of the diamond's freedom from imperfections. An imperfection may be an impurity or flaw inside the diamond or a blemish on its surface. Whatever the imperfection, it interferes with the passage of light through the diamond and lessens its brilliance. The freer the diamond is from imperfections, the greater its value as an inflation hedge.

The grading of a diamond's clarity is usually performed with a small 10-power magnifying glass called a loupe. If a diamond is perfect—no flaws, cracks, carbon spots, clouds, or other blemishes or imperfections of any sort visible under 10-power magnification—the diamond is called *flawless* (FL). (See Chart 5-2.) After flawless, the next best grade is *internally flawless* (IF). Internally flawless means a complete absence of internal flaws with only minor surface blemishes. The next best grade is *very, very slight inclusions* (VVSI). These are very, very small imperfections (called "inclusions") extremely difficult for a

CHART 5-1

GEMOLOGICAL INSTITUTE OF AMERICA COLOR GRADING SCALE

| D | E | F | G | H | I | J | K | L | M | N | O | P | Q | R | S | T | U | V | W | X | Y | Z |

| COLORLESS | NEAR COLORLESS | FAINT YELLOW | VERY LIGHT YELLOW | LIGHT YELLOW | FANCY YELLOW |

CHART 5-2

GEMOLOGICAL INSTITUTE OF AMERICA CLARITY GRADING SCALE

| Flawless• | VVSI 1•• | VVSI 2 | VSI 1••• | VSI 2 | SI 1•••• | SI 2 | I1••••• | I2 | I3 |

- • flawless under 10× magnification
- •• very, very slight inclusions
- ••• very slight inclusions
- •••• slight inclusions
- ••••• imperfect

qualified observer to find even under 10-power magnification. Next on the scale is *very slight inclusions* (VSI), then *slight inclusions* (SI). Least desirable are *imperfect* (I) stones.

Imperfections revealed under the scrutiny of a 10-power magnifying glass are not generally significant enough to affect the diamond's brilliance and beauty. Cut and color are much more closely tied to a diamond's attractiveness than minor flaws. But even though inclusions not apparent to the naked eye do not detract from the appearance of a diamond, the slightest imperfections do lower its value and prevent the stone from bringing the highest return.

Diamond buying advice: *buy only a diamond which is flawless (FL) or has very, very slight inclusions (VVSI).* These will rise the fastest relative to inflation.

4. *Cut.* The surface finish and polish of a diamond, as well as its proportions, also account for a diamond's beauty and hence its value. A diamond's cut, that is, its proportioning, faceting, and polishing, is therefore critical to its role as a storehouse of wealth.

Cutting of investment-grade diamonds is an art. Rough diamonds usually emerge from the mines in the shape of octahedrons, solid figures with eight plane surfaces. Master cutters then shape the rough diamond crystals into finely proportioned, highly polished gems that sparkle with fire and luster. This process plays a large part in establishing the ultimate rarity and price of a diamond, since skillful cutting will better display a diamond's natural assets to their greatest advantage.

Diamond buying advice: of the several popular shapes shown in Chart 5-3—brilliant (round), marquise, oval, emerald cut, single cut, pear, heart shape, and baguette— *your best investment is the round brilliant.* A brilliant round-cut diamond provides the greatest refraction of light because of its proportion, shape, and the angle of each of its fifty-eight planes. For this reason, it is the most popular cut throughout the world and hence the most "liquid," meaning easiest to sell.

Your brilliant round-cut stone should also be cut to ideal proportions because even two brilliant-cut stones of the same weight, the same color, and the same clarity can still vary by as much as 50 percent in value, with a major reason being the cut. Certain proportions are recognized

CHART 5-3

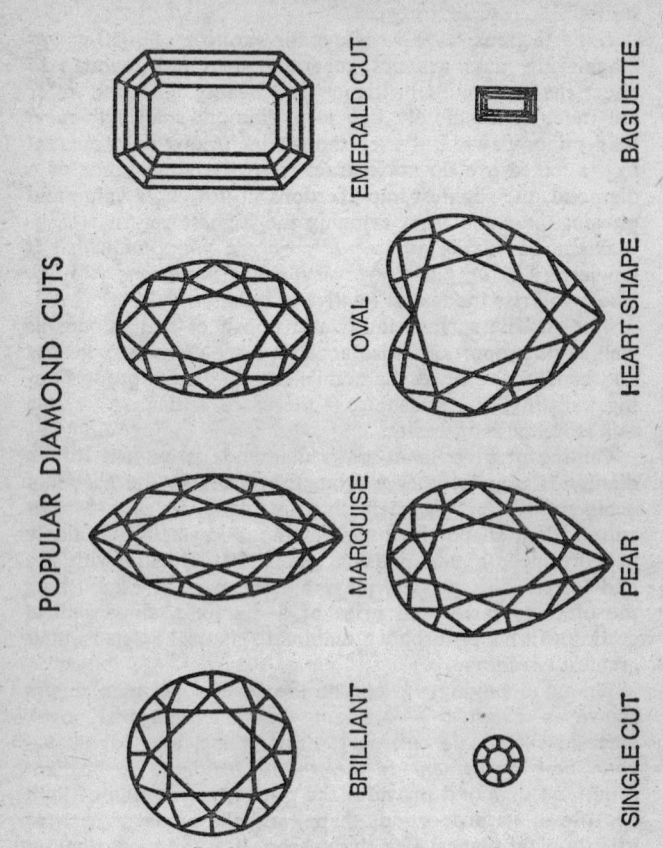

POPULAR DIAMOND CUTS

- EMERALD CUT
- BAGUETTE
- OVAL
- HEART SHAPE
- MARQUISE
- PEAR
- BRILLIANT
- SINGLE CUT

CHART 5-4

IDEAL DIAMOND PROPORTIONS

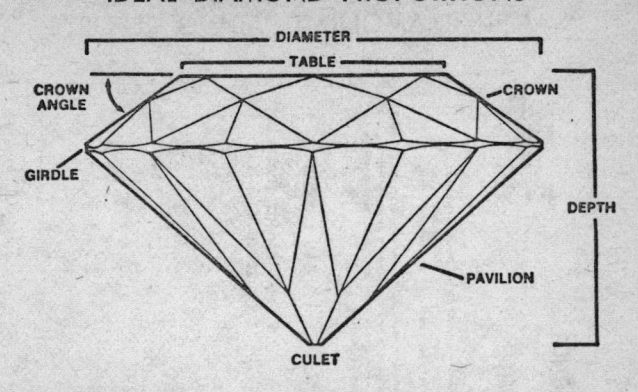

1. Depth percent — 57 to 63 percent
2. Table percent — 57 to 65 percent
3. Crown angle — 30–35 degrees
4. Girdle thickness — Avoid extremely thin or thick girdles
5. Culet size — Should not be large
6. Symmetry — Must be at least "Fair to Good"
7. Polish — Must be at least "Fair to Good"

as being within the range of ideally cut diamonds. Characteristics to be considered are illustrated in Chart 5-4, which shows you exactly what to look for when you buy.

5. *Certification.* When you buy your investment diamond, make sure you get a Gemological Institute of America (GIA) "Gem Trade Laboratory Diamond Grading Report" along with it (see Sample Diamond Grading Report, Chart 5-5). This certificate attests to your diamond's qualities and is the most powerful safeguard to ensure that your stone meets our investment diamond criteria:

   a. that your diamond weighs one *carat* or more,
   b. is H or better in *color* grade,
   c. has very, very slight inclusions (VVSI) or is flawless (FL) in *clarity,*
   d. is *brilliant* and *cut* to an ideal proportion.

CHART 5-5

SAMPLE DIAMOND GRADING REPORT

Gemological Institute of America
GEM TRADE LABORATORY
Scientific Identification of Gemstones and Pearls

Diamond Report No. NY123106
4/8/77

In the opinion of the Laboratory, the following are the characteristics of the stone, or stones, described on the attached report as based on measurements and also on observations made through the Gemolite (10X binocular darkfield magnification) and in the DiamondLite, utilizing master comparison stones. Mounted stones graded only to the extent that mounting permits examination.

(Red symbols denote internal characteristics; green, external. Symbols indicate nature and position of characteristics, not necessarily their size. Where applicable, setting prongs are shown by black symbols.)

Key to symbols
• -pinpoint inclusion
- -feather

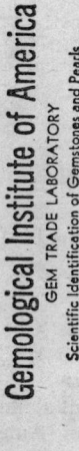

SHAPE AND CUT round brilliant
Measurements approx. 6.73 - 6.82 X 4.09 mm
Weight 1.15 carats

PROPORTIONS
Depth Percentage 60.3%
Table Diameter Percentage 65%
Girdle Thickness slightly thin to medium, faceted
Culet Size small

FINISH
Polish good
Symmetry good

CLARITY GRADE VVS$_2$

SAMPLE DIAMOND GRADING REPORT

COLOR GRADE F

Ultraviolet fluorescence — none

COMMENTS:
Minor hairline feathers in girdle and details of polish not shown.

GEM TRADE LABORATORY
Gemological Institute of America

By _____

SPECIMEN

GIA CLARITY-GRADING SCALE

| Flawless | VVS₁ | VVS₂ | VS₁ | VS₂ | SI₁ | SI₂ | I₁ | I₂ | I₃ |

Imperfect

GIA COLOR-GRADING SCALE

| D | E | F | G | H | I | J | K | L | M | N | O | P | Q | R | S | T | U | V | W | X | Y | Z |
| Colorless | Near Colorless | Faint Yellow | Very Light Yellow | Light Yellow | Fancy Yellow |

(Copyright 1975, GIA)

You can usually get a GIA certificate directly from your seller at no extra charge when buying the stone, or you can take (or send fully insured) the stone to the GIA, and for $50 they will certify it. In fact, this way is safer because you'll be sure your GIA certificate actually pertains to the stone you want to buy. The GIA has three main locations, which are listed in Chapter 24.

A GIA laboratory analysis offers you one of the most respected and widely used lab reports in the country. The oldest and most respected laboratory in the United States, the Gemological Institute of America is recognized by the trade for accuracy, dependability, and rigorous standards. All critical points regarding the carat weight, color, clarity, cut, and measurements of your stone will be described on the certificate.

WHERE TO BUY

Color, clarity, carat, and cut all have a bearing on a diamond's price. But where you purchase your gem also determines what you will pay.

A diamond investment makes the most sense when you purchase the stone at normal wholesale cost. Wholesale cost is simply the price a jeweler himself is willing to pay for the stone.

You can buy at wholesale in a number of ways:

Cousin in the business. Pity we don't all have a cousin in the business, because your best bet is to buy your diamond wholesale from someone you know personally. If you're fortunate enough to have a friend in the business or a direct line to a cutting house, there is no better source to use.

"Wholesale" investment diamond firm. Buying direct from a reputable wholesaler is the next best way to buy a diamond. A reputable wholesaler who is well connected—and is actually selling near wholesale—is an excellent source of supply.

Most investment diamond firms tack on 10 percent or 20 percent commission over and above the actual wholesale price. This is a perfectly acceptable way to buy if you don't know anyone in the business who can offer you a better deal.

Since the word "wholesale" will be tossed around like

salad by investment dealers to entice you, we must emphasize what it means. Again, the real wholesale price is the price a retail jewelry store is willing to pay for the diamond. When you buy you must pay as close to the genuine wholesale price as possible. This way, if you need to liquidate your investment you can sell to a jewelry store anywhere in the world and get your money out on very short notice.

Beware, if you buy at retail, which is about double the wholesale price, and then decide to sell. You'll have to wait years until the wholesale price a jeweler is willing to pay rises to the retail price that you paid before you can sell it to a jewelry store at the price you bought it.

If you decide to buy through a wholesale outfit, you have to be sure to deal with a genuine wholesaler who will pass savings and price advantages along to you. You can easily determine which firms are real wholesalers simply by comparing current costs of similar GIA certified stones.

After you have selected your stone, you have to ensure that the stone you want to buy is actually the stone the GIA certificate describes, rather than some inferior one. So get a statement from your wholesaler that he will refund your money if the diamond you buy proves to be a different diamond than the one described on the certificate. Together send the stone off for GIA inspection, then when the box comes back, unseal it together and compare the new GIA certificate with the one the wholesaler gave you. If they match, you have made a fine diamond purchase. If they don't, get a refund.

The integrity of your investment diamond firm is one of the most important factors to consider when investing. Before making any commitment to an investment diamond dealer whose integrity is in question, check with the New York State Attorney General (Securities Bureau, 2 World Trade Center, New York, New York 10047). New York State's special deputy attorney general, David E. Robbins, will advise whether the firm you propose to buy from is registered with his office. If the firm is not registered in New York, the financial capital of America, and you don't know the people you are buying from personally, it's best to seek out a different source.

Estate sale or pawn shop. An estate sale or pawn shop provides a good opportunity for a solid diamond investment buy, but to capitalize on it you must first develop some expertise in this area. Of course, if your cousin in the business or a qualified expert can accompany you, you might very well find a good buy.

DIAMONDS ARE FOREVER

Diamonds are such a fine long-term investment that many families prefer not to sell them at all, but instead pass their precious gems down from one generation to the next. Whatever you choose to do, however, the best strategy for diamonds is to make good buys, as close to wholesale as possible, then hold on for a number of years. It's this long-term-hold type of investment strategy that in the past has reliably beat inflation by more than twice the going inflation rate.

HOW TO GET THE BEST PRICE WHEN YOU SELL

It's when you sell that you will most appreciate the value of your GIA certificate or other written statement of your stone's quality. Instead of having to rely solely on the subjective judgment of the purchaser, you will be armed with a documented description of your diamond's quality.

But before you sell your stone for cash, you'll need some further ammunition to get the best price possible: knowledge of its approximate present value, and a dollar amount appraisal (the highest you can get) to help convince the buyer your diamond is very valuable. So call several wholesalers for a quote on their selling price for a similar stone. And take your gem to an appraiser. Insist on receiving full retail price appraisal and ask for the current wholesale price. Now with all your newly acquired estimates, one of which is high and in writing, you have three ways to sell:

1. *You can sell to a retail jeweler.* If you decide to sell through a jeweler, check out more than one to make sure you get the best price. Offers usually vary depending upon a jeweler's particular clientele, the season, and his own cash-flow situation.

Most jewelers are really out for themselves. Beware of the "submarine," a jeweler who will quote you an "underwater" price thinking you have no diamond smarts. Other submarines quote low prices because they are infuriated at the rise in wholesale diamond firms. Jealous that new firms are entering town and sweeping investors off their feet with wholesale diamonds, a retailer seeing someone walking into his or her shop with an unset investment-grade diamond may deliberately submarine you to discredit the investment diamond dealers. So make sure you don't get torpedoed. Get offers from several jewelers before accepting any of their proposals.

2. *You can sell through a diamond broker or diamond wholesaler.* Many of these dealers and wholesalers will handle your stone on consignment. You leave the diamond in their possession and they will sell it for you. In the jewelry business this is called a "memo." The procedure allows them to sell your diamond for a higher price than they would pay you for it.

When you give your diamond to a dealer on memo, you can choose to receive a percentage of the sale price, say 85 percent, 90 percent, or 95 percent, and let the dealer keep the rest as his commission. Or you can tell him the minimum amount you will take for your diamond and let him sell it for a price which also allows him to make a profit. A memo is actually a contract between you and a dealer and is legally binding. If a dealer who wishes to sell your stone doesn't have this type of form contract, contact another to handle your sale. Keep a signed copy of the memo for yourself.

3. *You can sell to your buyer directly.* You can also sell your diamonds through the classified sections in your local newspaper. This is when your retail appraisal will come in particularly handy. You can advertise in national publications like the *Wall Street Journal, Barron's,* or the gemological trade publications, such as the *Lapidary Journal.*

If you choose this approach, you can safely show your diamond to a prospective buyer in the safety deposit box area of your bank. At the time of sale, ask for full payment by cash, money order, or bank check; if you accept a personal check, don't give up your stone until your buyer's check has cleared. If you need to ship your diamond, mail it in a small, securely sealed box via registered mail. Your package can be insured up to $25,000. Be sure to ask for a return receipt.

Selling to your buyer directly will probably take you a

lot of time, but you will probably get a better price because you will reach more people interested in buying diamonds. You'll also save on middleman costs.

CONCLUSION

In recent years top-quality diamonds have outrun most other investments as long-term wealth multipliers. Naturally, no one can see into the future. However, the past is a pretty good indicator. For over thirty years, even through deep recessions, the value of diamonds has been climbing. And since diamonds have been celebrated through the ages, the across-the-board appeal of this investment vehicle is undeniable. If you can carefully follow the buying and selling rules outlined in this chapter, diamonds could be the ideal high return long-term investment. With diamonds as part of your long-term portfolio, you can rest assured that your capital will appreciate faster than the rate of inflation all around you.

6. COLORED GEMSTONES

While diamonds may still be every investor's best and safest friend, their dramatic price appreciation has caused the price of colored gemstones to climb. This is why, as a smart investor, you should leave no stone unturned.

Thrust into the investment limelight recently here in America, colored gemstones serve two wealth-preserving roles. First, they give the smaller investor, whose investment funds are modest (under $50,000), the opportunity to participate in gems without having to put a large sum into a diamond. Second, glittering gemstones give the large investor an opportunity to diversify.

With no De Beers cartel to steer their prices, however, colored gemstones are not as absolutely sure performers as diamonds. During deep recession or depression colored stones will tend to soften in price if you have to sell. But with continued inflation, which is what we should expect, their value will no doubt continue to soar.

The Colombian emerald you could have bought for $2,000 a decade ago has already tripled in price to $6,000 because of inflation. The three-carat Siamese ruby you could have snapped up for $150 a decade ago is worth $1,500 today. Both are still climbing.

Rises are not limited to the precious stones alone. Ten years ago you could have picked up top-quality aquamarines for a mere $50 per carat. Today they're worth $400 a carat. Almost every sort of colored gemstone imaginable from amethyst to zoisite is moving ahead in value at about twice the inflation rate. Both precious and semiprecious gemstones alike are following the lead set by diamonds, reaching record values as holders of dollars convert their paper to tangible assets.

Gemstones' colorings are among the richest, purest, and most beautiful in nature. And unlike flowers, their beauty is enduring and dependable. King Tut's treasures include necklaces of lapis lazuli, carnelian, and turquoise that still inspire lust in collectors and fashion mavens two thousand years after their creation.

Since scarcity is one of the chief qualifiers for the increasing value of fine gems, and since it appears that they are going to be even scarcer and more expensive in the future—very few major gem deposits have been discovered in the last generation—colored gems, like diamonds, will continue to be a reliable inflation hedge as paper currency loses its purchasing power.

WHAT TO BUY

Although the age-old distinction is beginning to break down because it serves little purpose, gemstones are still usually divided into two general classifications: precious and semiprecious. The diamond, ruby, emerald, and sapphire make up the royal four of precious stones. All the other stones are considered semiprecious.

Ruby. Color: varying shades of red. Ruby is the hardest gemstone after diamond. Its color varies with individual deposits, and the most desirable is "pigeon's blood," pure red with a hint of blue. The finest rubies known come from Burma where they have been mined for more than seven hundred years. Important deposits of rubies are also in Thailand, Cambodia, Sri Lanka, Tanzania, and Kenya. Clear rubies larger than one carat can sell as high as thousands of dollars per carat.

Emerald. Color: emerald green, light green, yellow-green, and dark green. Cleopatra's emerald mines in Egypt were worked as far back as two thousand years ago and provided many stones for ancient-world craftsmen. Some civilizations believed that the subtle change of color that emeralds sometimes displayed represented the incompatibility of lovers. The most highly prized emeralds are deep green in color with no tinge of yellow or blue; these may cost several thousand dollars per carat, even as much as $30,000 per carat in flawless condition. The best known localities for emeralds are Colombia, Rhodesia, and Zambia.

Sapphire. Color: blue in various hues, colorless, pink, orange, yellow-green, purple, black. The name sapphire comes from the Greek word for blue, but sapphires occur in almost every color. The most desired colors are cornflower or soft blue and "kashmir" blue, which can cost several thousand dollars per carat. Some of the world's most famous sapphires come from India, in the vale of Kashmir, high in the Himalayas. Cambodia, Australia, and the United States also produce these precious gemstones. In the case of star sapphires, the centering and sharpness of the star are important factors in valuation.

Amethyst. Color: light to deep purple, lavender. Amethyst is the most highly prized type of quartz, a brilliant crystalline mineral. Its color varies from pale lilac, which may be almost colorless, to a deep, rich, royal purple. Although the price of amethyst has tripled during the last decade, it remains less than a $100-per-carat stone even at retail.

Aquamarine. Color: blue, blue-green. Aquamarine, once used as a talisman for sailors, comes from a Latin word for water of the sea and is so named for its sea-water color. The color of aquamarine may vary from a pale blue to a deep blue or rich blue-green. Although in ancient times a light sea-blue color was considered the most desirable, today the deeper blue stones are more highly prized. There are aquamarine deposits on all continents, but the most important are in Brazil. The deeper blue stones have been in great demand in recent years and their price has risen steadily. Still, the best aquamarines generally sell for from $500 to $1,000 per carat wholesale.

Chrysoberyl (alexandrite; cat's-eye). Color: golden yellow, green-yellow, purplish red, blue-green, brown. Although the word *chrysoberyl* is derived from the Greek meaning "golden beryl," yellow chrysoberyls are not the color of major gem significance. The variety of great importance is *alexandrite*, which is most desired because of its dramatic change in color from red or violet in artificial light to green or blue-green in sunlight. The finest alexandrite changes from a purplish red to blue-green, both colors showing a minimum of brownish tint. Larger stones with good color change can cost thousands of dollars per carat.

The other type and best-known chrysoberyl is known as the *cat's-eye,* which contains parallel inclusions producing a silver-white line in a cut stone. Fine cat's-eyes weighing more than a few carats may sell for thousands of dollars a carat.

Garnet. Color: red most often, but may be orange, yellow, brown, pale green, deep green, violet, purple, or colorless. The name *garnet* refers to a group of minerals all closely related in structure and composition. *Rhodolite* is a garnet species of rose red or pale violet color found in the United States, Sri Lanka, Brazil, Zambia, Tanzania, and Kenya. *Grossularite,* the most colorful of the garnets, is typically found colorless, pale green, yellowish green, cinnamon-brown, orange, yellow, and deep green, resembling the color of fine emerald. Deposits of grossularite are known to exist in Pakistan, South Africa, Canada, Sri Lanka, Tanzania, the United States, and Russia. Vanadium grossularite, found only in Tanzania and Kenya, is extremely scarce, and stones weighing more than five carats may sell for more than $1,000 per carat. *Demantoid,* however, are the most valuable of garnets. They are found in the Urals. Rumor indicates that a nuclear accident has rendered further mining of these known deposits highly unlikely.

Jade. Color: green, white, pink, lilac, brown, yellow, red, orange, blue, black. Although jade and the color green are synonymous, the mineral occurs in many translucent colors, the most valuable being emerald green from Burma. The term *jade* used in the gem trade actually refers to two distinct and different minerals: *jadeite* and *nephrite,* the latter being more modestly priced.

Opal. Color: colorless, white, yellow, orange, various shades of red, yellowish brown, greenish blue, gray, black, violet. There are four varieties of gem-quality opal. *White opal,* an opaque white material that looks much like porcelain, is the kind most commonly seen in opal jewelry. Its colors can appear as flashes, speckles, or sheets of rainbow hues and may sell for a few dollars to hundreds of dollars per carat. *Black opal* contains fire similar to white opal, but the body color is black or dark gray. Black opals, extremely rare and costly, can command more than $1,000 per carat. *Water opal* is a transparent, colorless opal that contains brilliant speckles of color within. *Fire opal* has an orange or red body color and may be transparent or translucent. Because of their softness and fragility these types of opal are more suitable for pins and pendants than for ring stones.

Peridot. Color: yellow-green, olive green, brownish. Although peridot is a warm, soft olive or yellow-green mineral, it never reaches the intensity or shade of green characteristic of emerald. Good specimens are found in Burma with lesser deposits in Kenya, Norway, Arizona, and Mexico. The best material is green with no tinge of brown or yellow. The finest and larger stones may retail for more than $200 per carat.

Topaz. Color: colorless, yellow, yellow-orange, reddish orange, red-brown, sherry, blue, pink, pale green. Most yellow or brown gems were called "topaz" in ancient times and these are the colors by which topaz is known today. Although the most important color variety is the range from yellow to brown, with the golden brown commanding prices of several hundred dollars per carat, other colors are now becoming more popular. Because of the surge in aquamarine prices, blue topaz has begun to stand in as a substitute. Colorless topaz is also attractive and still inexpensive. The most important topaz supplies today come from Brazil, Sri Lanka, Burma, and Russia.

Tourmaline. Color: colorless, pink, red, yellow, brown, green, blue, violet, black, multicolored. Tourmaline, a general group of minerals with similar atomic structures and chemical compositions, displays the richest variety of colors of all known gemstones. The most desired colors are intense red, green, and blue. The most valuable tourmalines, red with a tinge of purple or violet, come from Maine, California, and Brazil and can retail as high as $200 per carat. Large blue tourmalines command similar value. Recently a poll conducted of dealers, merchants, and others interested in gems, unofficially selected tourmaline as the U.S. national gemstone.

Tanzanite (zoisite). Color: violet-blue, sapphire blue. In 1967 transparent crystals of violet-blue zoisite were found in Tanga province, Tanzania, to which Tiffany & Co. gave the name *tanzanite.* In a decade, the retail price of clear large stones rose from $100 to $1,000 per carat. Tanzanite is known to be found only in Tanzania, and decreasing production at the mines has made the finer and larger gems scarce and costly. The best tanzanites resemble blue sapphires; this is the reason they have been in such heavy demand and are so rare and expensive.

HOW TO CHOOSE THE CORRECT INVESTMENT GEMSTONE

In buying a gemstone, as with diamonds, always consider the five C's: carat weight, color, clarity, cut, and certification.

1. *Carat weight.* As a general rule, the larger your stone, the greater its value and the faster it will swell in appreciation.

Colored gemstone buying advice: *don't consider buying any precious stones under two carats (except diamonds) or any semiprecious stones under five carats.* Inflation will appreciate larger stones the fastest. Small stones do not carry similar inflation-beating value.

2. *Color.* While the most valuable diamonds have an *absence* of color, the value of a colored gemstone is determined by the *purity* of its color. The more valuable rubies, for instance, will be a definite red-red, not orange-red or pink-red. Any tinge of foreign color diminishes color purity and usually the value. The colors ruby red, emerald green, and sapphire blue have become so well recognized that they are commonly accepted as color designations in themselves. We have already seen the colors to look for in the previous section.

Colored gemstone buying advice: since the quality of a gemstone's color accounts for about 70 percent of its value and inflation-beating ability, you should *buy only "vivid" (intense color saturation) or "bright" (conspicuously lustrous) stones.* Avoid "dull" stones which have low color saturation or lack luster. Color "distribution" should be "even," which means there should be as little color zoning as possible; avoid "uneven" color distribution with noticeable color zoning. The words in quotations are gem trade descriptions. Use them when purchasing.

3. *Clarity.* As with diamonds, clarity is the absence of internal or external marks when viewed under a standard jeweler's loupe (a 10-power magnification glass). A clear, clean stone is, of course, the most desirable; anything less than optically clear is less valuable. Stones other than

flawless or clear quality may not serve you as well in the long run as inflation beaters.

Colored gemstone buying advice: *buy either flawless stones* (free from all inclusions and external blemishes under 10-power magnification) *or clear stones* (no inclusions visible to the trained, unaided eye).

4. *Cut.* Like a well-cut diamond, a well-cut colored gemstone will allow the most light to return to your eye and will account for your stone's brilliance. As the cut of a stone determines its brilliance, a stone that has been cut too shallow will permit light to leak to the bottom and cause the stone to appear watery. On the other hand, a stone that is cut too deep will permit light to escape to the side and cause the stone to appear dull.

Colored gemstone buying advice: *buy only stones of excellent or good cut. Avoid fair and poor cut stones.*

5. *Certification.* Be sure your seller certifies your stones for carat weight, color, clarity, cut, as well as for authenticity. Modern science has made it fairly easy for professionals to duplicate genuine stones to such a degree that some imitations even include similar imperfections. Since instruments are required to tell the difference, try to choose a dealer or broker who is a certified gemologist and will acknowledge in writing the authenticity of your stone. If you invest any substantial sums of money in gemstones, arrange to have the stone or stones certified by the Gemological Institute of America before you buy.

The GIA will not appraise the value of your stones, but will give you an identification and professional description of the gem. If the stone has minor imperfections, they will be noted accordingly, but most important, if the stone has been doctored or synthesized, you will be promptly advised in writing. The cost of the service is about $40 per stone, but the authentication is well worth the price when you are ready to resell.

WHERE TO BUY

Where to buy your colored gemstones is almost as important as which specific ones to buy, because the closer you can get to the genuine wholesale price the better the investment you have made. As with diamonds, if you have to pay retail, you have to wait until the wholesale price appreciates to the retail price you paid to benefit monetarily when you sell. While you can assuredly get your money out at a profit, you may have to wait forever and have not made the best possible investment. So avoid buying from retail jewelers, unless they will give you what you know to be a good price or you know you'll never want to sell. While retail jewelers are convenient and offer large selections, they are also quite likely to charge about double or triple the wholesale value of the stone. And since a relatively large part of what you spend in a retail store is likely to be for the setting, it may be more difficult to realize the profit you require on resale.

If you don't have a friend in the business, or have a friend who has a friend there, you should buy your gemstones from a wholesale stone dealer, a specialist who handles nothing but a wide variety of loose stones. Make certain that he is reputable and active in the type of stone you want. You should be able to buy from him at between 20 percent and 35 percent less than full retail value.

You can also hire a gem broker to check his contacts for what you want. A gem broker's fees are usually under the average retail markup, and a broker will provide expert advice. If you know what you want, he or she can save you legwork. Many dealers double as brokers.

It's also a good idea to shop overseas in the countries of excavation to save on costs of importation and high markup and labor in the U.S. So if you vacation or take a business trip to a country of a gemstone's origin, be sure to bring some extra cash for a possible purchase. Never buy in tourist shops, but rather from a local wholesaler. Just check the phonebook.

After your purchase, you might consider having your gemstone mounted in a ring, but be certain that the craftsmanship and quality of the material in the setting meet the quality of your new investment.

WHEN AND WHERE TO SELL

As with diamonds, many glittering gemstones remain "in the family," passed on from generation to generation tax free. So you don't get yourself into trouble with the IRS, it's best to check with a qualified tax advisor so you know the tax consequences of various kinds of legacies.

If you choose to sell, however, do so after holding on a period of no less than two to five years, to give your gems time to mature financially. When it's time to sell, preferably after five years, you have four alternatives.

First, you can sell to a *retail jeweler*. But remember, as with diamonds, beware of the "submarine." Check prices with three to five jewelers to make sure you're getting the best price possible.

Second, you can sell through a *gem dealer or broker* who has contacts throughout the gemstone industry. You will usually pay a 5- to 15-percent commission if you choose to sell this way.

Third, you may sell by means of a classified ad in the *Lapidary Journal*, the *Wall Street Journal*, *Barron's*, or a local newspaper. This will take the longest time, but you will probably get the best price because you'll be reaching the most people, and you are the one naming the price. You can show your stones in the privacy of your safety deposit box area.

Finally, besides selling your colored gems, you can also *trade* them. If you think you'd like to trade, just join a local gem club. Here you will meet people with a similar interest in buying, selling, and trading.

GEM CLUBS

Nearly all major cities in the United States have gem clubs. Most clubs are affiliated and sponsor not only swapping sessions but lectures, tours, auctions, field trips, and special exhibits. The larger clubs also sponsor shows, where dealers may sell their stones at booths. Such shows can be a real education as they offer you the opportunity to view hundreds of cut stones and to buy at prices well below retail.

To find out about gem clubs and shows, check the *Lapidary Journal*. Each year the April issue lists most of the clubs, including the name of the secretary, address, and where and when the club meets. Every issue contains a calendar listing of local shows.

KNOWLEDGE IS POWER

The more you know about colored gemstones, the easier it will be for you to profit. In addition to gem clubs, there are many fine books available on the subject. Several of these books are listed in Chapter 24.

Going to museums is also profitable. There is a fairly comprehensive gem collection at the American Museum of Natural History in New York City, another extensive collection at the Smithsonian Institution in Washington, D.C. There are also many other fine gem collections throughout the country.

If you have the time, consider a home study course. There are three excellent courses: "Diamonds," "Colored Stones," and "Gem Identification," offered by the Gemological Institute of America. Write to: GIA, 11940 San Vicente Boulevard, Los Angeles, California 90049 for further details.

When all is said and done, a carefully selected investment gemstone is a guaranteed bird in the hand. Arm yourself with a wealth of facts; then buy the very best you can afford. It's a straightforward strategy that works brilliantly.

7. SILVER

Investors who went into silver as recently as 1971 paid less than $2 per ounce. Within three years they'd doubled their investment. By 1978, silver had *again* doubled, going from the $4 to $8 range. Many doubled their money once again.

The precious metal then exploded! It was one of the most atomic price explosions in any metal's history, and by 1980 the sterling metal was solidly trading in the $10 to $20 range after once being thrust by a bunch of greedy speculators (trying to corner the market) into the $40 to $50 range. Never buy silver in violent markets. Buy when the waters are calm as you do with gold.

The silver opportunity will continue. There is strong indication that successive major silver bull markets will extend until at least the end of this century.

WHY SILVER WILL GO HIGH

Silver is a precious metal and, like gold, has served as mankind's money since coinage was invented. Like gold, it is a storehouse of value. Like gold, it is a medium of exchange.

Many monetary experts believe, in fact, that during periods of monetary crisis, silver is a *better* medium of exchange than gold because it is easier to spend. This is true because silver comes in smaller quantities. You don't want to buy a bottle of Perrier with a one-ounce gold Krugerrand worth about $500, nor with a tenth-ounce Krugerrand worth about $50. But you might with a *real* silver American dime, today worth approximately a dollar.

But the most compelling reason silver will rise—and why you should own it—has nothing to do with the fact that silver is a money substitute. The main reason you should own it is that industrial users will be forcing silver's price up for years to come. Silver's secret is out. Accelerating industrial demand for silver coupled with declining silver supplies will force the *real* users of silver, the IBMs and Eastman Kodaks of the world, who *must* have it to stay in business, to bid its price up and up. Unlike the gold bulls, the silver bulls have become the beneficiaries of a true industrial metal, the one metal most widely used of all the precious metals in industry.

"NOBODY" DOES IT BETTER

As one of the ninety-two natural elements, silver possesses chemical, physical, and atomic properties that make it unique. For this reason it is now one of the most critical materials known on earth. Of all the elements known to mankind, silver is: 1) the best conductor of electricity, 2) the best conductor of heat, and 3) the most reflective of light. Before the industrial revolution, these characteristics were facts only for scientists and tinkerers to fantasize about. Today these precious characteristics make silver indispensable in the electronic, photographic, and telecommunications industries.

With the electronics, computer, photographic, and communications revolutions still practically in their infancy, silver usage, and hence its price, is certain to swell in the years to come. Silver is in heavy demand as an essential part of electronic circuiting. It is required by all industrialized countries, especially by their governments, for electronic strategic defense. It is the key element in film and photography. Moreover, since World War II, hundreds of new industrial and military uses for silver have been discovered each year.

For these reasons, many precious-metals experts believe there is more profit to be made in silver during the next twenty years than in gold. To fully understand why the silver situation may generate a greater payoff than gold, we have to look at the monumental supply/demand imbalance the U.S. government created during its long history of silver manipulation.

THE SILVER STAGE

For more than one hundred years the government of the United States has maintained policies that enable silver today to be potentially one of the most explosive metals on any market in any country. Since the history of silver price manipulation by our government is long and involved, we'll only generalize the highlights.

Shortly after the Civil War, the U.S. government began purchasing $4 million worth of silver each month. The silver was purchased so that the government could mint coins. Because the $4 million purchases were required by federal statute, the government bought the silver whether it needed it to mint coins or not. This led to excess silver in the U.S. Treasury.

Even though by 1890 the United States was becoming silver rich, the federal program of accumulating silver was boosted to require $4.5 million worth of silver purchases per month. And by this time no minting of coins was required. As a result, the U.S. silver stocks were greatly enlarged.

The laws encouraging silver accumulation and silver production were passed by legislators from the western states who argued in Congress that it was in the "national interest" to mint silver as well as gold coins. In fact, it merely insured silver miners in their states higher profits as the government purchases were made at higher than prevailing prices. At the same time, Populist politicians back East supported the silver stockpiling and minting program because with silver backing the dollar, in addition to the existing gold backing, the government could print more paper money and thus bring more government programs to the people.

These actions by the government, the politicians, and the silver interests stimulated silver mining in the United States so greatly that literally millions of ounces of silver flowed into the U.S. Treasury from the western mines. Silver even flowed into the United States from abroad to take advantage of the high prices the U.S. government was paying for silver. America was now silver rich.

Decades later the United States was still silver rich, but by the 1950s, the electronic, computer, and photographic demand for silver exceeded new mine production. Silver's price started to rise.

By 1963 the government was attempting to suppress the rising price of silver at $1.29 an ounce. The $1.29 figure wasn't a lark. That's the price at which the silver content of a silver dollar is worth $1.00. If silver's price broke the $1.29 per ounce barrier, or the $1.00 per silver dollar barrier, people might melt their silver coins down and sell to industrial users, a practice that for some reason the government opposed.

Since the government by this time had accumulated well over 2 billion ounces of silver, it was easily able to supply enough silver to the industrial users to suppress its price. In other words, the government kept the market flooded to hold silver's price down.

By 1971, however, the government had flooded the market with all but 170 million of its 2.2 billion ounces of silver. It could not continue to hold silver's price artificially low. For strategic reasons it could not afford to deplete its remaining supplies. So the government stopped selling and silver's price began to climb. Even if the government tried to suppress silver's price today, it could not do it for very long. The government does not have enough silver to do so.

ADDICTS

As the government has discontinued flooding the market with silver to suppress its price and as industrial consumption continues to increase, silver's price will be forced higher.

There is no question that big business will remain in the silver market, no matter what silver's price. The reason the giants will continue to buy is that during the fifties and sixties they were convinced they could indefinitely obtain vast amounts of silver at artificially low prices. As a result, many companies invested heavily in processes that require silver. They became dependent on silver simply because they believed the government would be able to sell them all the silver they wanted at $1 or $2 per ounce for years to come. But they were in error and now they are hooked on the precious metal.

Besides miscalculating and investing heavily in these "silver processes," these industrial giants had no great success in developing programs to discover alternatives to silver. Their main disincentive seems to have been their belief that the government would supply them with cheap silver forever.

Today the reason for the dynamic price rises in this metal is that industries are addicted to silver and find it nearly impossible to give up their habits. They continue buying. Substitutes may one day be found, but the transition in each industry will have to be made slowly as each industrial user relies on a different one of silver's many valuable properties.

HIGHER PRICES WON'T REDUCE CONSUMPTION!

We can make a case for steadily rising silver prices for still another important reason. *Higher silver prices will not significantly reduce silver consumption.* Normally, when the cost of a product's vital ingredient climbs in price, the product will be priced out of the market. When the price of cotton rises substantially, for example, shirtmakers will switch to cheaper synthetics. Not true with silver. The companies that use silver require silver *only*. What's more, since silver constitutes only a small fraction of the price of most products that use silver, the price of silver could literally skyrocket with the underlying product moving up only moderately.

Examples abound. Silver costs constitute only a minute fraction of the costs of producing photographic film. This means the price of silver can skyrocket without breaking the film manufacturer's budget, or the manufacturer's demand for silver. When the price of silver quintupled during the early and middle 1970s, for instance, the price of film inched up almost unnoticeably, and the demand for silver by the film companies ran strong.

The same is true in electronics and defense. The U.S. Defense Department, for example, requires more than one hundred thousand ounces of silver for every nuclear submarine it builds. It obviously isn't going to stop building subs, planes, missiles, or tanks just because the price of a single component multiplies.

The same holds true for computer companies. The demand for computers by corporations and private individuals is so strong that large computer manufacturers have no alternative but to pay what they must for silver and pass the costs along in terms of higher computer prices. These companies are not going to stop this technology that makes our lives easier because the price of one small but vital component—silver—multiplies.

Normally, when the cost of a product's essential component rises, the product can be priced out of the market. This isn't the case with silver, because the people who use it have developed a dependence.

THE COMING SILVER SHORTAGE

Along with the greater and greater demand for silver, there are dwindling silver supplies. This further insures higher silver prices to come. Silver is a rapidly diminishing asset, like oil. It's easy to see why. Geologically, silver was deposited out of hot fertile waters in fractures of rock at relatively shallow depths. Because the precious metal is found only on or near the earth's surface, most silver veins exhaust themselves soon after silver mines reach maturity. It is said, for example, that at just about the time the railroad reached Tonopah, Nevada, to handle the great silver trove there, the shallow silver deposits petered out.

The shallowness of silver deposits also means that most rich deposits have already been found and exhausted. The fundamental force, as we can see then, is the imbalance between silver's supply and demand.

At the time of this writing the silver available for new production and from salvaging previously used silver—the *supply*—is about 300 million ounces annually.

At the same time, the *demand* is significantly higher. Industrial consumption alone is 350 million ounces to 400 million ounces annually. In addition to the industrial use of silver, governments also use silver for commemorative coins. Witness the Canadian commemorative coins minted for the 1976 Olympic games. Silver is being used up for commemorative coins at the rate of about 20 million ounces to 40 million ounces each year. So the total annual silver consumption (industrial and coinage) is approximately 400 million ounces. With consumption at around 400 million ounces per year and available supply about 100 million ounces less, the fundamental law of supply and demand dictates that silver's price must be bid higher.

LET THE BIDDING START

The question now becomes what will the price be at which supply and demand for silver are brought into equilibrium. In other words, how high can we expect silver to go? There will always be certain hoards of silver awaiting the appropriate moment to sell. (By far the largest is in India but Indian silver is usually mixed with alloys and is considered undesirable by many refiners.) Wherever these hoards will be found to correct the silver supply deficit, all we can say for sure is that it will take progressively higher silver prices to pry the dwindling hoards loose from their owners.

As the industrial users go to market bidding for silver, there will be progressively less available. So they'll bid against each other trying to pry those silver hoards loose. How high the bidding will go is anybody's guess. But the evidence is clear that no matter how heavy the bidding, none of the heavy industrial users will drop out. During the wild 1979–80 run-up into the $50 range when billionaire Nelson Bunker Hunt tried to corner the silver market, the bidding was as hot as it could get. But Hunt had to drop out—the industrial users proved they had the real staying power. Maybe next time it will take a silver price of $75 or $100 per ounce to slow the speculators and industrial giants down. No one can say for sure.

WHEN TO BUY SILVER

If you don't make a habit of following economic events and the silver market daily (in the *Wall Street Journal* or other business newspapers or magazines), you should buy silver for the long term rather than for quick profit. And unless you plan to be on the phone with your broker two or three times a week or more, you should buy silver and plan to hold it for a few years, confident that the worldwide silver shortage will work in your favor.

Buy when markets are calm and volume low. The *worst* way to proceed would be to buy during hot and heavy rallies when the industrial users are madly competing with the Nelson Bunker Hunts of the world in an attempt to corner the silver market.

Wait until the Hunt brothers and other silver speculators have either made their killings, taken their baths, or gone on their vacations. You'll know this has happened when you see the silver price fall after it rallies.

If you're planning on playing the big rallies, be warned: rallies could be relatively brief (lasting one to six months), and if your timing is off, you can stand to lose. Silver is not for the faint-hearted. So if you're the nervous type, don't play. Buy when silver is nice and cool; you can always sell out with a juicy profit when the big boys get into the action. You should buy silver, like gold, when its price is stable. It rarely makes sense to try to chase the precious metals as their prices are being thrust forward.

THE SILVER EQUATION

One last point about *when* to buy silver before we look at the *ways* to buy it. Many silver bulls you speak to will point to the historical sixteen-to-one gold to silver ratio and tell you it's okay to chase silver anytime gold's price exceeds silver's by more than sixteen times. In other words, if gold were selling at $500.00 an ounce they would argue silver is worth 1/16 of this amount, or $31.25. They argue this is a sensible strategy no matter how many speculators are in the market and no matter how wild the bidding for silver might become.

You should *not* be concerned with the sixteen-to-one ratio. This sixteen-to-one ratio they speak of was chosen by the U.S. government in 1792, and was probably based in large part on an old Roman fifteen-to-one ratio. The ratio game, while fun to play, merely gives a general idea of how the market has valued silver in the past, and has little bearing on silver's price today. (It is comforting to note, however, that at the time of this writing with gold trading at around $500.00 per ounce, the historic ratio *would* place silver at $31.25 per ounce.)

WAYS TO INVEST

Generally speaking, you have three main ways to invest in silver:

1. *Silver coins*—by buying American dimes, quarters, or half-dollars dated 1964 and before.
2. *Silver bullion*—by buying bars of refined silver.
3. *Silver stocks*—by buying shares of corporations that mine silver.

There are other ways of owning the metal that we will touch on, but for beginners it's best to stick to coins, bullion, or stocks.

SILVER COINS

Once U.S. currency was backed by real silver. In fact, it was *made* with the sterling metal. So, if you have any dimes, quarters, and half-dollars minted in 1964 or earlier, sleep well knowing they are 90 percent silver. You're richer than you think as each coin is already worth about ten times its face value. If you've saved any Kennedy half-dollars which were minted from 1965 to 1970, those are only 40 percent silver, but you're still doing okay. Anyone who owns these silver coins today actually has a miniature silver mine on hand. The value of these coins rises and falls with the price of silver.

Silver coins have been such a fine investment over the years that people now buy and sell *bags* of them in the investment markets. Each investment bag contains coins that amount to $1,000 in face value.

In other words, you can now invest in silver by buying a bag containing ten thousand dimes or four thousand quarters or two thousand half-dollars. The value of these bags is listed along with the price of silver in the business section of your daily newspaper. At the time of this writing each of these bags is worth about $10,000, and even at this price they are still excellent hedges against inflation.

Don't let the large quantities of coins scare you from

owning them. A bag of coins is only about the size of a basketball, weighing approximately fifty pounds. If the coins in the bag were melted down and the silver extracted, they would yield a net total of about seven hundred twenty ounces of the precious metal. (The Kennedy halfs would yield less.) But since you can buy and sell these bags of coins, *as bags,* there's no reason for you to melt the precious coins down in order to cash in. You just sell your bag.

You can buy silver coins through various coin dealers and silver brokers whose advertisements appear regularly in the *Wall Street Journal* and in the business sections of most major newspapers. Nearly all of the dealers who will sell you gold now also sell bags of silver coins. To let them know what you want, just specify "junk" silver. They'll know this means pre-1965 U.S. coins with no numismatic (coin collector) value.

Many people wonder whether they should buy junk silver on "margin"—paying 20 percent or 30 percent "down," and owing the rest. Of course, this creates a "leveraged" situation and can produce a quick bag of profits if the price of silver suddenly shoots up. But it's best to stay away from coin margin investments, not only because of high interest costs involved but because a major advantage of buying these coins is having them in your physical possession.

With today's economic conditions, you cannot help but take the threat of runaway inflation seriously (however small the chance may be). If the monetary system ever collapses completely, silver coins will have great value: you'll be able to spend them day to day for your necessities until the crisis is over. Thus, silver coin possession, in addition to being a fine investment, is insurance against a possible breakdown of your own means of exchange that might accompany a period of runaway inflation.

One last point on silver coins. The one type of silver coin you should avoid for investment purposes is the commemorative coin. These are usually minted by private companies, sometimes even by governments. You should avoid them because they will cost you much more than the value of the silver in the coin itself. The added premium can be as high as 50 percent or more and is most often far in excess of any scarcity value the coin might have.

SILVER BULLION

You can easily purchase silver bullion in almost any quantity. There are two ways to do it: 1) buy through a *dealer*, or 2) buy through the *futures market*.

Most dealers who sell gold will be happy to sell you silver bullion as well. In fact, many coin dealers now sell silver bullion, too.

If you buy from a dealer, you can make arrangements to have the silver shipped directly to you. Or, of course, you can pick the precious metal up yourself. Buying commissions vary from dealer to dealer but are generally around 2 percent.

If you're rich enough, or plan on winning your state's lottery, you can also buy bullion through the silver futures market. Just call up any commodity brokerage house or the commodity department of any large stock brokerage company and buy a silver contract for future delivery. Your broker can explain how you can take delivery on a futures contract—when the contract expires you're entitled to buy silver in lots of about $100,000 at a price you contracted for in advance. The commission you pay to buy the silver will be about $75, which should be no problem if you can afford the sterling metal itself.

STOCKING UP

One of the most potentially profitable ways of owning silver is to buy shares of stock in silver mining companies. As with gold shares, silver shares present you with a *leveraged* opportunity.

Leverage works to your benefit. We saw earlier how it works with gold. It works the same way with silver. If it costs a silver mining company $5 to find and retrieve an ounce of silver worth $10, the company's profit will be $5 per ounce. But with silver selling at, say, $20 per ounce, that same company will have a profit of $15 for every ounce it sells. The price of silver *doubled*, but the silver mining company's profits actually tripled. That's precious metal leverage.

The other major advantage (besides leverage) you have with gold stocks, however, unfortunately does not apply to shares in silver mining companies. While many gold shares pay extremely high dividends, the silver shares have not yet earned such a reputation.

Nevertheless, like the gold stocks, silver stocks offer the ordinary investor an opportunity to partake in precious metal bull markets once they have begun. Since the full significance of higher silver prices is usually not reflected by the stock price until some time after silver makes its upward move and after the mining company has officially declared its higher earnings, silver stocks present you with a chance to get into the silver market after a major move is under way.

As silver stocks often begin to climb days, weeks, or months after the sterling metal begins to streak on its own, the opportunities for latecomers are certainly there. But just because silver itself begins its acceleration doesn't mean that a wind tunnel will be created for all silver stocks. Forward momentum will develop for all silver stocks in general, but some will be carried forward faster than others.

When you buy a silver stock, as you do with a gold stock, you are betting on more than just bullion movement. There are special risks inherent in owning shares of silver mining companies. First of all, you are betting that the silver company stocks you are buying will not be adversely affected by strikes, natural disasters, adverse government regulations, or other turmoil. Second, remember that the same leverage that can make a silver stock's profits soar when silver is streaking upward can devastate that stock when company profits don't satisfy Wall Street's expectations.

To guard against these personal profit uncertainties, it's best to work with a stockbroker who understands the silver market. And it's surprising how few good ones there are. In addition to choosing a good individual, make sure he or she comes from a good firm, one with at least a precious metal research specialist. Fortunately, most of the larger brokerage houses have such specialists.

There are many large, relatively stable silver mining companies that you and your broker can choose from. These companies, listed on the stock exchanges, provide annual reports for your information.

As most silver is recovered as a by-product of other ores such as copper, lead, and zinc, you can also put your investment dollars into companies that specialize in base-metal mining. However, know that your silver investment dollar is diluted when you put it into a company with marginal rather than total silver capabilities.

PLAYING FUTURES

Playing the silver "futures" market is the best way to speculate in silver on low margin. Playing the futures market is also the best way to get burned.

The key to profitability in futures is *precise* timing, which is more often than not just about impossible for those not "hooked up" to the floor of the silver exchange by wire. My advice: stay away from futures (including gold futures), unless, of course, you want to take delivery of at least $100,000 worth of silver (or gold) bullion. More on the secrets of futures trading in the second part of the book.

SILVER SUMMARY

Silver will experience a series of bull markets between now and the beginning of the twenty-first century. Strong demand for the precious metal coupled with diminishing supply will necessarily combine to thrust silver values forward.

The uptrend will be irregular. Speculative buying and selling will cause exaggerations in price, both on the upswings and downswings. Expect to experience hectic rallies, followed by periods of resolution, then times of rest.

You'll do best by buying near the beginning of a rally and selling near the end. But there's no requirement to be exceptionally precise in your silver buying habits. If you ride silver for the long term, the odds are that you'll realize a handsome profit when you decide to cash in.

8. THE STRATEGICS

What oil was to the 1970s—a critical world resource in short supply and stiff demand—a whole host of strategic materials will be to the 1980s. As oil systematically and consistently swelled in value during the last decade, so did the fortunes of the farsighted smart enough to have socked their savings into oil stocks and drilling service companies. Similarly, as the strategic materials, from chromium to titanium, rise in value in the 1980s, so will the fortunes of those who are creative and aware enough to learn how to own them, and to recognize that major profits are nearly always made by those who own critical natural resources just as they come into vogue.

The strategic market is very new and the biggest mistake you can make with regard to getting into these critical resources is to let the newness of their markets or their exotic names scare you off. Don't laugh; once upon a time people thought of Xerox as a bizarre Greek god, hardly something they would want to rely upon to rapidly duplicate their money.

But Xerox has become a type of magic the world has come to love and need. Most of the world, however, probably won't recognize the strategics until the turn of the century. Without chromium, for example, which is indispensable in the production of stainless steel, we would have to rely on primitive hospital and surgical equipment. Without titanium, we'd have little aerospace or strategic defense capability. Without germanium or silicon to produce semiconductors, what would we do for pocket calculators and other digital equipment? Where would we be without cobalt for jet travel or without rhodium for pollution control? There's going to be a time in the not-too-distant future when the answer to these questions will be: "We'd be back in the Dark Ages." Incredibly, few people know anything about the strategic metals as investments.

HIGH FLYERS?

With the electronics, aerospace, computer, and consumer appliance industries born relatively recently, an accelerating demand for many of the strategic and critical resources will no doubt take off and fly through the 1980s and 1990s as these industries grow up. Never before in mankind's history has there existed such spectacular worldwide quest for the strategics. As society once learned to become dependent on the wheel, it has now learned to be dependent on strategics. And while our demand for strategic resources consistently grows, our supply sources are becoming increasingly fragile —which means, economically, values have to rise. This is why it is a good idea to consider investing a small part of your spare cash in strategics. As the markets are volatile, however, invest no more than 10 percent of your investment fund in strategics.

The case for strategics is strong. The United States is more than 90 percent dependent on foreign countries for a number of critical substances: chromium, cobalt, columbium, manganese, vanadium are only a few of the critical materials this country must import to function. Moreover, we are heavily dependent for our strategic resources on countries either unstable or unfriendly! For materials such as platinum, chromium, and vanadium, we rely heavily on the Soviets. For many other critical materials we rely on unstable areas of Africa that are subject to political embargo, social unrest, coups, and revolutions; when a supply source of a strategic material is interrupted, its price skyrockets.

The fragility of the supply side of the supply/demand relationship we are talking about was illustrated recently. In the late 1970s, for example, when Angolan guerrillas attacked Zaire and captured a mine that had been supplying well over half of the Free World's cobalt, production of the strategic material, critical to the aerospace and electronics industries, was suspended. Cobalt, which had been trading in the $6.50 range, was hurled into the $45.00 realm before calming down to $25.00. Investors astute enough to own the critical material and to sell as the crisis peaked (crisis peaks are the best time to sell) made seven times their money. Others who waited too long to sell still were able to multiply their wealth by four.

The Free World to a very great extent is dependent on just such an unstable area now, dubbed the "Persian Gulf of Minerals"—the region of Africa extending from Zaire to Zambia, Zimbabwe to South Africa. It's a region whose wealth and political instability both compare to the Middle East. This is also why we compare the strategics to oil in terms of potential price increase. We can't control supply.

THE SOVIET SQUEEZE

But the strategic supply squeeze goes further. The Soviet Union has abruptly begun a resource war directed at the capitalist community. This war is being waged not only by the Soviets' extending their reach into South Africa to control the strategics through the Cuban army, but by their own operations as well. The inevitable result of Soviet dominance in this area will be an even greater supply/demand imbalance resulting in even higher prices for strategics in the years to come.

But the Russian resource war goes further. Russia, rich in strategics itself, is ending its role as significant supplier of these critical resources to those whose ideologies it opposes. At the same time, it seems to be stepping up its own purchasing on world markets and stockpiling for an advanced military technology buildup.

The evidence is clear. Soviet selling of strategics has dropped off sharply, and according to Undersecretary of Defense for Research and Engineering, William Perry, the Russians have been outproducing us two to one or more in most categories of military equipment, which is no doubt making their stockpiling necessary, particularly of the strategic war materials such as chromium, cobalt, germanium, magnesium, tantalum, and titanium.

To make strategic price matters potentially more explosive, prior U.S. policies of neglecting strategic materials are coming under attack from a new and more conservative administration. Even as a presidential hopeful, Ronald Reagan had been sharply critical of his predecessor's policy on strategics. Now, as president, he says it's time for the United States to boost its own stockpiles, an act which can only drive prices in one direction—up.

WHEN AND WHOM TO CALL TO BUY

The best time to buy strategic resources is during a recession. This is the time when industrial demand for them falls. As a consequence, their prices are usually at their cycle lows. If you buy during recession, then hold on until the economy heats up and you can usually get out with a good profit.

Brokers now offer more than a dozen critical materials the world has come to depend upon. There are two types of brokers you can call upon: 1) your regular stockbroker, who can buy shares of stock in companies that mine the strategic natural resources, or 2) a specialized strategic metals broker (see Chapter 24 for listings of reputable brokers), who can advise you on which strategics you can own directly. Your strategic materials broker can actually buy, sample, store, and insure the strategic material for you.

THE STRATEGIC SMORGASBORD

Since you're probably not yet familiar with strategic forms of wealth as direct investment media, here, as well as in Chart 8-1 which follows, is a rundown of what you can now choose to buy if you want to own the precious resources directly:

Antimony. A silvery white, brittle metal easily reduced to powder, its largest use is in automobile batteries. Not too exciting, but antimony is now being used increasingly for its fire-resistant properties in fabrics and plastic products. It's sure to get a boost as the consumer revolution continues. Moreover, economically mineable antimony is concentrated mainly in politically uncertain regions (China, Bolivia, South Africa, USSR), so supply and price are likely to be volatile upward.

Beryllium. A very light, hard white metal, brighter than aluminum and widely used for aerospace technology and in nuclear reactors. Because use of beryllium can reasonably be expected to grow in the years ahead, the U.S. Federal Emergency Management Agency has recently upped its stockpile goals. Price is bound to rise.

Cadmium. Cadmium is a very soft bluish white malleable metal and was not discovered until 1817. Only recently has there been a strong upward trend in commercial interest. Primarily used in electronics, cadmium's demand is likely to grow. New uses are being found every year. Cadmium's ability to convert sunlight to electricity in photovoltaic cells should give it a good solar energy future. The United States intends to double its stockpile. Watch for rising prices.

Chromium. Chrome, a brittle, hard silver metal that can take a high polish, is indispensable in the production of stainless steel (and therefore aircraft, armaments, autos) and for surgical instruments, which contain as much as 30 percent chromium. With no known substitute in the manufacture of stainless steel, chromium should witness a steady and strong demand in the years ahead. The United States is 90 percent dependent on imports mostly from unstable or unfriendly sources: South Africa, Zimbabwe, and the USSR. An interruption of supply could easily result from either political upheaval in Africa or by a further reduction of Soviet volume on world markets.

Cobalt. A lustrous metal resembling iron, cobalt is magnetic and can take a high polish. It's vital to the aerospace business. We can't build jet engines without it. Cobalt is essential for electromagnetic components in electronic equipment. We use it in the radio, television, and communications fields. Since South Africa supplies more than half the world's needs, any political unrest there would almost certainly drive cobalt's price up. The United States, which is 90 percent dependent on foreign sources, has recently doubled its stockpile goal for the metal.

Columbium. Columbium is a shiny soft white metal which resists corrosion. Columbium, which turns bluish after long exposure to light, is employed for beams and girders in buildings and oil drilling towers and pipelines. Although the United States is 100 percent dependent on foreign sources, world supplies look relatively stable geopolitically. Brazil and Canada are large producers so the metal's price isn't likely to explode but rather experience more systematic movement.

Germanium. Lustrous, hard, and brittle, silvery in color, germanium is a semiconductor that has revolutionized the communications industry. Having permitted miniaturization of radios, televisions, and telephone dialing equipment, it is now used in pocket calculators and digital watches. Germanium's use in infrared night sights for guns will also make it much more valuable in the years ahead.

Lithium. Soft and ductile, lithium is the lightest metal known. Although the United States produces half the world's supply, contamination and pollution problems will require large capital outlays to solve them; thus, increased production costs will insure higher lithium prices. Presently used in ceramics, enamels, and in the production of aluminum, it will surely show increasing demand because of its potential use in electric car batteries.

Magnesium. Silvery white in color, magnesium is the extremely light metal used in aircraft, missiles, and other lightweight military equipment. But because of its great abundance in nature, its price potential in future years will be limited. It should, however, still outperform the inflation rate over the long term.

Manganese. This is a gray-white metal, hard and brittle, used in steel making. About half the world's manganese supply is controlled by the Communist bloc with about 40 percent controlled by South Africa. Although foreign supplies are abundant, the United States is totally dependent; any foreign supply surprises would no doubt drive the metal's price up.

Rhodium. Besides this silvery white metal's use in the optical and jewelry fields, this platinumlike substance is generating increasingly heavy demand in auto exhaust systems. Auto industry demand will most likely remain high as the U.S. and Japanese governments continue to tighten emission control standards. As America is nearly totally dependent on South Africa and the USSR for this precious metal, upward price potential could prove explosive.

Silicon. Silicon is a relatively light and quite abundant metalloid. But higher energy costs will make silicon more expensive to produce and when combined with the computer industry's mushrooming addiction to silicon, no doubt there will be steady price increases in the years to come.

Tantalum. It's a gray, heavy, and extremely hard metal named for being tantalizingly difficult to isolate. U.S. import dependence is 96 percent. Since tantalum's biggest user is the expanding electronic industry, no doubt consumption and thus price will increase in the years to come. In 1980, the U.S. strategic stockpile goal was raised to 8,400,000 pounds while presently inventory is less than 3 million pounds.

Titanium. Silvery white titanium, so strong and light, resists corrosion and as such is in heavy demand by the aerospace industry. U.S. aircraft manufacturers, who now buy their titanium three years in advance, say they will double their strategic metals use by 1985. With the arms race continuing and no titanium substitute existing, the extraordinary metal is practically guaranteed to rise in the future.

Tungsten. Because of its exceedingly high melting point, this silvery material is used extensively in electric lights,

CHART 8-1

THE STRATEGIC MATERIALS INVESTMENT FIELD SUMMARY

Strategic Material	Standard Unit Size	Packing
Antimony	5 tons	Wooden cases
Beryllium	2,500 kilos	Drums
Cadmium	2 tons	Wooden cases or drums
Chromium	1 ton	Steel drums
Cobalt	250 kilos	Steel drums
Columbium	2 tons	Drums
Germanium	20 kilos	Wooden boxes
Lithium	500 kilos	Watertight containers
Magnesium	5 tons	Shrink wrapped
Manganese	10 tons	Steel drums
Rhodium	20 troy ounces	Steel drums
Silicon	10 tons	Metal boxes or drums
Tantalite	200 pounds	Bags or drums
Titanium	500 kilos	Drums
Tungsten	1 ton	Drums
Vanadium	2 tons	Drums
Zirconium	10 tons	Drums

machine tools, and oil drilling bits. These and new technologically important uses will no doubt carry tungsten's value higher during the decade.

Vanadium. It's a silvery white malleable metal turning up most recently in jet engines and nuclear technology. Major oil and gas pipeline work should also spark new demand. If Reagan and the Republicans ever make nuclear energy acceptable again, the metal should take off. Vanadium should react well to government stockpiling.

Zirconium. This one's a metallic element and fairly abundant, more so than nickel and copper. It has a wide variety of uses but each one—from tanning agents to deodorants—is so small that its upward price will probably match the inflation rate only. It is also used in nuclear engineering, however, and a new national energy policy, favoring nuclear energy, could boost its upward price potential.

THE STRATEGIC INVESTMENT GAME

If one or more of the strategics sound interesting and you'd like to position yourself in any one of them *directly* (as opposed to buying shares of stock in companies that have strategic resource interests), the first thing you need to do is make a cash deposit with a strategic materials broker who can buy them for you. In most cases your broker will need your cash deposit to cover your intended purchases.

Because of the large lot sizes in strategics, a minimum purchase would be about $5,000 or $10,000. Now you're ready to place your order over the phone or by written instructions.

When you tell your strategic metals broker what you want to buy, he'll inform you of the most recent price of the critical substance you've decided upon. At this point, you can instruct your broker to do one of two things in order to acquire the material at a favorable price: 1) buy "at the market," which is whatever the going price is at the moment, or 2) place a limit order to be filled on a "fill-or-kill" basis. Your fill-or-kill request means that if the order cannot be filled immediately at your limit price or better, it will be canceled. This will prevent you from paying more than a certain predetermined amount.

If and when your order is executed by your broker, he

or you must take *delivery*. Standard delivery of your investment is usually in the form of the material deposited in a warehouse. Don't worry, it's insured by your broker against fire, theft, and other hazards. Or at least it should be—so check with your broker to make sure it is. Don't be surprised if the warehouse is located in Rotterdam (Holland), London, or elsewhere in Europe. (London is the major world trading center for strategics, so delivery and storage are usually nearby. This makes it easier to sell back.) If you wish to take delivery yourself or in another warehouse, in most cases you would be billed for any additional delivery costs. Usually, delivery will take place four to twelve weeks after the trade date. If you want immediate delivery, you may be charged a premium.

After you make your purchase, you'll receive several *documents* relating to the business transacted. Read them over to be sure you understand them. Here's the necessary documentation you should get:

1. *Confirmation of sale*. Issued by your broker, this document confirms the type of material purchased, quantity, minimum grade (quality), purchase price, and commission.

2. *Warehouse receipt*. Issued by the warehouse where your strategic material is stored, this document states the amount and type of material being held.

3. *Sampling certificate*. Issued by a warehouse inspector, this documents his sight inspection and his weighing of your strategic material in the warehouse.

4. *Assayer's report*. Issued by an assayer, this document shows your strategic material's exact chemical composition. It's based on a chemical analysis of the material stored in the warehouse. (The assayer's report and sampling certificate are often included on one document.)

STRATEGIC CHARGES

We just saw what you'll *get*. Here's what you'll *pay:*

1. *Cost of strategic material purchased*. This cost will be billed to your account based on the price per standard unit size of the material you ordered. Note that according to generally accepted industry procedures, your account may be subsequently debited or credited for small variances (up to about 2 percent) in the actual amount of the material

delivered. If you buy a material contained in alloy, oxide, or ore, you pay the quoted price times the percentage of the pure material contained in the alloy, oxide, or ore.

2. *Commission.* Your broker will, of course, charge a sales commission, which usually runs in the $100 to $200 range.

3. *Delivery charge.* Warehouses charge for acceptance of your strategic material and for setting it aside with your "name" on it. The charge, which varies according to the number of units and type of material you buy, usually runs about $50 or $75 per unit. It's usually paid by your broker, then billed by him to you.

4. *Sampling charge.* Charged by the warehouse inspector for his sampling inspection, the inspector's charge varies with the amount of material he inspects. Usually it will not exceed $100 per unit. It's paid by your broker, who will pass the charge along to you.

5. *Assaying charge.* Charged by the assayer for his chemical analysis of your strategic material, it varies with what he's looking for. This charge, which is also passed on from your broker to you, usually runs about $150 per unit.

6. *Storage and insurance charges.* Since your strategic material is held at the warehouse, you must pay to have it stored and insured. You can pay these charges in local currency yourself or let your broker handle it, for which he will bill you a monthly "maintenance fee" of about 0.25 percent (one quarter of one percent) of the cost of the strategic material you purchased. You will probably save some money, however, paying the storage and insurance charges directly. Ask your broker about it and he'll tell you how much it will cost and how to pay it.

WHEN TO SELL

Strategic resources are a long-term-hold type of investment. Over the years they should rise significantly faster than the inflation rate.

The market is relatively new, however, and strategic investments are much less liquid than investments in other tangibles such as gold and silver. Certainly you can liquidate your strategics within hours at your option; it's just that if you have to sell in a hurry, you might not get the best price possible—that is, you may have to take a loss.

With this in mind be aware that strategic resource investments are not proper vehicles for in-and-out short-termers, unless, of course, you and your broker follow the market daily. Strategics are not generally for short-term trading because of light trading volume on the strategic exchanges. As such, the market is often very "emotional," often subject to temporary highs and lows. The longer your holding period the more of these inevitable air pockets in the market you will avoid and the greater time your metals will have to appreciate.

So approach the strategics with a long-term perspective: try to hold on for three to five years to give your natural resources time to mature financially. You don't want to buy and sell too often.

Now, with your long-term perspective firmly in mind, note these best times for strategic resource liquidation: 1) at a peak period of high economic activity when demand for your strategic material is usually strong—such a period is characterized by booming business and a general feeling of economic prosperity, or 2) at the peak of a crisis, such as war or supply shortage, when the price of your strategic material has been bid up to unreasonably high levels. (You can always buy back when things quiet down.)

If you follow the buying, holding, and selling rules we've outlined, you should indeed do well, even prosper, by owning any one of a number of strategic resources—the prizes fit for the winners of the worldwide resources war that began with the oil crisis in the 1970s.

9. INVESTOR'S DELIGHT?

THE DISAPPEARING BOND TRICK

Okay, so you're sophisticated. No branch of the Bank of Inflationland for you. You own bonds.

If you feel warm and cozy when you think of bonds, you're probably like most other people. Most of us learned at Grandpa's knee that bonds were riskless, ideal for those who presumably knew little about money.

The rationale was simple. Bonds were supposedly the most secure and conservative investments we could make, Grandpa told us, because they were "senior" securities. This means that bond interest was paid before stock dividends in the event the company fell on hard times and couldn't fund both.

Times have since changed, however; bonds are still senior securities, but not quite as safe in times of rising inflation. To understand why, you really have to understand exactly what a bond is.

A bond is simply an IOU written by a borrowing corporation or government body: "IOU, Investor, $1,000, signed The Corporation." That's a bond. You lend your money and receive an IOU from the borrower, The Corporation. Your IOU is called a bond, because it legally binds the borrower to repay you, the lender.

That's what a bond is. Now let's see how you are supposed to profit. Generally, you buy a bond in a $1,000 denomination. If you buy a bond the day the borrowing corporation or government body first issues it, then redeem it, say, twenty years later at maturity, you will have received regular interest payments. Usually, you collect

120 MONEYSMARTS

your interest income by detaching and redeeming the interest-bearing coupons that are attached to your bond.

In addition, the corporation or government body that issued the bond will repay you the $1,000 face value when the bond "matures." (Bond maturity is the same as the IOU repayment date.)

Now we enter Inflationland.

Now the bond evaporation begins.

We're falling into essentially the same wealth trap with bonds as we do when we put our money in the bank. We receive interest payments several times a year, of course. But these fixed interest payments buy less and less every time we stop at a checkout counter. With consumer prices rising at double-digit levels, your bonds must yield those same double digits for you simply to maintain your present economic comfort level.

If you check your bonds—corporate, government, and municipals—you'll probably find that the interest rates you're receiving are lower than the current inflation rate. This means your living standard and net worth are decreasing through inflation rather than increasing as you had originally been led to believe when you bought or inherited the bonds.

The main point to remember here is that we can't raise our comfort levels or even maintain our current living standards with bonds—unless our bond portfolio pays a rate of interest that *exceeds* the inflation rate.

But that's not the end of it.

The second trouble with bonds is that if you want to cash one in for a car, vacation, or cosmetic surgery before maturity (not yours, the bond's), you might not be able to get all your money out. Financial Houdinis call this the "disappearing bond trick."

You've probably experienced this sort of black magic already. You bought or inherited a $1,000 bond yielding 7 percent interest. You or your rich relative paid normal face value, $1,000, to receive 7 percent interest or $70 interest every year. But then inflation burst on the scene and doubled bond interest rates from 7 percent to 14 percent, just as it doubled the price of a hamburger from 70¢ to $1.40. (This "interest rate" is simply the "price" of borrowing money.) The point is, with the current rate of interest inflated to 14 percent, you wouldn't be able to sell your $1,000 bond for $1,000—you'd have to sell it for $500!

The reason your bond's value dropped from $1,000 to $500 is that investors who want to buy bonds would rather buy the newer 14 percent bonds yielding $140 a year instead of your 7 percent bond. Therefore, you would have to offer your bond at *half price*—$500. Because at $500 the $70 interest a year your bond paid would yield a 14 percent return on the $500 invested ($70 is 14 percent of $500), the same inflated 14 percent investors could now get on the newer 14 percent bonds.

Tricky as the bond act is, the basic rule to remember is that interest rates rise with inflation, and as this happens, the market value of your bonds plummets. You lose a good part of your wealth to inflation automatically.

Inflation robs you whether you hang on for years or sell tomorrow. If you want to cash in *before* the bond matures, you will have to do so at a loss. If you need the money to buy something, you may have to go without. If you hold on *until* your bond matures, prices will have risen and you probably won't be able to afford what you wanted either. It's the same buy-less-go-without dilemma we face when we keep our savings in the bank, then take them out expecting to be richer. But only your bonds can actually disappear. Remember: don't own bonds during a period of rising interest rates. You can only lose.

THE SEESAW GAME

RULE: Since bonds lose value when interest rates in the economy rise, you should own them only after interest rates have reached a peak and are heading down. This way you take advantage of peaking rates and, incidentally, other people's disappearing bonds.

The money-making principle is exactly as we have seen. As rising rates of interest make bonds grow smaller, diminishing interest rates make them grow larger. It's merely the disappearing bond trick in reverse.

It's like riding a seesaw. Interest rates go down, driving bond prices up. Then, interest rates come up and bond prices go down.

Once you take the time to learn the motions, the potential for profit will be yours for the taking. The average person still thinks of bonds as very conservative vehicles that are purchased at an early age, held for the better part of your years, then redeemed at par. But now you know the better bond game. The modern way to own bonds is not for life.

GO DEEP

Given a nice long bull market, bonds can really go a distance. Even during a brief bull market some bonds can go a long way.

First of all, a bond's potential depends on its remaining life. Besides this, any individual bond's potential is also determined by the bond's "coupon" rate (coupon rate is the interest the bond pays as a percent of its face amount). The bond buyer's rule for the biggest profits is: the *longer* your bond has to live before it's redeemed by its issuer and the *lower* its coupon rate, the more its price can be thrust upward in response to interest rates on their way down.

To get an idea of the profit potential, just think of that $1,000 bond that lost half its value when interest rates shot up from 7 to 14 percent. The trick is, of course, to *buy* that bond for $500—in other words, to buy into a "deep discount" or disappearing bond by taking such a disappearing bond off someone else's hands as general interest rates are about to peak. Then as interest rates decline, your bond will rise. You can double your money.

Fortunately, there *is* an element of conservatism about bonds that makes doing this all the more rewarding. You don't have the sticky problem you have with the stock market in choosing the right performer in a rising market. Even in bull markets, some individual stocks are stubborn and will move against the strong upward current. This is usually not the case with bonds, however. In general, nearly all of the deep discount financial movers go and come in the same direction.

Of course, make sure not to get stuck with a bond that has a deteriorating credit rating. All you really have to do to profit in bonds—besides knowing which way the general interest rates in the economy are going—is to buy into just about *any healthy* company. Any intelligent broker or banker can help you out.

Keep an eye on interest rates yourself. The rate you will

be watching out for, in newspapers, on radio, and on television, is the *long*-term bond rate. Ninety-nine times out of one hundred it moves up and down with the prime rate, which nearly everyone follows these days. You *don't* even have to watch the interest rate situation *daily*. Just watch the long-term trend, over, say, the past three months.

If you're too busy to be concerned with interest rate movements and trendlines, just ask your broker or banker which way they're headed; and if he or she can't steer you in the correct bond direction, switch to someone who can.

Above all, remember the rule of bonds for big profits: buy at a deep discount when interest rates in the economy are peaking and are about to turn down, ride your bond's price up when the economy's general interest rate is going down, then sell when interest rates are low and your own bond price is high. The easiest way to accomplish this is to ask your broker or banker for deep discount bonds.

10. MAGIC PORTFOLIOS

This is a time of wealth renewal, a time to move into some of the tangibles you instinctively want to own. Gold, silver, diamonds, gemstones, art, antiques, and the strategics will be to the eighties what IBM, Xerox, and Polaroid were to the sixties. All of the Magic Assets (with the exception of the strategics, which are a more recent phenomenon) have earned their reputation as wealth multipliers throughout history. If you buy them according to the guidelines here, they will increase your wealth for years to come.

Common stocks are also important. Stocks are the Sleeping Beauties which will replace gold in your portfolio to multiply your worth when the inflation rate decelerates. Together these components of the Dollar Diversification formula will insure your financial safety in the years ahead.

We saw in the previous chapter how to use deep discount bonds to your advantage. As with gold and stocks, you have to know when to own bonds.

SUIT YOURSELF

Like any other recipe, the inflation-beating ingredients of our Dollar Diversification technique should be combined in appropriate amounts and correct proportion to bring *you* peace of mind through the inflationary wealth crisis as it continues to develop. They must suit *your* individual tastes and preferences, not mine and not your next-door neighbor's. They must capture *your* interest and imagination as they multiply your wealth and bolster your lifestyle.

Because your Magic Asset portfolio is personal, remember that the sample portfolios we will see in this chapter are just that: merely *samples* to give you some idea of the versatility of the Dollar Diversification technique. You will have to adapt them to your own lifestyle unless, of course, after careful consideration you find the portfolios we present to be exactly right for you.

No one can make your Magic Asset decisions for you, because only you can determine what suits you. Only you can take into consideration your short- and long-term objectives, your expertise, your emotions, your interests. You have to create an investment program that fits your way of life and that gives you confidence in your financial situation.

You are your best wealth management advisor. If you don't respond to art or antiques or react to diamonds or colored gemstones, you don't have to utilize them. If you're an avid stock market or gold chartist, you can ignore the other tangibles completely and use your instincts and expertise to your financial advantage in these areas. With Dollar Diversification, there is no requirement to invest in any of the Magic Assets, but only the *choice* to invest as you see fit.

IF YOU NEED STEADY INCOME

One reason you might decide to forgo art and antiques, gems and silver could be if you require steady income from your investments. In this case you should concentrate on high-yielding gold stocks as discussed in Chapter 2, common stocks that pay dividends as discussed in Chapter 3, or bonds as discussed in Chapter 9. We'll also see how to use money market funds to score high yields in the second part of this book.

GETTING YOUR MONEY OUT IN A HURRY

If you're going to have to use some funds on short notice, you would be best off invested in gold, stocks, and silver so you can quickly convert into cash. On the other hand, if you can set aside your funds and forget about them for several years, you can invest in a way of life by favoring diamonds, colored gemstones, art, and antiques.

HOW MUCH TO INVEST

The most important thing you have to do before you start to seek Magic Asset opportunities is to decide upon an appropriate amount to invest. The best way to determine how many dollars' worth of Magic Assets you can acquire is by adding up the current value of your nontangible investment assets. These are the ones now losing purchasing power and draining your wealth: your bank savings and certificates of deposit, and most likely your bonds. This will give you an idea of what must be protected from inflation's invisible hand.

You may not want to invest all of those funds in Magic Assets, so, from this total, subtract the amount of cash you want to keep on hand. We'll see how to earn about twice the going bank interest on this amount of cash you want to keep on hand in Chapter 19, "You Are the Best Cash Captain."

For now, the remaining amount will be what you will invest in the Magic Assets to protect you from inflation and multiply your wealth. This is the amount you have for your Dollar Diversification program.

It is unnecessary to convert all of your dollar denominated holdings into Magic Assets, but the amount you choose to invest will probably come close to one of the sample portfolio *sizes* below. These portfolio sizes break down into eight convenient investment levels:

Portfolio Investment Level	Dollar Amount
Entry	$ 500
Small	$ 1,000
Moderate	$ 5,000
Medium	$ 10,000
Large	$ 20,000
Advanced	$ 50,000
Substantial	$100,000
Institutional	$500,000

Don't worry if the amount you want to invest falls in between two of the investment levels given above. If you have $40,000 worth of bonds and savings you want to convert into Magic Assets, for example, you can double up on the "Large" $20,000 portfolio. Or, if you have $35,000 to invest, you can use the next smaller investment level as a rough guide. This will give you some spare cash to use at your investment discretion.

SAMPLE MAGIC PORTFOLIOS

We have two groups of sample Magic Portfolios: Accelerating Inflation Portfolios and Decelerating Inflation Portfolios. We use the Accelerating Inflation Portfolios when the inflation rate is accelerating. We will use the Decelerating Inflation Portfolios when the inflation rate is decelerating. The Dollar Diversification technique is as simple as this.

THE ACCELERATION/DECELERATION ADJUSTMENT

Your Magic Asset portfolio will be different when inflation is accelerating than when it's decelerating. When dollar erosion is rampant during accelerating inflation, your focus will be on gold. As inflation reaches its top speed, then begins to decelerate, you sell your gold as soon as possible to buy stocks. (Remember, those who sold gold during the first quarter of 1980 just as inflation peaked at 18 percent made a bundle.)

Everything else—diamonds, gems, art, and antique investments—may remain intact because they will rise over the long term in periods of accelerating or decelerating inflation.

Contrast, for example, the $10,000 (medium) Accelerating Inflation Portfolio with the $10,000 Decelerating Inflation Portfolio. When inflation is accelerating, $3,000 would go into gold and only $1,000 into stocks. When the inflation rate is decelerating, only $1,000 goes into gold and $3,000 into stocks.

We have already seen the logic. In Chapter 2, we concluded that gold rises with accelerating inflation as large international interests cash in dollars and stock up on gold

MODEL ACCELERATING INFLATION PORTFOLIOS

Investment Assets	Entry	Small	Moderate	Medium	Large	Advanced	Substantial	Institutional
Gold	$500	$1,000	$5,000	$10,000	$20,000	$50,000	$100,000	$500,000
	$500	$1,000	$2,000	$3,000	$ 6,000	$10,000	$ 20,000	$100,000
Diamonds	—	—	—	—	—	$15,000	$ 30,000	$150,000
Colored Gemstones	—	—	$1,000	$2,000	$ 4,000	$ 5,000	$ 10,000	$ 50,000
Art/Antiques	—	—	$1,000	$3,000	$ 6,000	$10,000	$ 20,000	$100,000
Silver	—	—	$1,000	$1,000	$ 2,000	$ 5,000	$ 10,000	$ 50,000
Stocks	—	—	—	$1,000	$ 2,000	$ 5,000	$ 10,000	$ 50,000
Total of Investments	$500	$1,000	$5,000	$10,000	$20,000	$50,000	$100,000	$500,000

First find the most appropriate size portfolio for you. Read down the column headed by your chosen portfolio size, and notice the amount of money allocated to each of the Magic Assets. Use this sample portfolio as a rough guide when the inflation rate is accelerating.

MODEL DECELERATING INFLATION PORTFOLIOS

Investment Assets	Entry	Small	Moderate	Medium	Large	Advanced	Substantial	Institutional
	$500	$1,000	$5,000	$10,000	$20,000	$50,000	$100,000	$500,000
Gold	—	—	—	$ 1,000	$ 2,000	$ 5,000	$ 10,000	$ 50,000
Diamonds	—	—	—	—	—	$15,000	$ 30,000	$150,000
Colored Gemstones	—	—	$1,000	$ 2,000	$ 4,000	$ 5,000	$ 10,000	$ 50,000
Art/Antiques	—	—	$1,000	$ 3,000	$ 6,000	$10,000	$ 20,000	$100,000
Silver	—	—	$1,000	$ 1,000	$ 2,000	$ 5,000	$ 10,000	$ 50,000
Stocks	$500	$1,000	$2,000	$ 3,000	$ 6,000	$10,000	$ 20,000	$100,000
Total of Investments	$500	$1,000	$5,000	$10,000	$20,000	$50,000	$100,000	$500,000

Again, find your portfolio size and read down the column to ascertain the amount of money the sample investment program allocates to each of the Magic Assets. Use this sample portfolio as a rough guide when the inflation rate is decelerating. Remember, these sample portfolios are guides. You must adapt them to your own lifestyle.

130 MONEYSMARTS

to prevent loss of dollar purchasing power. In Chapter 3 we concluded that stocks rise with falling inflation, just as the country comes out of recession. Gold and stocks are therefore "inverse" investments. Your investment *emphasis* is on one *or* the other.

HOW TO TELL WHETHER INFLATION IS ACCELERATING OR DECELERATING

Because we emphasize *gold* when inflation is accelerating and *stocks* when inflation is decelerating, we have to understand when inflation is accelerating and when it is decelerating.

The consumer price index is the most convenient indicator of inflation we have. You should note the monthly increases in the CPI as they are published in newspapers and magazines or broadcast on television and radio. Look for the trend over the previous three months. If the inflation rate, as evidenced by the CPI, is getting worse, this means inflation is accelerating. If the inflation rate is going down, then inflation is decelerating.

Better yet, monitor the wholesale price index (WPI) published monthly in the business section of most newspapers. The WPI serves as a distant early warning of erosion of dollar value and acts as a crystal ball. You learn to notice changes in the direction of the inflation rate before they actually happen. You can therefore act before others; having acted first, you will profit the most.

You can also monitor inflation by reading any of a number of daily or weekly business journals which are, incidentally, tax deductible. The *Wall Street Journal*, the most widely read business daily, is an excellent place to begin and is really not as fearsome reading as one might believe. More important, reading the feature articles on the front and back pages should give you some insight into where inflation is headed and what to do with your money. *Business Week* and *Forbes*, while admittedly not as exciting as *Newsweek, Time,* or *People,* can also clue you in to where the inflation rate is headed.

If, for instance, you read that Congress is about to pass a constitutional amendment to balance the budget, you know you had better sell gold fast and get into stocks. On the other hand, if through your reading you continue to believe

MAGIC PORTFOLIOS 131

military spending will add increasing billions to the federal deficit, you know inflation will be fueled as the government prints extra money to fund new defense projects.

Always try to *anticipate* the news. This way you will act before others, which means you will be getting in on the ground floor of both gold and stock market moves. There is an old saying on Wall Street, "Buy on the rumor, sell on the news." The point is to anticipate and to act *first*.

ACCELERATION/DECELERATION SUMMARY

You have to adjust your portfolio when you sense the inflation rate is about to switch direction, that is: 1) when the inflation rate is about to accelerate during a period when it has been decelerating, or 2) when the inflation rate begins to decelerate during a period when it has been accelerating.

In the first case, when inflation begins to accelerate, you will liquidate a portion of your stocks and buy gold.

In the second case, when the general inflation rate begins to decelerate, liquidate a portion of gold to buy stocks. The reason for these adjustments cannot be overemphasized:

1. In the first case, *gold rises with rising inflation*.
2. In the second case, *stocks rise with falling inflation*.

This is the way to diversification flexibility. You will never be caught off-guard.

BONDS

Try not to feel too warm and cozy when you think of bonds. Bonds can be helpful but are really not a necessary ingredient in the Magic Asset portfolio because in the past they have rarely outdistanced inflation.

If you want to use bonds, however, use them for both income *and* monetary appreciation. Buy a bond only when it yields higher than the current inflation rate. And remember the seesaw game (discussed at length in Chapter 9) for getting a good profit on the sale of a bond: buy a deep discount bond, collect inflation-beating interest, then sell after interest rates have declined and your bond's value has automatically increased. This way you'll have outdistanced inflation with high interest *and* generated capital appreciation on your bonds as well.

The easiest way to accomplish all this is to ask your

broker or banker for a deep discount bond with good potential. If your broker or banker hesitates at all to help out, find another one; there are plenty to choose from.

Bond concepts aren't the easiest things in the world for beginners to grasp. This is understandable. If you feel you still have trouble understanding when to buy, how long to hold, and when to sell bonds, go back and reread Chapter 9. It's all really very simple once you digest the whole picture. And once you understand how bonds work, you'll never be caught with disappearing or impotent IOUs again.

STRATEGICS

Since strategic and critical materials have not served as Magic Assets throughout history, but are rather more recent investment phenomena, we have not included them in the sample portfolios. This doesn't mean you shouldn't own them, rather that as newer and unproven financial vehicles compared with the others, they may carry additional risk.

Don't invest more than 10 percent of your investment funds in strategics. If you're going to buy strategics, buy them during a recession. This is when demand for these resources is at a cyclical low. It's the time when they will be reasonably priced.

Once you own them, wait for the economy and inflation to carry them up. In other words, hold on until the economy is racing ahead at full steam, or, of course, a time of economic crisis, such as a shortage of the strategic material you own. That's the time you'll want to get out with profits.

AGAIN, DIAMONDS ARE FOREVER

Diamonds are forever, but they aren't for everyone. Only those portfolios in the $50,000-plus category can comfortably diversify into diamonds.

As detailed in Chapter 5, if you are going to rely on an investment-grade diamond to outpace inflation, that diamond must be absolutely flawless or nearly so. These diamonds are legendarily expensive, generally beginning in the $10,000 to $20,000 range. An investment diamond ties up too much capital for the $20,000-and-under portfolios.

One emerging phenomenon in the diamond investment

field, however, is the development of syndicates comprised of individual investors who have joined together to buy an investment diamond. Such groups are somewhat like investment clubs or real estate partnerships, but are usually composed of family members. You could consider doing this.

Fortunately, there are also a wide variety of high quality, colored gemstones that fit the under-$50,000 portfolios.

BUILDING FOR THE FUTURE

It's quite possible that you expect to be able to convert more inflationary money into Magic Assets for your Dollar Diversification program within the next year or two. If that's the case, there are two basic ways you can build your portfolio:

1. Use a program appropriate to the amount you have now. As you receive more funds to invest, add to each of the investments to bring them up to proportions appropriate to a larger-size budget.

2. Assume you have the extra assets you expect to be able to use later, and establish your program now based on the assets you expect to have in the future. Number the Magic Assets in order of personal priority. Begin with the most important one and add the other investments as the funds become available. (This is a good way for those with a $20,000 portfolio to own an investment diamond.)

Your ultimate objective is to create a stockpile of assets that allows you to feel comfortable about your own future, knowing that you're protected against lost purchasing power and erosion of wealth, and that you've created a lifestyle you enjoy by acting upon wealth-multiplying opportunities you think are best for you.

PART TWO

THE WINNING LIFESTYLE

11. BARTERING, BARGAINING, AND BORROWING

THE CASHLESS CARRY

A good way to beat today's stiff price situation and develop some interesting relationships is to get into *bartering*. Barter is simply the act of exchanging goods or services without using money. In other words, you give something in order to get something in return.

Barter is one of the oldest forms of exchanging goods for services. Cavepeople bartered. The Greeks bartered. The Romans bartered. People bartered during the Renaissance and during the great German inflation. Today it is estimated that 8 million Americans practice some form of barter.

The most popular type of barter is the "swap"—a direct trade between two people. Cindi Tiger, a young, long-haired, blue-eyed, unemployed actress, doesn't have a car or much money. In Los Angeles, this is extremely inconvenient. But she knows the right people in Hollywood. She has access to all the private screenings of the soon-to-be-released major motion pictures. So she invites friends and acquaintances to screenings in exchange for transportation around L.A. This is barter. There's no need for money.

Most of us have swapped for something we wanted at one time or another. Maybe we've exchanged something for someone else's time and expertise, saying, in effect, "I'll do this for you and you can teach me so and so."

Marathon running tips, tennis lessons, and the like fall into this category of barter. Maybe it was a luxury item we exchanged because we would have felt guilty paying money—a mink coat for a friend's or relative's aquamarine ring, for example. Or it might be that we've needed something and a swap was the only way to obtain it, a summer place on the beach in exchange for flying instruction, perhaps. Or maybe someone made us a once-in-a-lifetime offer and we didn't want to pass it up—Mick Jagger tickets for something special in return.

Let's say you want to swap. How do you go about accomplishing this personalized and mutually beneficial deal? Although you can advertise your idea in swap columns or pin up notices at your local supermarket or copy center (explaining what you have and what you want), the very best way to find out if someone will swap with you is to ask the people with whom you interact every day.

One woman had always paid her psychologist in cash. But when she and her husband went their separate ways, she had much less cash on hand, and after summoning her courage, asked the doctor if he was interested in seeing any of her ceramics for a possible trade. At first the psychologist was stunned, but he quickly regained his composure to say yes. As it turned out, the woman hit her doctor's nail on the head. He was a gourmet cook who had been searching unsuccessfully for a set of special Chinese covered dishes. Although none of the pieces on hand pleased the doctor, she could easily design and make what he needed and in this way pay her doctor's fees for a year. The doctor got what he needed, saved time shopping and money on sales tax.

In structuring a deal such as this, and for barter deals in general, it is important to remember the simple parity rule of barter: parity between the bargaining parties is essential. In other words, it is important that the exchange be equal in value. But this does not necessarily have to be measured in terms of cash for cash equivalence. As long as both parties to the deal come to an agreement in advance, you have met the parity rule.

When lawyers trade with lawyers or artists with artists, it is fairly easy to assess equivalent values in advance. Here, the same criterion might apply to each other's work: one hour's legal or art work for another. But how do photographers and carpenters, for example, work out their equivalent values, or lawyers and gardeners?

There are three easy ways to ensure the parity rule is followed to establish a fair deal. Take your choice as to which you want to use on a case-by-case approach:

1. *Fair market value method.* Assign *fair market value* to what you want to trade, then trade items or services of *equal* fair market value.

2. *Equal time method.* Follow the rule *equal time equals equal worth.*

3. *Intuitive method.* Trust your intuition and make a deal with which you feel comfortable.

The fair market value method. The obvious method of computing what something is worth is to determine the regular *fair market value* of one's work or item to be traded and apply it directly to the trade. A fashion photographer in Boston reports, for instance, that she and her carpenter computed their services at the going rates in their city. The skilled carpenter worked at $20 an hour, threw in materials at his own cost, in return for a beautiful set of photos of his children that would otherwise have cost him $85. Most people feel comfortable with this method. The value of what each party gives and gets is easy to see and conforms to everyday business experience.

Besides trading services under this method of barter, you can also trade objects for objects, or objects for services. It is here, particularly for larger trades, that your diamonds and colored gemstones can come in handy. When trading your precious gemstones, always try to exchange them based on their fair market *retail* value to ensure you are getting the most for your money. And as long as you paid close to wholesale for them, you will have built a nice profit into your deal.

The equal time method. Many people are inclined to value *everyone's time and labor equally,* regardless of the going market rate. They subscribe to the social philosophy that all human labor is equal. Seth, a Newport Beach lawyer, was active in the human rights movement in both college and law school during the sixties and seventies and has been involved with many statewide legal programs. He now owns a cliff house that he is remodeling in Laguna Beach. Seth and the woman who shares his home believe that all labor should be valued on an equal basis. For them, barter is a way to break down some of the conditioning of modern life. When a Chicano renovator came into Seth's office wanting to file a claim against the state for a job-related injury, Seth swapped his time on an equal-labor-hour basis for a spiral staircase and sunroof. Seth's new friend was pleased his work was so highly valued; Seth felt he struck a bargain since he was not expert enough to do the construction himself. Nor was it something for which he wanted to pay cash.

The intuitive method. Still other people, like Miss Ichiebon in Chicago, who owns an antique clothing shop, determine parity *intuitively*. She likes to keep the swapping process natural and fluid. When Miss Ichiebon traded an Oriental kimono to have her portrait painted by an artist friend to send to her mother in Japan, it turned out to be a large mixed media work predominantly in oil and it had taken more time than her artist friend had anticipated. Miss Ichiebon felt that the red and black silk kimono she had traded was inadequate payment for so much of his time. So she gave the artist an open-ended $300 credit in her shop. She likes swaps to be flexible and spontaneous and to preserve relationships.

Are there any pitfalls to swapping? Sure. Many enthusiastic *swappers* are so pleased with barter as a way of life that they sometimes forget to earn enough cash to pay their weekly bills. When a young schoolteacher from Jackson Hole, Wyoming, moved there from the Bronx, he was so infatuated with his new lifestyle that he swapped for nearly everything—until he looked around and realized he didn't need that many cows and egg-laying chickens, but he did need more cash on hand for everyday bills. Now he's learned to swap for only what he needs.

Modern-day swapping is still a relatively new activity. Here are three general guidelines to aid you:

1. Check for opportunities in swap columns and posted announcements. A national newspaper, *Barter Communique,* can keep you current (see Chapter 24 for details). But more important, if you want to trade with someone, be direct. Ask.

2. Be precise in stating your expectations. What each gives and what each receives are vital quantities in striking your deal.

3. Agree on a fair evaluation of each other's goods and services so both people gain. The objective of your negotiation should be mutual satisfaction.

Above all, enjoy the interaction inherent in trading. In all likelihood it will probably take more time finding just the right barter deal than buying retail. But by bartering you don't pay extra for middlemen or tax. Once you begin to "cashless carry," you'll no doubt see opportunities everywhere. Without batting an eyelash you'll ask grocers, shopowners, doctors, innkeepers if they want to make a deal. Good trading!

"MONEY TALKS, NOBODY WALKS"

The art of *bargaining,* like the art of bartering, is now practiced by millions of people. Along with bartering, bargaining can be a key to beating the national price spiral. Bargaining is easy. You just have to know when and where you can bargain and how to go about it.

Comparison shopping opens the door, so be a comparison shopper. Once you know what the current prices are for the item you want to buy, you can try to influence your neighborhood merchant, no matter how big or small, to meet or beat the competition. You've probably been comparison shopping for years. If you've ever looked for a car, appliance, or stereo, you already know to go to several dealers to see what each offers. But you can also do this with other items as well—everything from suede jackets to bicycles. Always try to let one dealer know if another is offering you a better price, until you find the place that gives you the most product for your money.

Besides bargaining for the product itself, you should bargain as well for the best credit, delivery, and service terms. These extras can really raise your comfort level in life. Aftersale services can save you money, particularly if you are buying a car, dishwasher, or other electromechanical product.

But these aren't the only extras. More often than not it's easier for your seller to agree to certain bonuses than a discounted price. For example, an extra accessory, free clothing alterations, or free flower or plant delivery all can be just as valuable as simply a lower price.

Besides comparison shopping you can also negotiate a

better price on many items by offering to pay cash. This is an advantage to your seller as he can immediately convert your cash to more inventory and therefore more profit. So if your seller won't meet his competition, perhaps because he's giving you better delivery or service or free alterations anyway, pull out your green and start negotiating.

Buying goods in quantity, cases not boxes of food, for example, can also save you money. You'd be surprised how much you can save, especially at some of the new discount supermarkets. You can also bargain for goods off-season—an air conditioner in December, for example, or a fur coat in July.

Watch out for discount stores. Presumably you can't bargain there since the ticket prices are already lower than those of other retailers. But it's usually worth a try, especially in certain segments of the market, electronics, for example, where competitive pressures are keen.

The same is true in most department stores where prices are considered "firm." You usually can't bargain, but there are exceptions. Sometimes you'll be successful negotiating a lower "as is" price on a floor sample or a discontinued item, or on an item that is slightly shopworn or imperfect. So never rule out discount or department stores.

While bargaining is one of the oldest arts practiced, like bartering it too has only recently grown into a national pastime. These are the basic bargaining rules:

1. Be positive about what you want to buy. Some successful negotiating openers might be: "It's just what I want, but it's beyond my budget. Can you do better on the price?" or "I love it. Is it going on sale soon?"

2. Be discreet. Don't let everyone in the store know what's happening. Try not to negotiate within earshot of other customers. This may force the salesperson to defend the original price for fear of having to give everyone discounts.

3. Be reasonable. Give the seller a way to save face by presenting a rational case for a lower price to him or her. You can always rely on scratches, dents, mismatched or off colors, as well as floor samples and discontinued items to help the bargaining process along.

4. Be respectful. Don't antagonize the salesperson by belittling the merchandise or ridiculing the price. Remem-

ber, be positive because you can't bargain with someone you've antagonized—even if you are right on the facts.

5. Make sure you're dealing with someone who has the authority to make a concession—the store owner or a manager.

Once you put these rules into practice you'll find that negotiating a better price is often a matter of being at the right place at the right time, that is, finding a retailer who is ready to sell at a lower price to make an immediate sale. But more often it will be the direct result of your ability to persuade the person in charge to give you a better deal. You won't be successful every time, but you'll certainly become good at bargaining and save a bundle trying.

WHEN DEBT PAYS

The idea of running into a small and sensible amount of debt to outdistance inflation is now well accepted during certain economic circumstances. One financial expert after another has been suggesting that planned debt is a kind of thrift. The rationale is: when prices of the items you want to own are increasing sharply, it's ridiculous for you *not* to try to beat the price spiral by borrowing the money to buy now—if you can borrow at a good rate.

Drop your inhibitions about debts and about what is prudent. Today's world of inflation makes money matters different. If you can borrow now at an interest rate that is lower than the inflation rate it will be to your advantage to go into debt. Figure it like this: if your interest expense on the borrowed money will be *smaller* than the increase in the product's price from now until the time you can afford to buy it, then it is logical to borrow and buy now. And when you realize that not only inflation but the tax laws often favor the borrower, the borrowing-spending habit becomes all the more inviting.

Let's take a case study. Consider the young couple who have their hearts set on a $300 stereo. (Of course, they have bargained it down from $500 after barter has failed.) If they save $25 a month, they will have the $300 at the end of a year. At a 6 percent passbook savings rate, compounded quarterly, they will have earned about $10 in interest. If this working couple is in a 36 percent federal tax bracket, they will owe about $4 in federal taxes—having earned this interest—leaving $6 net interest after the tax bill is subtracted. In the meantime, the price of the stereo will have risen to $345, assuming 15 percent stereo inflation. So, the couple will have lost $345 minus $300, or $45, less the $6 interest, or $39 by waiting to save for the stereo—and they'll have had to spend the year listening to their tiny clock-radio.

But what if the couple gets a smart $300 cash advance on their favorite credit card and buys the stereo at their local Tech Hi-Fi store immediately? If, for example, they have to pay 12 percent interest on the advance, their total interest cost at year's end when they pay off their debt will be $36, which is lower than the expected increase in the cost of the stereo. So figuring it this way the consumers stand to benefit by $9.

By borrowing, the couple has avoided the price increase on the $300 stereo, and scores a net benefit equal to $9. But there's still more to be gained. If they itemize their deductions on their tax return they'll get an additional tax benefit. They can deduct the $36 interest expense for tax purposes. Since they are in the 36 percent income tax bracket the $36 interest expense will save them another $13 ($36 times 36 percent) for tax purposes. That's still not all. They'll be able to dance in front of their new system for an extra year.

So remember when the simple "debt pays" rule applies: debt pays when the interest expense on the debt will be less than the price inflation of the item you plan to buy.

12. OUTSMARTING OPEC

When the gasoline crunch flares up, you sleep in your car or rise with the sun to get near the front of a line at the gas station. People are very imaginative in attempting to beat the system. One woman feigns pregnancy with the aid of pillows to win her way to the front of the line. Others use their charm. Still others are less creative. Some threaten physical violence and in a few cases a fistfight actually erupts. One short-tempered motorist at a station in Sacramento was critically wounded by gunfire during one panic. A driver in Denver forced a station attendant at gunpoint to sell him $10 of gasoline despite a $5 limit during another panic. Police reported stabbings at gas stations in San Francisco and New York as tempers ran hot and tanks low.

But the energy crisis goes further than gasoline panic. Sometimes we can't get enough oil to heat our homes in the winter and cool them in the summer. And we're asked to voluntarily freeze—or sweat.

Since 1973, our confidence has been shaken by one energy catastrophe after another—natural gas shortages, a major coal strike, the meltdown at Three Mile Island. And on a larger scale—OPEC.

Middle Eastern political instability in particular has shown that Americans can no longer be sure from season to season how much imported oil—which is our major source of energy as we can see in Chart 12-1—will be available. Nor do we have any idea about oil's potential price. For all we know it could zoom up another $10 a barrel within the year.

As the Shah was being ousted in Iran, we saw a stoppage of Iranian production followed by a partial recovery and then another stoppage and embargo along with the Hostage Crisis. We have seen variations in Saudi Arabian production as large as a million barrels a day. The only thing we know for certain is that OPEC production is volatile, the price of oil is skyrocketing, and periodic fuel shortages make themselves felt.

We don't know how long our energy-wasteful lifestyles will depend upon OPEC oil. Reliable sources predict that OPEC will be with us for some time, perhaps fifty or seventy-five years, and new and far worse crises will develop. According to Saudi Arabian oil minister Ahmed Zaki Yamani, future shortages could make past energy shortages seem like "mere passing events of trivial consequence."

The petrosqueeze, grave as any crisis we have faced since the Vietnam war, presents a dilemma of such scope and complexity that it is beginning to take the wind out of our sails of affluence. In many sectors of the economy it has already forced changes in the American lifestyle and

CHART 12-1

U.S. ENERGY CONSUMPTION, 1977

Source	Percentage of Total	Quantity in Units Commonly Used for Each Source	Millions of Barrels Per Day of Oil Equivalent
Oil	50%	18.4 million barrels per day	18.4
Natural Gas	25	19.2 trillion cubic feet per year	9.2
Coal	18	625 million tons per year	6.7
Nuclear	4	251 kilowatt hours per year	1.3
Hydro	3	230 billion kilowatt hours per year	1.1
TOTAL	100%		36.7

Source: Department of Energy.

undermined national confidence. Yet for all the commotion we make about our energy future, we Americans have taken few steps to ameliorate the energy crisis that threatens our way of life.

GET TOUGH, AMERICA

In our reluctance to come to grips with energy gluttony we have already paid a king's ransom. For a decade, we have stood by while the price at the gas pumps has soared by dimes and quarters from forty cents per gallon in the early seventies. Moreover, we have watched our country's bill for foreign oil increase from $1.3 billion to $60 billion. Meekly, we have accepted this massive annual OPEC oil tax on our purchasing power; an oil tax that spreads inflation and cripples American confidence and prosperity.

If as individuals we do not begin taking advantage of a whole host of energy media we have at our disposal—for travel, heat, light, air conditioning—our dependence on OPEC oil will stunt our affluence for decades to come. Moreover, the economy will be plagued by chronic double-digit inflation as the Middle East sheikdoms exact their unprecedented toll on all of us. Above all, our self-determination and free spirit might erode, possibly pitting one segment of the American economy against another in a terrible age of energy scarcity.

THE LECTRIC LEOPARD

When Benjamin Franklin discovered electricity, little did he realize it might one day be used to help cure the gasoline blues. Imagine your "second" car without a gas tank. Imagine how many of the 100 billion gallons of gasoline could be saved if *everyone's* second car had no gas tank. Imagine how much money on gas you'd save. Imagine these cars also without mufflers and exhaust systems, radiators and cooling systems, spark plugs and carburetor and you quickly get the picture of a gas-free electric automobile.

Twenty-three high-technology car makers in the United States are now manufacturing electric cars according to a national directory published by the *Electric Vehicle News*. Ben Franklin would be proud. With only one moving part in the power plant and a once-a-year check of the motor brushes the only important electrical concern, these new electrical wonders offer you the essence of carefree economical driving. Although most of these manufacturers, including the giants, are still doing experimental work, at least five will now build short-range electric cars to order, or supply kits for you to convert gasoline-burning cars to electricity. Some of these firms are ready to put you in the driver's seat of a fully licensable, battery-powered car in as few as eight days.

Most of the new electric cars don't *look* like electric cars. They are actually electrified conversions of cars built by major U.S. and foreign auto firms. The small companies that manufacture them say it's less expensive to buy existing bodies that meet existing federal safety requirements than to design and build them from scratch.

You save money on the outside through the use of these standard bodies, but on the inside these electric cars are truly a technological innovation. Operating solely on battery power, electric cars produce no air pollution, neither engine noise nor exhaust emission, and require only a fraction of the maintenance of gas-engined autos.

If you're tired of waiting on lines to pay exorbitant gasoline prices, rediscover electricity. Electric cars are easy to operate, and meet all federal safety and Department of Energy standards. Most are attractive. To purchase one, all you have to do is call one of these companies (see also Chapter 24):

Electric Vehicle Associates (216 524-5992) offers a four-passenger car based on an American Motors Pacer Wagon. The standard price is $13,838, and delivery is eight to twelve weeks after an order and deposit are placed. Driving range is estimated at thirty to fifty miles—perfect for trips downtown. Top speed is in excess of 55 mph. Recharge time is ten to twelve hours (overnight) on 110-volt household current, or five to six hours on a 220 circuit.

U.S. Electricar (617 249-2177) says it can have an electrified Renault Le Car, called a Lectric Leopard, ready for you in eight working days. The Leopard comes in four models ranging in price from $7,495 to $8,995, and boasts a range of sixty to eighty miles. Top speed is 55 mph.

Jet Industries (512 385-0660) offers four models primarily as commercial vehicles. They start with a four-passenger mini-van on a Japanese body priced at $8,000. Delivery time is thirty to sixty days. Range is forty to sixty miles and recharge time is eight hours on household current.

Marathon Vehicles (703 280-1717) builds two commercial vans from the ground up—a six-wheeler that sells for $12,500 and a four-wheel C-300 that sells for $6,800.

Electric Passenger Cars and Vans (714 272-8288) is the only U.S. firm that offers an electric hybrid—a battery-powered vehicle that also has a small auxiliary gasoline engine that runs an on-board DC generator. It comes in two models: a Hummingbird Mark IV based on a Ford Pinto, and a Hummingbird van based on a Volkswagen. The car is priced at $11,975 with the hybrid feature and $9,975 without. The van goes for $12,750 with the hybrid and $10,000 without.

SAVE THE TIGER

If you decide to wait for G.M. or Ford to satisfy your every designer desire before you go electric, why not become a gasoholic in the meantime? If you could replace with alcohol 10 percent of all the gasoline you burn up each year, and if everyone did the same, we would save 10 billion gallons of imported oil annually. This is the theory behind gasohol. Moreover, energy economists reveal that gasohol will reduce air pollution and increase your fuel efficiency and gas mileage as well.

Besides saving money on gas, gasohol would increase our dollar purchasing power in other ways. First of all, we would diminish our dependence on OPEC. This would narrow our country's international balance of payments deficit and thereby increase the purchasing power of our dollars vis-à-vis foreign currencies.

Gasohol, a mixture of 10 percent alcohol and 90 percent gasoline, is hardly a new technology. Henry Ford, who introduced the country to gasoline on a large scale, originally promoted a way to help us kick that habit. Perhaps instinctively anticipating the formation of OPEC and the petrosqueeze, Ford promoted the use of gasohol as fuel for his cars as far back as the depression. During the late thirties, in fact, gasohol was used as auto fuel in some parts of the Midwest. But unfortunately it never caught on because it was too expensive to produce. Gasoline was more economical. But today, technology and skyrocketing OPEC prices have changed the economics of auto fuel. After forty-five years gasohol is now being produced again and beginning to trickle through the pumps at ordinary filling stations.

If you're still not sure about trying it, consider how much the country will benefit. As the cost of OPEC oil increases further, the rewards of the new gasohol technology and production will increase. Not only will widespread use of gasohol result in greater dollar purchasing power but greater American energy self-sufficiency as well. Many gasoholics also applaud the new and expanding American farm markets for corn and sugar, the raw commodities used in the production of gasohol. And gasohol production will develop new fuel distribution systems and increase national employment; estimates range as high as $15 billion worth of new distillery work alone.

So next time you're out at the pumps, why not try some gasohol.

SCARSDALE ENERGY DIET

Since World War II, we've lubricated our lives with free-flowing oil. We've grown accustomed to using all the oil we've ever wanted. For years, oil was so cheap that many of us took for granted our mobile, two-car family life. All of us have taken for granted electricity rates so low that the real price adjusted for inflation actually fell during the fifties and sixties.

The unfortunate result of our self-indulgence has been that we Americans as a group are now one of the world's least efficient energy consumers. One thought of skyrocketing fuel costs and our paramount energy question becomes whether we will continue to feed or put on a diet the voracious consumption monster we have created.

Many people see going on an energy diet as curtailment —something un-American. Some see conserving and cutting back as living in the past. Some see conservation as the product of an antigrowth crusade led by a group of "100 percent natural" flower children. This is wrong and, unfortunately, far too much of the language we have heard in recent years, such as one president's insistence on "austerity" and "sacrifice," has strengthened some of the unpleasant and misleading imagery many people have of conserving fuel.

We should think instead in terms of *productive conservation*—conserving money on fuel so we can spend it in more pleasurable ways. Productive conservation promotes energy savings on the roads and in our homes in a manner that is economically and socially beneficial. Productive conservation will also lessen our reliance on oil and free investment capital for production of more desirable forms of wealth through higher levels of employment. Productive conservation is safe for the environment. Here's how we can benefit:

MORE MILES PER GAL

As motorists, we Americans consume one-ninth of all the oil used in the world every day. Or, more accurately, our gas-guzzling cars do. If we could use some of the money we spend on gas for, say, Persian rugs, books, or concert tickets, just think how much more rewarding life would be.

By far the *most* promising area for saving money on auto fuel economy is built-in vehicle efficiency, not driving slow as many would have us believe. As citizens, it's time to tell our Congress to require Detroit to increase fuel efficiency. Fuel-efficient automobiles would probably save each of us hundreds of dollars a year on gas. Congress has passed the Energy Policy and Conservation Act to establish the following fuel economy standards.

Year	*MPG*
1978	18.0
1979	19.0
1980	20.0
1981	27.5

But we can save much more if we each let Congress know we want it to raise auto fuel-efficiency standards far higher —to at least 35 or 40 mpg by 1990. This way we could save about 30 percent on gas bills.

Higher mileage standards are not really as onerous as the manufacturers would have us believe. Volkswagen's diesel Rabbit *already* gets 40 mpg and even higher fuel efficiency is not impossible Technological innovation in automobile materials, engine, and body design is a must. Detroit claims to have the world-class technology in them, so let's put this technology to the test. This will not only lead to improved fuel economy but will also make Detroit more competitive with the energy-conscious Japanese automobile industry. For the first time, Detroit would be positioned to meet the foreign fuel economy challenge. As in using gasohol, competing in the transnational auto market would also strengthen the U.S. balance of payments, which in turn would increase the purchasing power of our dollars.

One way automotive engineers and designers can build in fuel economy is to construct cars light enough to obtain good gas mileage, but still roomy enough to comfortably transport four or five passengers. This can be achieved with lighter materials, such as carbon fiber plastics—graphite reinforced epoxies, in which long filaments of pure carbon are molded with a plastic, providing great strength and light weight—cousins of Fiberglas. These are the materials that are turning up in rockets, satellites, and Boeing 737s. With

CHART 12-2

HOW TO DOUBLE GAS MILEAGE

1979 Ford LTD	Weight in Steel	Weight in Graphite	Weight Savings
Body-in-white	461.0 pounds	208.0 pounds	253.0 pounds
Frame	282.8	207.2	75.6
Front End	96.0	29.3	66.7
Hood	49.0	16.7	32.3
Trunk	42.8	13.9	28.9
Bumpers	123.1	44.4	78.7
Wheels	92.0	49.3	42.7
Doors	155.6	61.1	94.5
Miscellaneous	69.3	35.8	33.5

Source: Ford Motor Co.

the strength of carbon reinforcement, lightweight plastics are beginning to replace aluminum and steel.

An experimental LTD Ford built with carbon fiber wherever possible (see Chart 12-2) weighed one-third less than the same vehicle built with conventional materials. The weight-saving allowed the use of a lighter engine; gas mileage doubled.

There are also other ways Detroit could build fuel economy into cars. The manufacturers could provide us with "free-wheeling" gearing mechanisms. Few cars we drive have gearing mechanisms or setups that enable us to get the most miles per gallon. Most cars now on the road are built so that any time you turn on the motor and start to drive you burn gas. Cars today are built with the engine rigidly connected to the wheels. This means a car must continue to work and waste gas unnecessarily even when going downhill. Engineers in Detroit could save us money by designing a free-wheeling gearing mechanism. Such a device would keep the engine from holding back the car and wasting gas when natural momentum and gravity would otherwise let it roll on its own. So the technology is available. We have to encourage Detroit to use it.

FREE HEAT AND AIR CONDITIONING

About 40 percent of the money we spend on energy in America goes to heat, air condition, light, and provide hot water for our homes, commercial and government buildings. Our homes alone consume 20 percent of all American energy.

In general, the newer the residential or commercial structure you live or work in, the more energy it requires and the more it costs. New York's World Trade Center's twin towers, for example, require as much electrical generating capacity as does all of Schenectady, with more than one hundred thousand residents.

Our hope for the future lies in the fundamental reversal of our present commitment to live and work in sealed buildings with massive plants for manufacturing air and delivering it at predetermined temperatures and velocities. The same applies to bulky lighting apparatus that utilizes a central control in place of individual office switches.

Why not choose instead to work and live in more intelligently designed buildings? A newly planned, unsealed IBM facility at Southfield, Michigan, will use only 51,000 BTUs per square foot, a fifth of what the building might have used had it been erected as a completely sealed office building of the sixties and early seventies. In IBM's case, fuel savings can be passed along to employees in terms of higher salaries and to shareholders in terms of higher dividends.

While the new IBM building's energy consumption drop is dramatic, there is nothing dramatic about how IBM plans to do it: double-glazed windows that open and close, increased insulation, and an abundance of natural lighting.

Some constructions are even more efficient. The twenty-story Ontario Hydro headquarters in Toronto provides warmth entirely by capturing the waste heat given off by lighting, office equipment, and employees.

Similar changes are likely to follow in new residential construction as well. A test house constructed by the Oak Ridge National Laboratory required only 20 percent as much electricity for space heating, cooling, and water heating as would a conventional house. Again, better absorption and reflection of heat, increased insulation, and natural lighting did the job.

The trend toward energy-conscious design is promising, but unlike the auto stock, which rapidly "turns over" and needs constant replenishing, the nation's building supply turns over slowly—at less than 5 percent per year. At this rate it would take twenty years to give the nation's homes and buildings energy efficiency. By that time, OPEC oil could be $1,000 per barrel.

For this reason, now is the time to mount a "retrofit" campaign. Retrofit is something you can take part in yourself. It's simply the upgrading of your home through the insertion of more efficient windows, insulation, thermostats, and other components.

A study conducted by Standard Oil of California showed that with an insulation investment of $981, Portland homeowners could save $245 in energy a year. This was a 25 percent return on the $981 investment, a return of about twice the rate of inflation! The study concluded that similar energy savings are possible in a substantial part of the national housing stock.

Utility companies are now getting into the home improvement act and will give you advice on how you, personally, can save energy. Many will even arrange for local contractors to do the necessary jobs and check to make sure your retrofitting has been properly done.

The Washington Natural Gas Company, serving Puget Sound, for example, began by selling "conservation kits" for attic insulation. The "kit" meant that the company provided and installed the insulation, guaranteed and financed it, all for about $200. The overall reduction in heating energy, 22 percent, was so successful that by November 1977 the utility had sold almost 15,000 such kits, and it estimated that its advertising and promotion created a demand that led to more than an additional 40,000 jobs for *other* insulation contractors. The whole economy benefited. Now the utility sells a more elaborate kit—attic insulation, pilotless natural gas furnace, and automatic day-night thermostat which will reduce heating energy by an estimated 36 percent. So check with your local utility company to see what kind of money you can save in your area. The general belief is that if simple insulation packages such as six-inch ceiling insulation, storm windows and doors, caulking, and weather stripping were installed in the estimated 20 million homes that need them, we could save as a nation on home fuel bills by about 25 percent.

You can also boost your cash flow and save energy dollars in less profound ways. Turn off lights, change temperature settings, and shut down your kitchen motors when not in use. All this can go a long way in saving up for Magic Assets.

Whatever way we save energy—in our cars, at home, or at work—the benefits of putting ourselves on a crash energy diet are clear. We can cut oil imports, lessening our nation's reliance on OPEC. This will reduce the deficit in the balance of trade. Economically speaking, this means we'll have more purchasing power left for ourselves, more capital left for investments. Employment and national prosperity could begin its lift-off.

THE ULTIMATE ENERGIZER

Since the taming of electricity, only scientists, tinkerers, and dreamers have seemed interested in catching the sun's rays for heat and electricity. Now solar energy has been propelled into the mainstream of U.S. energy planning by this nation's ambitious commitment, which aims to generate 20 percent of our heat and electricity from the sun by the year 2000. *Energy Future*, the authoritative report of the Harvard Business School Energy Project, declares our goal—and more—to be attainable.

Many people still think that solar energy is a science of the future, something awaiting a technological breakthrough. This is simply not true. Solar heating is a present-day alternative to OPEC oil and by the turn of the century, according to some estimates, sun rays can replace 3 million barrels of OPEC oil a day.

Of the two major types of solar energy, it is solar heating rather than solar electricity which can be your own most immediate fuel saver. Solar heating, actually an ancient science, represents a return to old world technology. Most societies have had sense enough to incorporate the sun into the design of their architecture for heat. The baths at Pompeii, for example, demonstrate the use the Roman people made of solar energy for heating. Channels carrying water to the baths were built open to the sun and lined with grooves to help heat the water.

Today, a design that manages to capture the sun in a similar way is called "passive" solar heating. Passive solar captures the sun's energy through design techniques without the use of fancy "collectors," plumbing, or pumps. You can easily make use of it.

The next time you consider buying or building a home, why not have the building sited and landscaped to be, in effect, a large solar collector? To capture the sun's rays, it would face south. In winter, its special large double-glazed windows would capture the sun's heat. Its walls would retain the heat at night. This type of system involves only one moving part: the earth moving around the sun.

Another type of solar system you can install in your home involves more than just the sun and the earth. You can now buy heat collectors and other paraphernalia to warm your home. This is called an "active" solar system. For the 1980s, solar heating will make its principal impact in this active form.

Because solar heating is well suited to most new residential and commercial buildings and to about one-third of the nation's 35 million existing dwellings, its potential is quite vast.

You can receive tax credit information, free brochures, and the names of solar installers in your area by calling the National Solar Heating and Cooling Information Center (see Chapter 24 for toll-free phone numbers). The solar companies sell and install solar systems and can tell you how big your long-run cost savings can grow.

GOING SOLAR

When you consider a solar heating investment, you have to look at the percentage return on the purchase price. In other words you want to recoup in a few years the money you spend on installing your solar system; you do this by adding up the dollars saved on fuel costs, as the fuel savings will eventually make up for the purchase price and the cost of installation of your new solar system.

Consider the home economics of a possible solar investment. You pay in the $2,000 range for a passive hot water system for a single family home. For a passive space heating system you pay from a few hundred dollars to $5,000. For an active space and hot water heating system, $5,000 to $13,000.

Assume a solar hot water system costs you $2,400 including installation and all accessories, and that it saves you $200 a year on home heating oil costs. With a simple analysis, $2,400 divided by $200, the payback is twelve years, a return of slightly over 8 percent.

But consider taxes, and the advantage is greater. The $200 saved per year can be considered tax-free income. In a 33 percent bracket, the return is equivalent to a pretax 12 percent return; and in a 50 percent bracket, 17 percent. Depending on your tax bracket these returns can be better than the highest yield bonds. And assuming fuel costs rise faster than inflation (visualize a system purchased at *today's* prices and saving energy at *tomorrow's* prices), solar energy becomes even more favorable.

If you need more convincing, Congress has made solar heating even more attractive by providing an additional incentive. At the time of this writing you can get a credit against your federal income taxes of 30 percent of the first $2,000 you spend to buy and install solar equipment plus 20 percent of the next $8,000 you spend. Thus, your total credit can be as high as $2,200.

If you're still not convinced, you can now get *state* tax credits as well. At least thirty-two states have granted property tax relief for solar installations. Fifteen states have income tax credits or deductions and six offer exemptions from sales tax. All this is in addition to Uncle Sam's tax rebate.

The biggest tax breaks are in California and it's no coincidence that the state accounts for a majority of solar sales. Californians may deduct 55 percent of the cost of a solar system from their state income tax bill, up to a total tax credit of $3,000. Combining this with the federal credit could reduce the cost of a solar water heater by about 80 percent.

NEW AMERICAN CHALLENGE

The greatest challenge we face during the rest of this century is an economic one—finding and applying the most cost-effective forms of energy to make the nation run smoothly and to regain our lost affluence.

Fear not. Energy in stupendous quantities is all around us and corporate America is busily searching for ways to harness it. In one day enough sunlight falls on California to power the entire country for days. And as long as the moon revolves around the earth and exerts a pull on the oceans bordering America's coastlines, the tides will ebb and flow with phenomenal power. There is also energy in the wind, which we can harness and utilize. There is geothermal energy deep in the earth. And there is the prospect for controlled fusion power, which would literally allow us to use the same mighty forces that are at work in the sun. All told, the sources that guarantee freedom from OPEC are practically inexhaustible.

For the immediate future, however, Americans face a great economic challenge. We cannot count on any single solution. On a personal level, a winning energy policy includes a variety of elements: electric cars, support of *productive* conservation at home and on the road, and solar energy. The energy renaissance will not come about automatically, nor will it be accomplished overnight. But at least we have begun.

13. INFLATION-BEATING HOBBIES

If you want to travel the cash-flow improvement path and meet interesting people along the way, there are several profitable routes to take. Each, by the way, more educational and entertaining than most top-rated television programs. If your tastes run to the exotic or your imagination to the nostalgic, you can now begin cashing in on rising returns in any of a growing number of inflation-beating hobbies.

Take a lesson from Margaret Woodbury Strong. When the largest single stockholder in Eastman Kodak died some years ago at the age of seventy-two, she had accumulated what seemed like the most extensive collection of exotica ever amassed under one roof. Among her 300,000 possessions were 27,000 dolls, 600 doll houses, and Winslow Homer's personal library. She also managed to put together 473 varieties of Japanese calligraphic brushes and 2,000 paintings, along with myriad doorstops, fossils, bells, bicycles, napkin rings, jars, thimbles, canes, and ship models. In addition, at the time of her death, Margaret Woodbury Strong had in her collection a total of forty bathtubs. During the master collector's lifetime, the exotica she owned increased her net worth by hundreds of thousands of dollars. Her survivors still benefit.

As a collector of memorabilia, you can get in on the ground floor, as Margaret Woodbury Strong did, in the area of "preantiques"—artifacts of the twenty-first century. Now is the time to begin, just as the inflation explosion is beginning to propel exotica values forward. The idea is to collect what you can afford now with the knowledge that the collecting community will soon rally round in recognition of your personal choices. As values are continually rising, you always have the option of selling out.

You can't go wrong with tangibles that climb higher than inflation. Collect Indian relics, pre-1900 whiskey bottles, Judy Garland or Joan Crawford bric-a-brac, or old cameras. On a "softer" scale, collect vintage comic books, old cigar-box labels (actually miniature lithographs), famous newspaper headlines ("Man Lands on Moon"), baseball cards (a favorite), even so-called worthless stock certificates. If you have the space, collect vintage bubble gum dispensers, Pachinko machines (the original pinball) or barber chairs. You don't need to stick with the tried and true, either. Hobby magazines of all kinds show that collectors' clubs of every description have sprung up across the nation to bring you together with other buyers, sellers, traders, and interested parties. There's a whole galaxy of double-digit annual risers to collect.

For most collectors, the hobby begins as its own reward. But these days have brought a recognition of monetary profit besides the acquisitive gratification. And when memorabilia collectors get together now, there is usually discussion on "where the profits will be the greatest." While the shrewdest don't give away their best cards, it's widely known that the largest payoffs will likely be found in those areas in which the forces in the marketplace have organized to create a growing demand that has not yet grown large enough to force prices up too high. Quite simply, then, the trick is to be in an "emerging hobby." Wall Streeters call it being in the "right industry." Happily, there are many emerging growth areas you can choose from.

NOT FOR BASEBALL FANS ONLY

Baseball heroes may have left the diamond years ago, but today their cards are rounding the bases at a different game, baseball's profitable inflation game.

Take Hank Aaron. His 1954 baseball card sold then for a penny new, but at one recent baseball card traders' convention on the campus of Montclair State College in New Jersey, Hank Aaron's card knocked in $100. "Only three years before," says *Baseball Hobby News* publisher

Vivian Barning, "the card was worth $15, and a lot of people thought that was too high."

In the years to come, baseball cards may prove to have been one of the grand slam hobby hedges against inflation and economic hard times. Nostalgia and renewed interest in America's favorite sport have begun to send the value of baseball memorabilia soaring. The huge increase in the value of Hank Aaron's card over the past three years as well as hundreds of similar experiences are sending hobbyists to their closets, attics, and basements, then heading for card conventions to trade the long-forgotten treasures of their childhood. But even those who have never collected as children are now getting into the popular and lucrative hobby.

One great attraction is that collecting these colorful cards is within the budget limitations of practically everybody. You can still buy millions for a penny apiece. Another thirty thousand are worth around 10¢ or 20¢. Only three thousand to four thousand are considered valuable and sell for a few dollars. Very few, only about two hundred cards, are worth more than $10. If you stick with the three thousand to four thousand valuable specimens, you're almost guaranteed a clean sweep.

Buying cards beats "putting your money in a bank," said one Radcliffe graduate at a recent convention in Atlanta. She should know. In the early 1970s, this penny speculator paid a quarter for a 1910 card of Philadelphia A's pitcher Eddie Plank. She later sold it for $300. As the hobby is still taxiing down the runway preparing for takeoff, however, it has become apparent that she sold too soon. Collectors are now offering between $2,000 and $3,000!

"It's a classic case of inflation. More and more people chasing fewer and fewer cards," explains one San Francisco Bay money manager who four years ago invested $625 in a 1933 card of the Cleveland Indians' famous former second baseman Napoleon Lajoie. Today his card is worth more than $4,500, "beating almost any other investment I can think of."

Because the baseball card market is growing by leaps and bounds, it is still suffering growing pains and is not yet particularly structured. So you'll have to attend card conventions to buy, sell, or trade, until you have established working group relationships with other collectors. This is best since your knowledge will be multiplied by the people you meet.

A decade ago there were only a handful of conventions each year. Today there are conventions, shows, coffee or cocktail meetings somewhere in the country almost every week. Your local neighborhood newspaper should have dates, times, and places. But also check your town bulletin boards and listen for public announcements on radio.

Besides exchanging signals at baseball card conventions, you can also score prices and potential buyers and sellers in other ways. One way is to read the baseball trade magazines and newsletters. *Baseball Hobby News, The Trader Speaks,* and *The Sporting News* subscriptions can help make you an expert in no time and are available at the conventions (also see Chapter 24). Reading these will make learning, buying, and selling a snap.

What makes one baseball card worth more than another? Scarcity, the superstar status of the player depicted, mint condition, and a card's "tale" or history. In general, heroes like Ty Cobb or Mickey Mantle command higher prices than less well-known players. The most valuable card, for example, which is commonly traded in the $5,000 to $10,000 range, is one that a cigarette company released in 1910. That's one of Honus Wagner, a Pittsburgh Pirates Hall of Fame shortstop. Tale has it that the card was "recalled" when the old superstar, a nonsmoker, threatened to sue, which left just a handful of cards in circulation. Superstar and scarcity really says it all.

Among collectors of the baby boom generation, Topps's 1952 Mickey Mantle ranks high and is still moving fast. Mantle, in fact, is the reigning glamour boy of baseball cards, even more than Babe Ruth, Joe DiMaggio, and Ted Williams, who all trade in the $1,000 range. In 1978 the Yankees superstar's card sold at auction for $680, up from $400 the year before. But its 1979 price was, get ready: $2,000. Both collector and slugger are profiting from the Mickey Mantle craze. In April 1979, the bomber was paid $3,000 for a five-hour autographing session at a card convention in New York City. More than two thousand people paid $2 (a once-in-a-lifetime bargain!) to get the switch-hitter's autograph.

On top of whatever value a card may innately possess, bloopers can bring home more. A quick look at coin or

164 MONEYSMARTS

stamp collecting will tell you the destiny of mistakes, misprints, or recalls. The value of the disputed stamp or misminted coin takes an immediately astral climb. If you're lucky enough to catch the error, you soar right along in potential earnings.

But unlike the increases in the value caused by mistakes in stamps or coins, baseball card premiums to date have not been as great. In 1959, for example, as a lark or perhaps as a dare from his teammates, right-handed pitcher Lew Burdette posed as a southpaw. The Topps's card photographer pictured him in the middle of his windup wearing the glove of his left-handed teammate Warren Spahn. To make matters even more strange, Topps misspelled his name. It was spelled L-o-u on the card. Still, it fetches only $2, which is just above the average for 1959 cards but less than you would now have to pay for All-Stars Willie Mays, Sandy Koufax, Yogi Berra, and Warren Spahn himself of the same year.

Before you invest even a penny in America's favorite pastime, you should pick up a copy of the *Sport Americana Baseball Card Price Guide*, the nation's foremost cardcollecting authority. It will tell you what individual cards are worth.

While most of the action in baseball memorabilia is in cards, you can also consider the long ball. Whatever has anything to do with baseball, collectors will make a market in. Buy programs, scorecards, uniforms, autographs, photographs, and similar items. A series of rain checks from the 1924 World Series recently went for $95; a set of Coca-Cola caps with baseball memorabilia under the lids was auctioned off for $20. Remember, prices of just about everything are climbing.

Among the hottest items and certainly the largest percentage gainers in recent years have been the hand-painted plastic figurines we could buy at the games as recently as the early 1960s. While you could buy them originally for under $2.75 or $3.00, the prices of some of these plastic moneymakers today hover in the $300.00 realm. This $300.00 was recently paid for the scarce figurines of Rocky Colavito and Dick Groat.

Watch also for steady increases in World Series programs. Those from the 1944 World Series, played by the St. Louis Browns, for example, are valued at $75 to $100 and are moving up well. Just a few years ago you could have bought them for $10 to $20 each. So don't ignore the double play. Cards are not the only tangibles rising.

If you weren't into baseball in the thirties, forties, fifties, or sixties; don't know Ty Cobb from Joe DiMaggio; and don't even care that Mickey Mantle won baseball's Triple Crown in 1956, it's not too late or too difficult to profit. Your best strategy is to stick with the present and look to the future. Pick up on the superstars of today. Reggie Jackson's 1969 rookie card commands about $10. A 1970 Johnny Bench now costs about the same. You can bet dimes to doughnuts a sharp increase will accrue in anticipation of today's superstars' induction into the Baseball Hall of Fame. The investment and risk are small; the potential rewards are great—even if you've never kept track of hits, runs, or errors. So get a copy of *Baseball Card Price Guide* today and start playing.

THE GOOD FIVE-CENT CIGAR-BOX LABEL

The secret is out. It's nothing new. America has been into cigars for years. While inflation has killed the good five-cent cigar, however, it's been working wonders for some of the country's rapidly growing number of cigar-box label collectors. These people are ecstatic.

Those turn-of-the-century cigar-box labels, fine specimens of the commercially defunct art of stone lithography, have burst onto the booming collectibles scene as the latest in exotica. Many originally picked up for $10 to $20 only a few years ago are now netting shrewd collectors as much as $100.

The climb will continue, say the leading collectors, because the growing demand from both old and new buyers alike will far outstrip the limited supply in the years ahead. No one prints more *old* cigar labels, obviously, and the available supply must be spread thinner and wider—leading inevitably to a bounty for every specimen. You could double your money in a relatively short time in a market like this.

As inflation beaters, the little lithographs are a natural. "They're rare," explains Clevelander Joseph A. Davidson, who has parlayed his label collection into a thriving business. The labels are rare because they are limited editions

—limited by history. Just as with old baseball cards and old coins, the clue is *old*. If it's yesteryear's hobby, it's tomorrow's surefire antique.

The history of the cigar-box label itself is intriguing. Between 1860 and 1920, when cigar smoking was at its peak, competition among makers was fierce and cigar manufacturers had to strive for ways to draw customers away from their competitors' brands. Most candy stores that displayed cigar boxes did so with the covers flipped back and the cigar purposefully exposed; the manufacturers designed cigar boxes with eye-catching lithographs on the inside covers to entice customers. For this early form of point-of-purchase advertising, manufacturers wanted the showiest, most colorful lithographs.

Coming up with the blockbuster design wasn't all that easy. It was quite an art. To produce a cigar-box lithograph the cigar-box artist would draw a design on a special stone surface with a wax pencil. Then he'd delicately chip away a thin layer of the surrounding stone, leaving a slightly raised design. When he was satisfied with the raised design, the artist would apply water and roll a single color of ink across the stone. The ink adhered only to the raised design and the artist then made an imprint of this single-color design. For every color in the design the artist required a separate stone. When he completed the lithography process, he added the finishing touches. Sometimes he sprinkled bronze dust or even gold or silver leaf over carefully applied shellac. Then he embossed his colorful creation with a forty-ton press.

That was the old way of doing things. These days cigar-box labels are printed using a much speedier, less expensive four-color method. The painstaking craft of commercial stone lithography has been elevated to an historical art.

As a first-time investor, you may find it more convenient to purchase at the retail level. This is perfectly acceptable, as long as the price you pay is in line with other retail prices in your area. You should pay in the range of $5 to $50. But remember, prices are rising all the time. Only time can tell how much more you might have to pay.

At Gregorie Galleries, the Cleveland print dealers, individual labels mounted on matteboard sold for $5 to $15 in 1978. Today the price has doubled. At Higbee's, one of several department store chains in which labels retail, you can buy them now for up to $40 apiece. Antique dealers throughout the country—Smolin's Prints in New York City for one—have sold several hundred at undisclosed prices during the past year.

To get the best bargains in town, go to the lesser-known antique markets and the hobby shows where you can buy larger quantities at a discount. It is at these places that the most astute collectors are amassing sizable collections through buying and trading. So check your local newspapers and bulletin boards for times and places. And don't forget hobby magazines.

A word of warning. Collectors will moan that it can be time-consuming attending all the relevant antiques shows and keeping up with all the latest information. But ask them if the monetary rewards are well worth their effort for an investment of practically nothing.

GOING "BANKRUPT"

One flamboyant financier raises many eyebrows on Wall Street with some of his "investments." Rumor has it that a few years ago he shelled out $600 for stock in the Pierce-Arrow Motor Car Company. With Chrysler's financial difficulties so often in the news, he certainly should have been aware that Pierce-Arrow lost its wheels in the 1930s.

Before you try to contact him to sell him your bankrupt stock in a cable T.V. venture or your pre-Communist-rule Chinese bonds, there's one thing you should know: those same certificates the financier bought three years ago for $20 each sell today for $120. So his original $600 investment is now worth $3,600. A 600 percent gain in three years. That's a return unmatched by any money manager anywhere.

What shrewd financiers from Southampton to Beverly Hills are cashing in on is a little-known but fast-growing hobby—collecting "antique" stock certificates. Long treasured by European collectors, ancient and not so ancient stock certificates have begun to emerge as bona fide collectibles here in the United States. Sparked by the quest for tangible collectibles, the new fascination has been complemented by a growing interest in the history of American business.

168 MONEYSMARTS

Most certificates people collect have been issued by companies that existed in years past. The vintage certificates are worthless in the sense that their issuing companies can no longer redeem them because they have gone under or been acquired by larger fish years ago. They are in great demand, however, and some are quite valuable to the collecting investors.

Certificates are like stamps, but the top quality engravings are bigger and the colors are more vivid. They have beautiful vignettes, a dollop of history, and even a teardrop of nostalgia going for them. An 1897 stock certificate of the Isabella Gold Mining Company, for instance, has a bright orange engraved border and an ornately detailed vignette in the upper left corner which features an eagle perched atop bunting. The company—formed in the gold rush days of the 1880s—was declared worthless after World War I. But its certificate lives again.

Even newer certificates too are valued for their historic significance and unusual designs. Certificates issued by Ringling Brothers and Barnum & Bailey just ten years ago picture a full-color circus parade. They go for about $350 apiece. As the circus was acquired in the early 1970s there will be no more Ringling Brothers certificates, a sure sign the existing ones will soar.

What collectors do with their worthless stock certificates illustrates the variety of people who collect them. They hang them on their walls. They paste them in albums. They squirrel them away in safe deposit boxes to be cashed later. Today it's estimated that there are between five thousand and ten thousand collectors.

Called "scripophily," pronounced scri-PAHF-i-li, certificate collecting was first named in England where approximately half the certificate-collecting public resides. Whatever they call themselves, a lot of scripophilists are former numismatists (coin collectors) and philatelists (stamp collectors) who have broadened their here-a-penny, there-a-penny horizons. They enjoy stock certificates because of their unique characteristics.

Some certificates bear unique and valuable signatures. Early shares in the stock of the American Express Company dated 1857 were signed by company founders Henry Wells and William Fargo and sell for approximately $650.

So far the highest price for a certificate actually signed

by pen and ink sold at auction for $3,000. The certificate, one thousand shares of the New York and Harlem Railroad Company, was signed by Commodore Cornelius Vanderbilt and dated 1885.

While many of the colorful certificates that left the gate at the gun are now worth well over $100, many slower starters are catching up fast. You can find some with fine potential for as low as $10. A 1954 certificate for one hundred shares of the Mission Development Company, a sure shot for the price, is worth $10 just for the facsimile signature of oil baron John Paul Getty.

As the "worthless" stock certificate market is not particularly structured, you'll have to attend scripophily conventions to buy, sell, or trade, until you have established relationships with other collectors. But this is easy. Join the Bond and Share Society. It's a British scripophily club with only one U.S. chapter in New York City. Dues are $25, which includes a newsletter. You can also subscribe to the monthly newsletter, *Friends of Financial History*, from R. M. Smythe and Company. Smythe will also sell you financial memorabilia on consignment. See Chapter 24 for further details.

If you think some of your old stock certificates decorating your closets, attic, or vault box might be worth something on the noncollector market but aren't sure, you can now call upon someone to verify their value. For a relatively modest sum, Tracers (212 558-6550) will tell you what they're worth on the actual stock market. Smythe, mentioned above, can make the same evaluation and can give you the collector value as well. You merely send in a *copy* of the certificate.

Recently, a retired schoolteacher did just this. In 1958 she had invested a few thousand dollars in a hot Massachusetts stock called Metals and Controls. She had Tracers research their value. Within weeks the financial detective firm reported some important news. Her company was bought out by Texas Instruments. She was now a quarter of a million dollars richer.

14. THE ROBEY AFFAIR

Early on the morning of May 14, 1918, W. T. Robey rushed into a Washington, D.C., post office to buy a sheet of 24¢ airmail stamps. The new issue he desired was made on the occasion of the first experimental airmail flight between the nation's capital and New York. The mail clerk had only a few sheets of what Robey wanted—blue airplanes set within red circumferences—but all were poorly centered. The clerk told him to return at noon when better specimens might be available.

When Robey returned around lunchtime, he was shown a freshly produced sheet of a hundred stamps. Robey's heart stopped. He did a doubletake. Each of the stamps in front of him had an inverted airplane! Robey hurriedly bought them. He then asked for more with the upside-down airplanes, but the rest were normal, as were the stamps Robey was to see at the other post offices he visited during that day.

As word of the first upside-down airmail flight reached the postmaster general's office, sales were stopped and supplies reviewed. Soon Robey was visited by postal inspectors who desperately attempted to reobtain the stamps. But Robey refused to part with them.

A collector offered Robey $500 for his new acquisition. But Robey knew they were worth much more. He received a first approximation of the stamps' value when Percy McGraw Mann of *Mekeel's Weekly Stamp News* offered him $10,000. But Robey wasn't selling out so fast, and within a week the new collector had his sheet of 24¢ stamps sold to a Philadelphia collector, Eugene Klein, for $15,000!

Since that incredible spring of 1918, the sheet of red

and blue airplane stamps has been broken up for the benefit of other collectors. Pity we all don't own one. Almost sixty years later to the month, in April 1978, a *single* upside-down airplane stamp from Robey's original sheet of one hundred was sold for $72,500 at auction in New York. Today it is valued at more than $100,000. Not a bad increase for a 24¢ airmail stamp.

W. T. Robey's fame is unique, of course. Discoveries of philatelic printing errors—the stuff stamp collectors' dreams are made of—are rare. It's not often that a one inch-square 24¢ stamp blossoms into a $100,000 treasure. But when you realize that nearly all other *rare* stamps you can easily buy have been swelling in value by 20 percent or more a year recently—and making their owners substantially richer —you realize that stamp collecting is a serious investment alternative.

HIGH FLYERS

By starting to pick up certain brightly colored pieces of magic investment-quality paper now, you can become impervious to coming inflationary storms and economic recessions.

When Salomon Brothers, the prestigious Wall Street investment banking house, recently tallied the performance of various types of investors, it found that over the past twelve years rare stamp collectors came in *third*—behind gold and silver bullion owners, and well, well ahead of stock and bond holders. However, unlike gold and silver owners, rare stamp collectors have not been subject to violent price fluctuations. As a group, stamps have never decreased in value.

The rare stamp boom will continue for as far into the future as we can see. There is strong evidence, practically beyond a shadow of a doubt, indicating that we can expect the market to soar.

First of all there are only a finite number of investment-grade stamps in existence—most printed before 1930 when stamps were first mass produced. So the supply side of the rare stamp equation is fixed. And while no *old* stamps are being printed anymore (and the total supply of a particular issue declines over time due to damage and loss) the quest for these investment-grade inflation beaters is growing. The inevitable result will be a skyrocketing stamp market.

Demand sending prices soaring comes from several respectable sources which aren't bound to go away. There are 25 million stamp collectors in this country, about 1 million of whom are serious investors. Millions of collector and investor dollars, then, are flowing into the stamp market every year, guaranteeing increased values. Further, besides the traditional stamp enthusiasts we have additional funds flowing into the colorful stamp market by a new wave of people in stamp syndicates. High income investors who know the rewards stamps have been yielding have been investing $10,000, $20,000, or $30,000 per person into syndications organized by dealers. Moreover, these syndications look like they are here to stay and are spreading fast.

In addition, both pension and mutual funds now include stamps in their portfolios—sure signs that the money pros are looking into stamps to better their financial performances. Some are looking to stamps to eventually become the darlings of Wall Street.

KNOWLEDGE IS MONEY

You'll probably have a great time acquiring the knowledge and making the contacts you need to profit in stamps. And it's easy. For starters you can subscribe to *Linn's Stamp News,* a weekly stamp newspaper, or to *Stamps,* a weekly magazine. Once you glance through a couple of copies of either, you'll have a pretty good feel for the stamp market.

One of the great attributes of collecting is that you'll have the opportunity of joining one of the hundreds of local or national stamp clubs in your area. This way you'll meet other people and dealers interested in buying, selling, and trading stamps. The largest group in the country with more than fifty thousand members is the American Philatelic Society. Second largest and growing fast is the Society of Philatelic Americans. You can check your phonebook for local branches, then call to find out when and where their meetings are held, or write to the main branches (see Chapter 24).

As you drop in on club meetings and exhibitions, you'll

find yourself making more and more friends in the colorful stamp field. You're now in an excellent position to acquire.

YOUR OWN SPOT

There is a galaxy of three hundred thousand individual stamps issued by one hundred fifty countries, at your fingertips. However, only *some* of these are moneymakers and are considered *investment* quality.

Your best investments are the "classics" such as 1840s through 1900 U.S. (and British) issues—these are comparable to the Old Masters in the art world. (But don't worry, they are a lot cheaper.)

Next best are the "middles" which run from 1900 to 1940. For beginning collectors middles are the right place to start because prices are more modest. For a couple of hundred dollars, you can get off to a great mini-collection.

There are also the "moderns," stamps that you should avoid for investment purposes; the moderns have been mass produced, and won't rise as quickly or with the same assurance as the "classics" and "middles." While demand for the moderns may be high, they are in abundant supply, so their price potential is limited.

Because you'll find so many different types of stamps to invest in, it's a good idea to choose a specialty or theme for your collection. We call this "topical" collecting. Simply choose a topic of life that excites you and start looking for stamps that picture it. Try to pick a topic with good investor support. The more people who end up in your particular specialty the higher the values of your stamps will rise.

The investment field along topical lines is wide open. You can collect, for instance, pictures of wild animals such as tropical fish or snow white polar bears. You can collect sleek metallic airliners or stuffy old politicians. To help you decide on a specialty and invest along topical lines, always feel free to call upon the American Topical Association. They can send you dozens of booklets on various topics listing the stamps you could collect illustrating your subjects. You can also get the ATA's magazine with articles on topical collecting and ads from the many dealers who specialize by subject matter.

Collecting along topical lines can be fun. A Harvard entomology professor was once showing off his collection in the classroom when he came across a Turkish stamp issued at the end of World War II to commemorate the U.S.S. *Missouri*'s visit to Istanbul. Suddenly, one wise guy student burst out, "Oh, I see it, a cockroach on deck." "No," replied the instructor, "the ship is in the *mothball* fleet." The class roared. A few pages later was a stamp commemorating the centenary of the game of baseball. "I got it," the same clever lad cried out, trying to even the score, "a *fly* in centerfield." "You got it," commended his prof.

GET THE BEST: THE $50 RULE

Once you choose your topic, pick up a few stamps of the *highest quality* you can afford. Generally stamps selling for more than $50 are your best investments. The biggest blunder a novice investor can make today is to buy low-cost stamps in the under-$50 range.

Stay away from cheaper stamps—including the highly touted new issues. While the new issue and cheaper stamp strategy has worked well for collectors in the past, you have to remember that today you are an *investor* in *rare* stamps not merely a stamp collector. You want the *greatest* appreciation on your collection, dollarwise when you sell, not just *some* appreciation.

Stick with the tried and true of *investment* stamps; these are generally the ones selling for at least $50 apiece. Only these will bring you the financial rewards we are talking about in this chapter. So before you buy, check the *Scott Stamp Catalogue,* the bible of stamp prices, for current prices.

If you can afford more than the $50 or so per stamp we are suggesting, by all means take advantage of the fact that the more expensive stamps will appreciate the fastest. There's no good reason *not* to spend $100, even $500 or $1,000 or more for stamps which will appreciate fastest, if you have the money. Just remember that the higher the quality of the items you buy, the faster your own net worth will rise into the future.

Most of the rare investment stamps in the over-$50 range you should concentrate on were issued before around

1930. Many experts, for example, suggest buying the early U.S. airmail issues of 1918 and 1923 (totaling six stamps and costing around $1,000 for the set). U.S. commemoratives issued before 1920, such as the 1898 Trans-Mississippi and the 1912 Pan-Pacific issues, are also sure winners. These stamps, of course, run significantly more than $100 per stamp, but these are the ones expected to rise at speeds of two and three times the inflation rate; in other words, they could double in value for you in three to five years!

GETTING INTO THE RIGHT CONDITION

To double your money twice in this decade, however, you will not only have to buy the right stamps, you have to buy them in either "superb" or "very fine" condition.

All stamps are ranked on a physical quality scale. These are the gradations: Superb, Very fine, Fine, Good, and Fair. Your cardinal *investment* rule for stamps is: *buy only "superb" or "very fine" stamps*. These will appreciate the fastest.

The physical condition of the stamps you buy and sell is an important investment point. Prices quoted in most catalogues (including *Scott*'s) refer to stamps in "fine" condition. In nearly all instances, "very fine" (also called "extra fine") and "superb" copies—the ones you should buy for investment purposes—will cost you more money. So don't think your dealer or seller is taking unfair advantage by charging you more than the *Scott Catalogue* price. You'll have the same advantage over your buyer when *you* sell. It's a seller's market.

The back side of a stamp is also an important point to consider in evaluating condition. Always check a stamp's gum. In most cases unused or "mint" stamps with *full* original gum on the back sell for more than copies without gum or with partial gum. Prices given in most catalogues for unused stamps are for specimens which have part of the original gum, except, of course, those varieties which were issued without gum. So, again, if you pay higher than catalogue price because you've bought a rare specimen with *full* original gum, rest assured that you've bought the best and that the stamp will appreciate to a greater extent percentagewise than a similar copy with less gum.

176 MONEYSMARTS

For investment purposes, you should avoid stamps with defects, even slight defects such as off-center images, missing perforations, heavy cancellations on used stamps, or faded or stained specimens. While these may sell for as little as 30 percent of the price of superb specimens, they may also have far less than 30 percent of the appreciation potential. Also avoid damaged, torn, or mutilated stamps which seldom bring more than a minute fraction of the price of superb or very fine specimens.

But, of course, this isn't to say you should avoid "valid errors" collectors love: inverts—including but not limited to upside-down planes, boats, or trains. Once you begin to collect, you'll understand.

DEALING WITH DEALERS

Although you'll be buying and selling many stamps from friends you make at club meetings, or at auction, your primary stamp source will be dealers. So meet as many as you can. But not just any dealers will do.

As more and more ordinary people now hold themselves out as stamp dealers, it becomes increasingly important to stick with those established dealers who have been in business the longest. *Try to deal with the elder generation—preferably those whose families have been in business for fifty years or longer.*

One of the major benefits the older dealers have over the newer ones is their reputation for honesty. The other major benefit is their obvious experience in detecting philatelic fakery—counterfeits and alterations.

It's not a perfect world; the main type of alteration today that an experienced dealer should be able to detect is what's called "regumming." When a new layer of gum on the back of a $100 stamp will make it appear to be worth $500 or even $1,000, there is strong incentive for some individuals (including dealers) to go into the stamp regumming business.

Sometimes, however, even an experienced dealer is fooled with regard to regumming, so it's best to have your dealer provide you with a "statement of quality" that includes a guarantee to refund your money if the stamp you buy proves to differ from its description in the written statement he or she issues you.

After you have purchased the stamp, send it for verification to the American Philatelic Society (APS). Send it insured, return receipt requested. APS will arrange expert inspection of your stamp and return it within sixty to ninety days. The charge to you is only $8 for a stamp catalogue-priced under $200, $11 for a stamp up to $1,000, and $15 for higher priced stamps. A similar service is performed by the Philatelic Foundation in New York.

HOLDING PATTERNS

The longer you wait before selling to another stamp enthusiast or dealer, the more money you'll make on any individual stamp. This is the general rule and will apply to your entire collection. This brings us to the subject of storing your stamps before you're ready to cash in.

If you'd like to display your stamps for all to see, it's a good idea to use specifically made protective mounts that have clear windows and black backgrounds. The black backgrounds will show the stamps' color more vividly. Whatever you do, *never* moisten the back of a stamp (as some stamp collecting guides suggest!) as this will only devalue it by ruining its original gum.

When placing your stamps in stamp mounts or in glassine envelopes as some people do, you should get in the habit of dusting the gummed back lightly with talcum powder (any kind will do) to preserve it. Just spread an extremely fine layer of the powder around with your fingers or a very fine paintbrush. This will help keep stamp gums young and ensure a maximum increase in value over time. It's especially important to do this in humid areas of the country. Spreading powder is an effective and inexpensive means of insurance against a stamp's gum sticking.

You also might want to be good to your stamps in another way. Keep a few mothballs around your stamps—even if you keep them in the safest place of all, your bank vault. There's a good reason for this. There are microscopic insects such as mites and somewhat larger silverfish which love nothing better than to feast on stamp gum, which is, after all, made from potato, cornstarch, or even sweet potato. The better the condition in which you keep your stamp gums, the more they will increase in value into the future.

If you find yourself investing in rare mint sheets make sure you keep them in philatelically approved mint sheet files, which you can buy from most stamp dealers. Don't use wax paper as some people do to store them. In warm weather the wax may melt and transfer onto the sheets of unused stamps. Then they'll hardly appreciate at all.

As your collection grows and you find yourself with different types of albums, store the books vertically rather than horizontally. Stamps are organic. They must breathe. If you place one album on top of another, there will be so much pressure on the bottom albums that air will be unable to reach the stamps. While in all likelihood no severe damage will be done, as with most things in life, your stamps will rise to higher plateaus without such heavy pressure.

No matter how and where you keep your rare stamps, however, you don't have to worry about them. Stamps show superb history. If you spend more than $50 for pre-1930 stamps in superb or very fine condition, these paper darlings will be as certain and steady moneymakers as anything you can buy.

15. RIGHT ON THE MONEY

King Farouk definitely had his faults, one of which was excessive attention to his rare coins. The portly monarch, an avid numismatist, was given to polishing his already radiant collection to a dazzling glare. All things considered, this wasn't the wisest habit since this caused his coins to sell at a considerable discount after his death.

With all his money, the king should have been better advised. He knew that gold and silver coins were countercyclical to paper investments, but he did not realize that cleaning and polishing precious old coins softens their definition and thus makes buyers swift to lower their offers.

Valuable coins should be handled most delicately. Old Farouk's elbow grease produced fingerprints, erasures, and hairline scratches, devaluing his coins by hundreds of dollars.

Overzealous cleaning is just one of the pitfalls of collecting inflation-beating coins. The pitfalls are worth knowing because inflation, according to Wall Street's Salomon Brothers, has been increasing the value of even the average rare coin by over 25 percent a year since 1971. That's three times the inflation rate for the same period.

The rarest coins are spinning up in worth even faster. The so-called Brasher doubloon, a gold colonial, was produced in 1787 by a well-known goldsmith, jeweler, and neighbor of George Washington—Ephraim Brasher. It sold for $3,000 in 1922. In 1979 it was purchased by Walter Perschke, the Chicago dealer, for a tidy $430,000. As of this writing, this is the highest amount to date paid at public auction for a single coin, and at its current rate of appreciation the Brasher will reach the million-dollar mark by about 1984—the world's first coin to reach the heady seven-figure stratum. Recently, Manfra, Tordella & Brookes, the large coin dealer, purchased a 1927-D $20 gold piece for $250,000. Within a week, it resold for more than $300,000.

Don't let the big numbers scare you. You don't have to buy the Brasher to beat inflation. For a few hundred dollars you can get off to a pretty good start, secure in the knowledge that average annual compound gains since 1971 —28 percent—have tripled the average inflation rate during that period.

No one has to explain, of course, that the more money you invest, the better buying opportunities you have. But note well that you don't have to go to dealer schools or be a Croesus to win. Anyone can get into the rare coin field.

PENNIES FROM HEAVEN

People clamor for rare coins because of their limited supply. Numismatic coins have acquired scarcity value above their intrinsic precious metal value which makes them increasingly valuable with time. What is minted by the United States government in any year is all that will *ever* be minted. A coin issued in 1898 will *never* be struck again.

Starting with the total number of coins issued in any particular year, the numismatic countdown begins. Millions of coins disappear from circulation every year for a multitude of untold reasons. Add to this the fact that very few coins remain in good enough condition to please collectors.

The result is that only those coins hoarded by investors and collectors can ever become available to present and future collectors. And while the supply steadily decreases, the demand is dramatically rising. The population of collectors has grown from approximately half a million in 1954 to over 12 million today. As with art and antiques, there is the growing awareness of collectibles. As always, any increase in demand leads to an upsurge in prices.

AGAIN, KNOWLEDGE IS MONEY

It is relatively easy to acquire the knowledge you need to profit in gold and silver coins. Networks of thousands of coin dealers and enthusiasts across the country are linked by clubs, magazines, newspapers, and newsletters, which makes it fairly simple for you to learn the basics.

Start by skimming through the monthly coin magazines on your local newsstand. They contain all the hobby news that can possibly affect your collecting habits—facts and photos presented in a way that makes learning fun. The ads in each issue allow you to choose from thousands of inflation-beating coins for sale. *Coin World* and *Coin Prices*, the leading trade papers, as well as the other coin magazines, will keep you up to date on who's selling what to whom and for how much.

You should also pick up a copy of *A Guide Book of United States Coins (The Redbook)*. Recognized as the most authoritative pricing reference, *The Redbook* gives standard prices for all U.S. coin issues, up-to-date information on private state and territorial gold issues, as well as proof coins. This is the best coin collection reference book there is, and it costs only $4.

GRADING

One of the things you'll soon realize from your reading is that the pricing of coins is as much a science as it is an art. Numismatists have a precise system for grading coins. A coin's condition can range from "about good" (AG-3), which is barely recognizable, to "perfect uncirculated" or "mint state" (MS-70). The better the condition the higher the price you pay and the faster inflation will push up its value.

Chart 15-1 describes the essential elements of the American Numismatic Association grading system. Both the grading descriptions and numbers designating a coin's state of preservation are given, not for you to memorize, but rather to illustrate how coin prices are determined.

Intermediate distinctions are important. An 1897 U.S. silver dollar, for instance, recently sold for $300 in MS-60 condition. The same mintage in MS-65 condition fetched

CHART 15-1

GRADING STANDARDS

Perfect Uncirculated	MS-70	Perfect new condition, showing no trace of wear. The finest quality possible, with no evidence of scratches, handling, or contact with other coins. Very few regular issue coins are found in this condition.
Choice Uncirculated	MS-65	An above average uncirculated coin which may be brilliant or lightly toned and has very few contact marks on the surface or rim.
Uncirculated	MS-60	Has no trace of wear but may show a moderate number of contact marks, and surface may be spotted or lack some luster.
Choice About Uncirculated	AU-55	Barest evidence of light wear on only the highest points of the design. Most of the mint luster remains.
About Uncirculated	AU-50	Has traces of light wear on many of the high points. At least half of the mint luster is still present.
Choice Extremely Fine	EF-45	Light overall wear shows on highest points. All design details are very sharp. Some of the mint luster is evident.

Extremely Fine	EF-40	Design is lightly worn throughout, but all features are sharp and well defined. Traces of luster may show.
Choice Very Fine	VF-30	Light even wear on the surface and highest parts of the design. All lettering and major features are sharp.
Very Fine	VF-20	Shows moderate wear on high points of design. All major details are clear.
Fine	F-12	Moderate to considerable even wear. Entire design is bold with overall pleasing appearance.
Very Good	VG-8	Well worn with main features clear and bold although rather flat.
Good	G-4	Heavily worn with design visible but faint in areas. Many details are flat.
About Good	AG-3	Very heavily worn with portions of lettering, date, and legends worn smooth. The date may be barely readable.

a whopping $4,500. The difference? The eagle on the MS-65 coin had all his breast feathers, but the feathers on the lesser MS-60 example showed a number of contact marks and lacked luster.

Obviously damaged coins, such as those that are bent, corroded, scratched, nicked, stained, mutilated, or oxidized, are worth less than those without defects. But manufacturing defects do not lessen value as much as other damage. Examples such as colonial coins with weakly struck designs, as well as early gold and silver coins with weight adjustment file marks, can be perfectly fine investments.

Your profit potential varies with your collection's condition. Concentrate on *investment-grade* coins, in mint state, which are the "uncirculated" and "brilliant uncirculated." These are the flawless ones that will appreciate most rapidly.

Since you will be concentrating on flawless coins, your chief source of rare coins will be dealers and private collectors. So don't get too excited about stumbling across a valuable coin from your change at the local hamburger joint. Your chances of this are nonexistent. Even if you do find an old date on your hamburger tray or tucked away in an old bureau, the likelihood of its having great value is remote. As soon as a coin becomes circulated, it loses a substantial amount of its value. And remember, uncirculated coins appreciate the fastest.

DEALERS

Now you're set to profit in coins. With the foregoing as background, consult any reputable coin dealer. These dealers will be happy to advise you and to suggest a start-up of the proper investment specimens.

One of the several investment dealers you may want to contact, even if you choose not to buy, is Littleton Rare Coins (see Chapter 24). It's a family-run business. You can send for their Rare Coin Investment Kit and a copy of their monthly newsletter, the *Coin Investment Reporter*. Both are free of charge. You'll get a hot-off-the-press analysis of what they believe looks best and where the market is going. (Up, of course.)

You can also contact Manfra, Tordella & Brookes or Investment Rarities for recommendations and to procure and sell coins for you. Besides these firms, *The Coin Dealer Newsletter* and *The Fortune Teller* (also listed in Chapter 24) are excellent newsletters to keep you up to date.

THE MIDAS TOUCH

There are a variety of ways to get off to a profitable start. U.S. gold coins offer excellent potential. They combine rarity, gold content, and historical romance. For these reasons gold coins enjoy significant value far above their gold content.

During most of the nineteenth century and the early part of the twentieth century, the U.S. Treasury minted gold coins in $1.00, $2.50, $3.00, $5.00, $10.00, $20,00, and $50.00 denominations. Some of these gold coins, in fact, particularly the flawless $5.00 Gold Liberty, $5.00 Gold Indian, $10.00 Gold Indian, and the $2.50 Gold Indian, have appreciated as much as 300 percent since 1975. Their low mintages have made them increasingly hard to find. In addition, remember that during the 1930s, thousands of U.S. gold coins were melted down for their bullion content. That is why they have great appeal to collectors and investors.

Here are examples with common dates and the *approximate* prices U.S. gold coins fetch today in uncirculated condition:

Face Value	Type	Years Minted	Dealer's Price
$20.00	Saint-Gaudens	1907–1933	$ 600
$20.00	Liberty	1849–1907	$ 575
$10.00	Indian	1907–1933	$ 575
$10.00	Liberty	1803–1907	$ 300
$ 5.00	Indian	1908–1929	$ 750
$ 5.00	Liberty	1839–1907	$ 210
$ 3.00	1 Major Type	1854–1889	$2,800
$ 2.50	Indian	1908–1929	$ 300
$ 2.50	Liberty	1840–1907	$ 465
$ 1.00	3 Major Types	1849–1889	$600 to $4,000

Remember King Farouk's rub-a-dub and the steep descent of the value of his collection? Prices go down sharply if coins are not in almost untouched condition. A $10 Liberty type, for instance, worth $500 if flawless, might bring only $250 if it showed signs of marks, scratches, or rubbing. Always, always buy the best you can afford.

Whatever gold coins you choose to buy, avoid buying commemorative medallions from private mints. Commemorative medallions will rarely be worth more than their precious metal bullion value. They will never command big premiums from coin collectors precisely because they are being coined by the millions. Private mints sell as many as they can in order to make a profit. Their coins rarely have any collector value, and you generally pay too high a premium over and above their precious metal content.

SILVER IS SUPER

In case inflation accelerates and a total collapse of the paper money economy results, silver coins will not only skyrocket but may be your only acceptable means of exchange for the purchase of necessities. During periods of runaway inflation and paper money collapse, precious coins usually replace the fallen currency. Even in China, after World War II when paper money was rejected nearly everywhere, silver coins circulated freely. People accepted them as a medium of exchange. Gold coins obviously serve the same purpose, but gold coins are the equivalent of $500 and $1,000 bills and do not take the place of small denomination silver.

Besides protection against real runaway inflation, silver coins are rising at rapid rates due to normal inflation. Silver prices have risen dramatically, and classic American silver coins naturally are following suit.

The American silver dollar offers some of the most exciting and interesting investment opportunities available anywhere. Minted from 1878 to 1935, there are two types you can buy: the Morgan type, minted from 1878 to 1921; and the Peace type, struck from 1921 through 1935. The Peace-type silver dollar is worth slightly less, because it is more common, especially the 1922 date.

You can capitalize on silver dollars in a variety of ways. Most beginning collectors pick them up individually, one at a time, while many collectors who specialize in silver coins acquire them in *roll sets* containing twenty of each date. Some even buy silver in *mixed bags* of one thousand pieces bearing different dates.

Besides owning silver dollars you can take part in the smaller denomination silver coin arena. These dimes, quarters, and half-dollars, minted before 1965, are the coins particularly convenient for buying your necessities. If our paper money economy collapses, you will be able to purchase goods and services at approximately the same prices as before the collapse with silver coins. A quart of milk might cost $500—or one silver dime.

You can buy silver dimes, quarters, and halfs individually, in rolls or by the bag, and hold them for an emergency. Even if inflation remains at current levels, these coins should continue their upsurge.

Before 1965 you could have entered a bank with $1,000 in silver certificates (pre-1965 dollar bills) and walked out with a bag of dimes, quarters, and halves in silver. Today, the same bag of "junk" silver is bought and sold at a premium above the face value for about $8,000. If you fear runaway inflation, buy a bag now. Your investment will be protected by the face value of the coins as well as the actual silver content.

Consider also *clad bags*. "Clad" is the term for certain fifty-cent pieces minted by the government between 1965 and 1970 as the United States was abandoning the gold and silver standards. Containing 40 percent silver, they are sold in bags of two thousand pieces. Face value is $1,000. They serve the same purpose as bags of junk silver, but cost about half as much.

Pre-1933 U.S. coins minted in uncirculated or proof condition in limited quantities are also becoming prime investor targets. These specimens are disappearing into collector vaults quite rapidly and have carried an annual compound appreciation rate of over 25 percent a year during the last decade.

THE PROOF IS IN THE MINTING

Proof sets have also had 20-percent to 25-percent rises. They make excellent investments. Proof sets are U.S. coins especially minted for investors and collectors in 1936 through 1942 and again through the fifties and early sixties using especially selected highly polished dyes. They are sharper than circulated coins and have a mirrorlike quality, a highly reflective surface.

The proof coinage operation is unique. Proof coins are minted at slow speeds with extra pressure, then individually inspected and handled by gloves or tongs. They also receive a final inspection by packers before being sonically sealed in special plastic see-through cases for investors.

CASHING IN

Buy your gold and silver coins or proof sets with long-term rather than short-term profits in mind. Try to hold on to them for at least two to five years. This gives them time to mature. If you want to sell only a few coins, you can sell through a dealer. Check with several dealers to ensure you are receiving the best possible price.

If you are selling an entire collection or a very rare coin, it will pay to call one of the large city auction houses as well as to check with dealers. The auction block is the choicest place to sell your coins. Although you have to pay the auctioneer 10 percent or 20 percent, chances are your coins will bring you top dollar. If you have something very rare and valuable, you should get about 25 percent more at auction than you would from a dealer.

If you follow these general guidelines, educate yourself minimally, and acquaint yourself with a few good coin dealers, your potential for profit and your comfort during inflation is outstanding.

HIGH ROLLERS BEWARE

Wherever potential profits are high, you can pay dearly for mistakes. Collectors, especially beginning collectors, should beware of the small number of charlatans in the coin collecting business.

On occasion an inexperienced collector will lose money on the purchase of a "Farouked" coin. A fly-by-night dealer may buy a 1941 Walking Liberty half-dollar in "fair" condition for $4, then "dip it" in a substance to make it shine and resell it to a novice collector as an "uncirculated." Another possibility is that a dealer might offer a collector a counterfeit coin, either because the dealer is dishonest or because he or she was unprofessional in screening procedures.

The most important thing to remember is: be scrupulously careful about your dealer. It is also a good idea to find out if your dealer is prepared to take a coin back when a mistake has been made.

If, in fact, you do suspect a coin in your collection to be counterfeit, you should know that coin authentication and certification is available at a fee through the American Numismatic Association or the International Numismatic Society. They will verify any coin you send them. Coins must not be submitted without first requesting mailing instructions and a schedule of fees charged for this service. Inquiries should be accompanied by a self-addressed, stamped envelope.

COIN FUNDS

For the average investor, taking part in the rare coin boom will be even easier and virtually error-proof in the days ahead. If the Securities and Exchange Commission approves a prospectus in registration at the time of this writing, your stockbroker may soon offer you shares from the first public offering of a limited partnership in a rare coin fund.

The fund will be similar to a mutual fund, and is to be managed by New England Rare Coin Management of Boston, which will buy and sell such ever-appreciating specimens as U.S. 1848 quarter eagles and 1907 "high relief" Saint-Gaudens U.S. gold pieces. This will serve as a convenient "in" for the wholly unknowledgeable investor, since the fund will administer, buy, and sell without the investor having to know anything at all beyond the buy-in price.

With growing awareness of rare coins as a prime inflation hedge, other rare coin experts will soon, no doubt, offer you their shares too. And with the influx of millions of fresh investor dollars into the coin market, be assured that these pennies from heaven will help keep your comfort level up for years to come.

16. FUTURES

Lured by stories of incredible untold fortunes since the go-go years, tens of thousands of American speculators have been flocking to the commodity futures market. People today are buying and selling "future contracts" in everything from coffee to cattle, cotton to corn.

Trading on the nation's ten futures exchanges has tripled since 1975. These futures exchanges are similar to the stock exchanges, simply marketplaces for buying and selling. Instead of buying and picking up cattle, for example, you pay 10 percent of the purchase price when you place your order and get a "contract" which represents your cattle. If cattle prices go up, you can make a killing; if cattle goes down, you can lose your shirt.

But be warned if you're tempted to flirt with commodities. There are sharks—with sharp teeth—in the waters. They'll do anything for money and they range from slightly unscrupulous to the fraudulent beyond the shadow of a doubt. Unless you learn to spot the Jaws, you can be bitten badly.

The most abundant species of commodity rip-off you are likely to encounter is the classic "boiler room" operation. Here, you'll be called by a fly-by-night man, a pleasant but forceful talker, employed by a firm with a strange name. He'll use a sophisticated, high-pressure pitch and well-modulated voice to get you to send in your money. But because some quite legitimate brokers may also have occasion to call you on the phone and ask for as much as $10,000 to open an account, it's imperative to learn to tell the legitimate from the less than legitimate.

For starters, the boiler-room man is likely to be peddling

a commodity much discussed in the news, such as oil during an oil crisis or OPEC pricing meeting. He'll also paint a rosy profit picture without warning of the thorns. In other words, if your salesman all but guarantees there's big money in your future, tell him to take a cold shower.

No matter what you tell him, he'll probably follow up with a deluge of beautifully printed promotional literature with alluring photos of bars of gold, silver, oil rigs or whatever it is he's selling. And this mailing will be followed up by a "courtesy" call to see if you have any questions. This second call is the one specifically designed to make you want to send in your money. Be doubly on guard against a demand for quick action in a market "ready to move" or "breaking out," and a request that you *wire* your money the same or next day, "early." Unlike your checks, which you can stop with a telephone call to your bank, your wired funds would clear your bank the day your bank wires them for you. You'd have no time for second thoughts.

A friend of mine, a lawyer, wired a $5,000 down payment for a crude-oil contract to an outfit during one of the recent annual meetings of OPEC. The salesman on the phone told him that oil prices obviously weren't going down and that he'd be both crazy and chicken *not* to invest at least $5,000. He invested, figuring it was better to take the path less traveled than to miss the boat completely. As it turned out, the company was named in a New York oil complaint, and he has been unable to reach the firm ever since.

Don't make my friend's mistake. The best way to check out a firm is to call the Commodity Futures Trading Commission's (CFTC) hotline (see Chapter 24) in Washington, D.C. This is the agency that regulates the futures business.

BEYOND THE BOILER ROOM

Even assuming you avoid the boiler man and his host of illusory products, there are plenty of less-than-honest ways you can be taken for a ride by a commodity futures man:

1. He can "bucket" you. An unscrupulous commodities broker might accept your order for a futures contract over the telephone and then fail to execute it. In other words,

he'll hold your money without actually buying the cattle or coffee contract. If the commodity you're betting on to go up in fact goes down, he'll take your "loss" and pocket it himself. If the commodity you've bought actually goes up and you want to take your profit, he'll blame a back office foul-up for not executing your order.

2. He can "churn" you. More difficult to spot than the bucket man is the churner, the guy who trades your account so often he is the only one who makes money. A gifted churner can talk you into a market, then within a week scare you and talk you out of it. Even reputable commodities firms have salesmen who push their clients to trade too often, and even the most upright brokers sometimes get carried away by minute-to-minute new analysis and trade too often. If a broker converts 10 percent to 20 percent of your account equity into commissions over the year, you're okay. But if he's converting 30 percent, 40 percent, or 50 percent of your equity into commissions over the year, you're likely to be getting poorer, not richer. He's talking you into too many trades.

3. He can "spread" you. The spread is a form of churning and is a difficult habit to break once you are into it. Spreads are legitimate trading techniques that reduce risks (and also potential profits) by allowing you to hedge your bet once you've taken a position. For example, you can *buy* a cattle contract in January for delivery in June, then spread by *selling* another cattle contract for delivery in September. This way you gain on one and lose on the other no matter whether cattle goes up or down. The idea, of course, is to have the gain end up greater than the loss. Your broker will probably want you to spread in a falling market when you already have one contract on your hands and it's losing value. Instead of simply getting rid of your contract before it loses more of its value, he'll want you to spread by selling another contract "short." Once in a while it makes sense. But not if it happens every time a market turns against you.

4. He can "trade ahead" of you. Here, a broker executes his own order just ahead of yours. Trading ahead is illegal and is done in thin markets where a few contracts bought or sold can make a commodity price jump way up or down. This is how it works: your broker may call all his clients, talking up cotton at the start of a cold winter by telling

them sweater demand is expected to rise because of an anticipated oil shortage. Meanwhile, he buys his own contract first, and profits as his own clients drive the price of cotton up. Finally he sells out before his trusting clients. To detect this pet device, watch for suspicious patterns of rising markets that break right after you've taken your own position.

5. He can "weigh you down" in his commodity pool. A commodity pool is analogous to a mutual fund that offers expert management and diversification for the speculator with not enough risk capital to open a regular commodity account, which commonly requires $5,000 or $10,000 as a minimum investment. Many unscrupulous brokers will accept as little as $2,000, throw you in a pool with other unsophisticated investors, and let their sky-high fees and commissions eat away your capital. Well-known brokerage firms have their own pools and there's nothing wrong with throwing in a few thousand dollars if you have the money to play with. Fees should average about $50 for a complete buy-sell transaction and in no case should you pay more than the standard commission, around $70. Beware of churning.

Rarely should commissions exceed 20 percent of the pool's managed equity in any year. If you pay higher, especially higher than 30 percent, you're probably being churned. Reasonable management fees are 0.5 percent per month and reasonable incentive fees for reaching certain prestated profit levels can be 10 percent to 25 percent per year. Be careful of pools that tell you incentive fees are unscrupulous but then take you for high trading commissions. This means the pool manager has no confidence in his ability to trade commodities and is merely interested in generating commissions for himself and his brokers.

SIX SIMPLE STRATEGIES IF YOU CAN'T RESIST FUTURES

Even if you're not bitten by the futures sharks, odds are that you'll lose time and money speculating in commodities. Prices rise and fall for complex reasons. The professionals themselves sometimes lose money on more than half their trades. If you must speculate, the trick is to *stop your losses fast on the wrong guesses and let your profits run.*

You'll improve your chances of coming out on top by following some simple rules:

1. *Cut your losses fast.* Many uninitiated traders will stubbornly and emotionally stay with a losing position for so long they wipe themselves out. The sensible thing to do and cardinal rule of speculating in commodities is to set a downside limit, 20 percent, for example, of your deposit, and sell out immediately and as soon as your loss hits that downside limit. Don't try to be a hero by waiting and waiting for a losing trend to turn around. It may never happen. The earlier in the game you take your medicine, the faster your financial condition will improve.

2. *Let your profits run.* "You can never get hurt taking a profit," your broker will tell you. That's true, but in general, a trend in motion tends to stay in motion. So don't sell out until the tide turns against you. That way you'll have a chance to make the bundle you need to offset your losses on other transactions.

3. *Commit only a small amount of capital.* By committing only small amounts of your speculative capital at a time you are less likely to be wiped out by an inevitable streak of bad luck. Losing streaks happen more often than winning ones. There's no better way to avoid them than to cut those losses fast or to keep a good part of your speculative capital in reserve.

4. *Trade as infrequently as possible.* There are so many fast-talking brokers in the commodity futures business that the temptation is great to buy or sell a commodity future *every* time you talk to him. Don't do it. The only person you'll make richer if you trade too often is your broker. Stay clear of brokers who put your money into something abruptly on the prospect of a fast rise, then pull out as quickly on the way down. This is a form of churning.

5. *Take advantage of selling short.* Selling short is merely betting that the price of some commodity will go *down*, instead of up. Shorting plays an important part in commodity futures trading. Short selling is the only way to stay in the game when prices are trending down. In fact, it's the best way to make money in falling markets.

6. *Don't play catch up.* Catch up can get you into trouble. Speculators who wait and wait through bull markets often wind up trading at the tail end of a price trend and suffer most when the tide turns. If, for example, you missed

the sustained copper or sugar rises in the 1978–80 bull markets that literally made millionaires out of some average middle-class people, don't speculate by trying to get into what you think may be the tail end of the price explosion.

My best advice is to stay clear of futures.

17. SELF-RELIANCE

Today, when our president and the Congress run out of our tax dollars to spend, they authorize the treasurer of the United States to print billions more—for everything from defense to welfare. Then they spend it into existence, which causes consumer prices to begin their lift-off.

Although most law-abiding citizens don't finance their operations in the same way, many of us play an important role in keeping prices orbiting once the government has launched them skyward.

In large measure, skyrocketing consumer prices are our fault and will accelerate until we adapt our lifestyles to slow them down. For some time, we consumers have been fueling the prices we pay by spending too much money. A new national buy-in-advance-of-price-hike psychology has mushroomed and growing numbers of economists are beginning to fear that this consumer spending now plays a significant part in prolonging the soaring price crisis. The inflationary thrust created by big government, according to these economists, is given added force by the billions of consumer dollars rushing through the economy.

Although neither consumers nor businessmen are singularly at fault, both play opposite leading roles to keep prices up. Corporate creditors encourage the current orgasmic spending sprees by equipping almost anyone who can sign his or her name with all sorts of financial elves. These helpers instantaneously expand our buying power to "bid" prices up: department store charge accounts, charge cards, and household finance loans. Flash cash. We dare not leave home without them.

Credit, when used wisely, can be quite beneficial (see

Chapter 11), but now we're hooked, seduced by more than a half billion plastic cards in circulation, spending ourselves into inflationary oblivion.

The symptoms are not difficult to recognize. Shopping and buying, the modern national pastime, is apparent in all of the American marketplaces. Although more colorful examples might be the young men and women who flash plastic in chic department stores, life at the gas pumps is more widely recognized. The first symptom of excessive consumption is the gas-thirsty customer on a long pump line as supplies are choked off by those cars already filled up. Sometimes the long lines are eliminated by price hikes, as customers abstain from buying at the higher price. But more often, panic and greed set in and buyers demand as much as they can get at whatever the cost for fear of being caught without as much as everyone else. This sort of insecurity, sometimes known as "catching up" or "topping off," played a major role in the 50 percent consumer increase of gasoline during 1979.

If we do not now take measures to prevent them, symptoms we have experienced on the gas lines can be expected to spread to other sectors of the economy. Increasing numbers of consumers have already been driving the prices of designer clothes, electronic paraphernalia, and bottled water sky high. This may only be the beginning.

As to why we Americans are fixating on designer clothes, electronic gear, and packaged life, economists, sociologists, and psychologists all hint at a similar explanation. Could it be that we still can't see through Madison Avenue? Has media imagery mesmerized us into overconsumption? Can professional image makers now manipulate our desires at will? This seems to be the case and corporate America knows it. U.S. business now allocates billions to the print and television media yearly—and it's paying off. We're buying it all—from foreign bottled water to tight jeans—and paying the hidden advertising costs, too.

Big business has been so extraordinarily successful at selling us packaged life—the "right way to live"—that most of us are incapable of visualizing life without props. Like the main character in *1984*, we have come to love, if not our Big Brother oppressor, then at least his designer line.

Question: Are our self-images so dependent on Madison Avenue that we couldn't be or obtain what we want from life without its help? With all our sophistication, it's time we realized that overconsumption is not going to put us where we want to be. The real way to obtain what we want from life is through self-reliance not self-adornment.

With an attitude of self-reliance, the emphasis would shift from inflationary spending to personal enrichment, from the mad chase of evanescent self-images to the joy of mental and physical achievement and the thrill of creative effort. Sports, crafts, conversation, music, romance, the arts, books, and other satisfying areas would stimulate and enrich our existence. A rebirth of these more instinctive pursuits of happiness could replace images and facades as the new standard of success. Our own spirits and sense of worth to family and friends would be renewed.

Getting back to basics could be the best thing that ever happened. Smokers once relying on cigarettes would be less likely to contract lung cancer and heart disease. Drivers once relying on gasoline for short trips would take up walking, jogging, or bicycling. This would produce healthier, stronger, and more alert minds and bodies and cleaner air to breathe. People who were once consumed with keeping up with the image makers' images would have more meaningful relationships with friends and neighbors. Less fast and funny foods, more meals prepared at home, would mean a better nourished family at less cost.

What we are talking about here is obvious: setting aside the materialistic crutches we have that can be seen supporting current consumer prices. The most important task now ahead of us is to complete the economic transition—already begun for us by inflation—of conscientiously rejecting the unnecessary in favor of more natural, physical, mental, and psychic growth.

18. UPPING YOUR SALARY

You should view your *career* as one of your primary inflation-beating investments. Your talent and professional value, if managed wisely, can be among your most important hedges against inflation in the 1980s.

Hopping up the career ladder is one of the best longterm strategies you can use to stay ahead of inflation. The value of a single job change can be enormous. A $10,000 salary differential invested in a money market fund at today's interest rates could be worth well over $156,000 in ten years; over $498,000 in twenty years. This extra career money can help you go the distance in outpacing inflation.

HOW TO BE YOUR OWN BEST INVESTMENT

If you take the time to shop around for a better job with higher pay you'll find it. And if you invest your additional earnings wisely, you will be well rewarded. You'll live more comfortably in the future.

Finding a better position to keep your earning capacity at its highest level possible is *not* difficult. Since most employers are constantly looking for fresh blood, higher paying jobs are nearly always available. You can learn about such higher paying positions by turning to local newspapers, close friends, and probably a half dozen (depending on your city) employment or executive placement firms. Attending a trade show or professional convention is also a good way to meet people who can put you in touch with contacts who have positions open in your field.

Look for a salary that will keep pace with inflation. This way you won't have to change jobs every year or two. Generally speaking, well-run, growing companies do keep paychecks in line with prices. It helps to be in an industry that has flexibility in the pricing of its products. Those industries that have a ready market in the forefront of technology can usually keep up. Banks can raise interest rates. But avoid utilities because their prices are regulated. Beware of government and teaching positions: taxpayers today are unsympathetic.

Fringe benefits can help beat inflation, too. Look for benefits stated as a percentage of a growing salary rather than as flat amounts. For instance, group life insurance that will grow with your salary is preferable to a fixed amount policy. (More on inflation-beating life insurance in Chapter 22.) Benefits such as dental insurance or subsidized cafeterias transfer some of inflation's damage from you to your company. They can help greatly to conserve your cash outflow.

PUTTING YOURSELF ON PAPER

In most cases, a future employer will want to *read* about who you are before granting you an interview. So you'll need a resume—a sketch of your job desires, education, and experience. Think short; telegraph your story, preferably on one page.

First, the essentials: your name, address, and telephone number. If you don't want your present employer to know you're planning a job change and salary jump, put only your home phone number. Then put down any personal information you would like your future employer to know, such as your age, marital status, your height and weight. None of this personal information is *required* (and the Equal Employment Opportunities Act prohibits employers from discriminating against applicants on the basis of age, sex, race, or marital status), but it is most often to your advantage to provide a complete picture of yourself.

Next, state the kind of job you're looking for. "Job Objective" and "Career Goal" are good headings. Although this section is optional, employers are most impressed with individuals who know exactly what they want. Include in your goal statement such specifics as willingness to relocate or desire to change fields, from advertising to publishing for example. Don't make this section long. One or two sentences are enough.

Next, list your previous work experience and education, under those headings. Which comes first depends on your strongest point. If you've graduated within the last year, put your schooling first, and then whatever summer or part-time jobs you've had. However, if you have a full-time employment history, start with that. In either case, the list should be in reverse chronological order. Start with the present and work your way back. If there are any suspicious-looking gaps, such as your year off to travel in Europe, you can explain it under a special heading: "Travel Experience," for example.

Your work experience section should have names and addresses of previous employers, your job title, if any, and a brief description of your duties on the job. Emphasize your competence by using action verbs: "prepared sale and purchase documents, managed hotel boutique, performed statistical computations." Omit the pronoun "I."

Your education section starts with your most advanced degree. Include name and address of high school or college and graduation date, or dates attended if you didn't graduate. Mention your grade point average only if it was exceptional. If you're fresh out of school, embellish your resume with a list of extracurricular activities and mention any courses that make you more qualified for the job.

Finally, add special categories if they seem important. These might include "Membership in Professional Organizations," "Licenses," "Publications," "Hobbies," "Military Service," "Volunteer Work," "Prizes and Awards." Then, put down "References: available upon request." That way, you only need to supply references to employers who show a definite interest in hiring you.

Resume writing is an inexact science. There are many formats. But whether you underline your headings or capitalize them, list dates at the left margin or after your job descriptions, remember to leave a lot of "white space" —large margins and double spacing where possible to make your resume more attractive and readable. After you have a satisfactory original, have it reproduced by offset, photocopy, or multilith process. You can find these services in the Yellow Pages.

CREATIVE CONTACT

If your employment history does not mesh entirely with your new job expectation, don't rely solely on a resume to realize your full salary potential. In a situation such as this, develop your new job campaign around an initial contact letter. In it, outline your interest and emphasize the skills that you can transfer to your new job.

Your contact letter should be no longer than two pages. Address the letter to a person, not just to "Personnel Director." If you don't know the name of the person you're applying to, call and ask. (Of course, if you're answering a "blind" newspaper ad with only a box number, no greeting is necessary.) Don't be afraid to use the first person too often in your letter, but don't be wordy. Recruiting experts suggest keeping paragraphs to six or seven typewritten lines and sentences to sixteen words.

Tell why you're writing: in response to an ad, on the advice of a friend, or simply because you admire the company and hope they'll find an opening for you. Avoid mentioning present or expected income in this letter and end with a note that you will follow up with a telephone call at a specific time and date.

There are many creative approaches you can use in making the initial contact. You can buy a small amount of stock and write the president as a concerned stockholder during these tough economic times; you can study the company product line and generate a promotional idea or product modification; you can even suggest a new category of job opening if you are sure they need it, and that you have the necessary skills to fill the new position.

READY TO ROLL

Interview day is near. If you are invited out of town, concentrate on getting more interviews in or near that town on the same day. This will keep your job search costs (which are tax deductible) down.

Wherever the interview, however, be assured that you are one of the select few whose resume or contact letter has been chosen from possibly hundreds. In New York, for instance, many small companies pull one hundred resumes a day with *New York Times* classified ads no bigger than three lines. The fact that you've gotten the interview means you are qualified for the job.

About a week before the interview, send the company official a brief fact sheet stating your relevant capabilities and experience. Handwrite a personal note somewhere for maximum impact.

THE INTERVIEW

The first five minutes of the interview will probably be as important as all the other minutes combined. Initial impressions are crucial so be sure to look your best and focus your attention on your interviewer from the beginning.

Among other questions, he or she will ask you why you want the job and why you believe you are qualified. Know the answers to these questions and state them directly and concisely. Emphasize your personal talents and give examples of how you've used them.

Your personal characteristics are important. A few moments of reflection now and right before your interview can give you the confidence and courage to land that higher paying job:

1. *Stability.* Do you work steadily toward definite goals and show firmness of purpose and character?

2. *Industry.* Do you have sound work habits, accept responsibility, and show evidence of following a job through to completion?

3. *Cooperation.* Do you have the ability to get along with others? Are you congenial with family, friends, and associates? Do you accept company policies without challenge or skepticism?

4. *Self-reliance.* Do you show evidence of assuming responsibility and handling your own affairs well by taking on projects and completing them without constant prodding or direction?

5. *Maturity.* Do you have regard for the results of acts, take responsibility for your own actions, and accept blame for your mistakes? Do you make your own decisions with an adult outlook? Do you have self-control?

6. *Perseverance.* Do you set up reasonable goals, then follow through and complete the projects you undertake? Do you stick to goals when the going gets rough?

7. *Loyalty.* Are you faithful to family, friends, and associates? Are you discreet in your comments about others?

MONEY TALK

Sooner or later the conversation will turn to our favorite subject, money. If the interviewer asks you to specify a salary, try to turn the tables and say, "What is the range that this position offers?" This will give you a bargaining range. Remember, your salary base with your present employer has little bearing on your potential value to your new employer. It is merely a launching pad that you will leave behind.

If you receive an offer during an interview, it is often better *not* to accept on the spot, no matter how much you want the job. It's better to ask for time to think it over. Then, if you want, you can try to negotiate a better financial package. This also gives the impression of negotiating from strength.

After your interview, drop a note of thanks to your interviewer.

HIRING YOUR OWN PERSONAL MARKETING FIRM

A few years ago you might have had to play the salary game solo. Today, you can get help climbing the corporate ladder from a number of personal marketing firms. These firms are specialists in finding you a specific job suited to your present career pattern. Their function is to position you against a specific job market and help you to sell your personal talent and professional value for higher pay. Just check the Yellow Pages for firms in your area.

Most personal marketing firms will help you prepare and compose a resume and letters of introduction, will assist you in finding out where the jobs are, will coach you on how to handle interviews (which can include putting you through a videotaped test interview), and advise you on handling negotiations. Some of these firms now offer complete programs consisting of one- or two-day seminars. These seminars generally offer personal help in preparing your resume and contact letter plus step-by-step advice for your interviews.

The charge for all this can run as high as 7.5 percent to 15.0 percent of your new annual salary. (The more work, letter and resume writing involved, the higher the percentage.) In other words, it costs around $3,000 for a $30,000 a year salary. But the money you spend for the new job and new salary will probably return more over the years than most other investments.

One recruitment company, Performance Dynamics International (PDI), will soon begin selling mini-programs that consist of day-long seminars and kits for launching an inflation-beating job campaign on your own. Costs for these packages will range from $500 to $1,000 depending upon the amount of time the recruitment company spends in generating a suitable list of prospective employers for you.

Whatever way you choose to boost your salary, going it alone or seeking the help of the professional job recruiters, some of the advice that PDI gives its clients is spelled out in *The Professional Job Changing System*. It's available in bookstores or through PDI (see Chapter 24). Another valuable guide is a popular paperback, *What Color Is Your Parachute?* Good hunting.

19. YOU ARE THE BEST CASH CAPTAIN

Noted British economist John Maynard Keynes advised us years ago that inflation can burn up our ready cash and life savings in so many invisible ways that only one person in a million could detect them all. But even though nearly everyone in the financial world knows that inflation is raging, not too many financial institutions stand ready to help us—particularly if we are small investors.

During violent inflation in years past when interest rates soared along with prices, average Americans with moderate nest eggs had to settle for a significantly lower yield on their savings than Mr. or Ms. Millionaire. Few could afford, as the Millionaires could, to put money into a diversified portfolio of high-yielding $10,000 Treasury bills; $25,000 pieces of commercial paper; and $100,000 certificates of deposit. But at long last you can do just that—and earn the same high interest rates on your savings as the very rich.

All you have to do is pull your money out of your savings and checking account and sink it into a *money market mutual fund*. With the advent of the money market mutual fund, individuals and families with as little as $1,000 cash on hand can sometimes generate yields of 15 percent and higher on their savings. So instead of keeping the money you use to pay your monthly bills in a traditional checking account (which yields no interest) or a savings account (which yields *almost* no interest), you can now keep it in one of the more than twenty professionally managed, high-yielding money market funds and watch your money swell along with inflation. You can even get your money out on a moment's notice without any interest penalty *and* write checks on it too.

Before we learn to profit from the money market mutual fund, however, let's understand one thing. Banks, in general, are hazardous to your wealth. Banks are the one inflationary trap nearly everyone recognizes by now. Bank savings won't get you richer, but can make you poorer.

Consider the $100 you saved up and socked away in a passbook savings account ten years ago. It happens to be worth less today than it was worth then in terms of real purchasing power. You could have bought more with the $100 ten years ago than you can buy today with that same $100 *together* with its earned interest.

So if you're thinking about depositing some money in your neighborhood branch of the Bank of Inflationland, first consider your family's potential loss of wealth.

You'll earn interest on your money, of course. But prices are rising so quickly that when you withdraw your money along with your money's earned interest, you won't be able to buy as much as you could have bought with your original deposit. The interest you'll earn won't make up for the purchasing power you'll lose to inflation.

You want to profit from inflation in the years ahead, not lose to it. In order for you to profit from inflation (after all, you are entitled to profit for investing your money), your bank's interest rate must be *higher* than the inflation rate. Again, that's not a common occurrence these inflationary days. A look at Chart 19-1 shows that banks rarely present you with such an opportunity. So you can't profit by keeping your money in the bank, not until banks begin to raise their interest rates. The chart also shows what you stand to lose by keeping your money there. *Your* move!

If you have any significant amount of money tied up in a bank, it's a good idea to consider putting it into a money market fund. At the current inflation rate, the money you leave in the bank in an ordinary savings account will be worth about fifty cents on the dollar by 1990 in terms

CHART 19-1

DON'T BANK ON IT
(Inflation rate calculated midyear to midyear.)

Year	Interest Rate	Inflation Rate	Percentage Gain to Saver	Percentage Loss to Saver	Purchasing Power Gain to Saver per $1,000 Invested	Purchasing Power Loss to Saver per $1,000 Invested
1967	5.00%	2.88%	2.12%		$21.20	
1968	5.00%	4.20%	.80%		$ 8.00	
1969	5.00%	5.37%		—.37%		—$ 3.70
1970	5.00%	5.93%		—.93%		—$ 9.30
1971	5.00%	4.30%	.70%		$ 7.00	
1972	5.00%	3.30%	1.70%		$17.00	
1973	5.25%	6.23%		—.98%		—$ 9.80
1974	5.25%	10.97%		—5.72%		—$57.20
1975	5.25%	9.14%		—3.89%		—$38.90
1976	5.25%	5.80%		—.55%		—$ 5.50
1977	5.25%	6.50%		—1.25%		—$12.50
1978	5.50%	7.70%		—2.20%		—$22.00
1979	5.50%	11.30%		—5.80%		—$58.00
1980	5.50%	13.50%		—8.00%		—$80.00

Note: Interest rates on savings accounts were the maximum allowed rates cited in the *Savings Banks Fact Book*, 1980, Savings Banks Association of New York State.

of real purchasing power. If inflation really gets going, you can lose everything.

The post-World War I German inflation fiasco provides a vivid example. In 1913, there were 19 billion marks (German currency) on deposit in German savings banks. By November 1924, prices had leaped so dramatically that all that money was almost worthless.

Now let's talk more about this concept of the money market fund. The money market mutual fund, into which you can now put your money instead of a bank, is nearly as convenient and flexible as your bank checking account and is one of the most useful concepts ever developed by Wall Street. By pooling your dollars with those of many investors across the country, your fund can afford to buy what Mr. or Ms. Millionaire does—high-yielding large denomination Treasury bills, certificates of deposit, commercial and other very high-yielding, short-term financial paper. Together with other investors, your fund's professional money managers buy these financial obligations in large denominations, usually lots of no less than $100,000 that would ordinarily be out of your reach. As interest rates fluctuate, your fund's management shifts its portfolio to take advantage of these magnificent financial instruments to obtain the highest rates possible—usually about double what you would earn on a savings or checking account.

Generally, the yield on a money market fund parallels the inflation rate. When inflation really got going during the first quarter of 1980, for instance—running wild at 18 percent—the money market funds had no problem keeping up. Most of them managed to outdistance inflation by a small amount. Then, as inflation tapered off during the second quarter of the year, settling into the 10- to 15-percent range, so did the money market fund yields. But still they had no problem matching or beating the inflation rate by a percentage point or two over this period.

While the money market funds can't outdistance inflation all the time, they usually come very close. Let's take a slightly longer look at the history of the money funds against inflation. The average rate of inflation for 1978 was 7.66 percent, and for 1979 it was 11.26 percent. Here's how some of the funds performed during the same two years:

Money Market Fund	1978 Yield	1979 Yield
Cash Reserve Management	8.1%	10.4%
Dreyfus Liquid Assets	7.4%	10.4%
Fidelity Daily Income	7.8%	10.7%
Intercapital Liquid Assets	7.6%	10.0%
Merrill Lynch Ready Assets	7.7%	10.7%
Moneymart Assets	7.4%	10.4%
Reserve Fund	7.4%	10.7%

Source: *Money* magazine's "Fund Watch."

The conclusion is obvious. The money funds are great places to park cash you're going to need soon or while you're deciding on something better to do with it. But don't leave it there and expect it to double overnight. Money market funds are not long-term investments. They just do a whole lot better than bank savings or checking accounts in protecting your short-term savings.

The money market funds can do well during inflationary times because they take advantage of high rates caused by the government's anti-inflationary policy. During periods of alarmingly high inflation—over 10 percent—the president and his economic advisors get nervous about the economy. When they think it's about to fly out of control, they hike interest rates up to cool inflation. When interest rates rise, so do money market fund rates.

Many, although not yet all, of the funds offer the convenience of check-writing privileges for drafts over a certain size. When the first funds began operations about ten years ago, some permitted checks but usually no smaller than $500. Now because of competition among the many more money market funds available, many of them permit you to write checks as small as $250; and stiffer competition between the funds will probably lower this minimum further.

You should use your fund's check-writing privilege to pay your rent, mortgage, property taxes, tuition, or to finance your family vacation—any bill as large as the fund's minimum check allowed. Continue to pay your small bills, however, by your normal bank check, of course, but replenish your funds by writing a large check on your money market fund. Your money will earn high interest right up until the day your check clears.

Because smaller investors have been pulling out of banks, and because there are laws setting maximum interest rates banks can pay, the banks are worried about competition from money market funds. In their advertising they have tried two ways to make the money funds seem unattractive. So be on guard.

First of all, bankers emphasize that only bank deposits are covered by federal deposit insurance. By implication, they are telling us that any other kind of investment is so risky it borders on the insane. The savvy investor will recall, however, that much of any money fund portfolio consists of Treasury bills. And if Treasury bills aren't safe, neither are the banks. The other investments of money funds are very respectable bank certificates of deposit and highly reliable commercial paper backed by the country's largest corporations. In many cases, the funds restrict themselves by charter to these three types of investments. Anyone who is not willing to accept this level of risk is, quite frankly, not willing to keep up with inflation.

The other argument used by the bankers is more subtle. There are times when the money funds' rates of return are slightly less than on the bank certificates (time deposits) offered to small investors. But don't be fooled. This usually occurs when inflation and interest rates are on the upswing and exactly when you should not tie up your money at a fixed return in a bank.

Money funds can quote only their actual rate of return over the previous months. Let's suppose that the average money fund return has been 11 percent over the last three months but that Treasury bills are now going up again and are yielding 14 percent or more. Banks can easily offer six-month certificates for a fixed 12 percent and expect to make a handsome profit (at your expense). The 12 percent sounds like a good deal until you realize that over the same period the money funds are almost sure to return 13 percent or better. Besides, with a money market fund you can take your money out right away and lose no interest. With bank certificates there's an interest penalty if you pull out early and you can't write checks on your money.

Later, we will discover another use of your money market fund: to escape the taxman. Since tax laws allow you to give your children tax-free gifts, you can give your money market fund investment to each child and let the money accumulate at a low-income-bracket rate, perhaps completely tax-free.

So if inflation is still raging and you're still earning only 5 percent or 6 percent in a passbook savings account, or even 8 percent, 10 percent, or 12 percent on a savings certificate or time deposit, call your broker today about investing in one of the money market funds. It'll help make inflation work for you.

20. GIMME SHELTER

To paraphrase an old ad jingle: we're making more now, but enjoying it less. Despite the big bucks we see on our paychecks, today's wage and salary figures are like the cool water mirage in a bone-dry desert. They are more illusory than real.

Because of higher Social Security and income taxes, we're having trouble keeping up with living costs, even as we receive wage gains that match increases in inflation. While higher living costs are eating up paycheck purchasing power, the folks from the Internal Revenue Service are taking us to the cleaners as well.

The tax ax is pointed up by a *Reader's Digest* study which reports that if you earned $20,000 annually during the late 1970s, you will need to earn $52,000 by the late 1980s to keep up with inflation. If you want to maintain your current *aftertax* purchasing power, however, you would require almost $68,000 per year by the end of this decade. This is because your higher income (due to inflation) would have pushed you several tax bracket notches higher, making you forfeit a bigger chunk of your paycheck to Uncle Sam. Economists call this less obvious phenomenon "tax bracket creep." No matter how much your salary advances, your taxes never stop sparring with your hard-won dollars.

What we are saying is that higher wages and salaries have bumped us into higher tax brackets, meaning a higher percentage of income to the bureaucrats in Washington. This son-of-inflation built-in tax increase known as tax bracket creep *automatically* raises our taxes.

OPTIONAL READING EXAMPLE

Look back to 1967. Young Ms. Moneydollar, a bank teller, earned $6,000. Married, with one child, Moneydollar took the "standard" deduction that year. The result: her take-home pay after federal income and Social Security taxes was about $5,200.

Suppose, to make up for inflation, her employer, Moneybank, doubled her pay to $12,000 by 1978, by which time inflation had doubled consumer prices. That *sounds* fair. With inflation doubled, and her pay doubled, Moneydollar now had the same purchasing power as before. Right?

Absolutely wrong! This is the tax bracket creep phenomenon—the hidden side of inflation Moneydollar can't readily see. It results in even more of her purchasing power being confiscated than meets her eye.

Even though Moneybank doubled her salary, Moneydollar continued to fall behind in purchasing power because her federal tax bill had *more* than doubled since 1967. Even though her employer, Moneybank, matched inflation dollar for dollar with salary increases, Ms. Moneydollar continued to lose aftertax buying power.

Specifically, bracket creep shrank Moneydollar's 1978 take-home pay to about $10,300. This $10,300 Moneydollar took home in 1978 bought less than what she could purchase with the $5,200 she took home in 1967.

Confusing as Moneydollar's financial dilemma is, it is compounded by the fact that she must also pay state and local taxes over and above federal taxes. In over half the states, property taxes have at least doubled since 1967. Had actual property taxes and other state and local levies been included in Moneydollar's calculation, her true loss of aftertax purchasing power would have been even greater.

Moneydollar is all of us. Owing to the tax bracket creep phenomenon and high inflation, we Americans were richer in 1967 than we are today. Half the dollars bought us far more materialism in 1967 than they do now. But look at Chart 20-1. It illustrates that we don't have to wait years to experience a loss in buying power. We can feel the effects of tax bracket creep right away.

CHART 20-1

INFLATION, TAXES, AND A 10 PERCENT PAY RAISE

1977 Gross Pay	1977 Take-home Pay	1978 10% Pay Raise	1978 Gross Pay	1978 Federal Income + Social Security Taxes	1978 Take-home Pay	1978 Take-home Pay Adjusted for 10% Inflation	1977 to 1978 % Increase in Take-Home Pay	1977 to 1978 % Increase in Federal Income + Social Security Taxes	1977 to 1978 Decrease in Buying Power
$10,000	8,800	1,000	11,000	1,465	9,535	8,582	+8%	+22%	—$218
$15,000	12,586	1,500	16,500	2,864	13,636	12,272	+8%	+19%	—$314
$20,000	16,324	2,000	22,000	4,298	17,702	15,932	+8%	+17%	—$392

Note: Chart 20-1 assumes:

10 percent rate
Married filing joint federal income taxes
3 exemptions
Standard deductions
Pay listed is the only source of income
State and local taxes not included

Anyone who received a $1,000 raise on a $10,000 base in 1978, for example, would have lost ground to inflation and the tax man to the tune of $218 in terms of actual buying power during the course of that year alone. Chart 20-1 also shows that a raise of $1,500 from a higher salary base of $15,000 in 1977 to $16,500 in 1978 resulted in a $314 loss in buying power.

The higher your salary the more you lose. And if you are so well compensated that you think you've escaped bracket creep's gravity altogether, some recent studies by the Tax Foundation may change your mind. One study showed that during a recent seven-year period, the family with an income of $50,000 that climbed to $67,500 suffered a drop in purchasing power of over $3,000—the equivalent of a week in Paris at a fine hotel, including transportation, meals, and sight-seeing. It's no longer a secret. High-powered $50,000 executives getting gold-lined pay hikes are really taking pay cuts. The bracket creep syndrome is the reason why economists call inflation "the hidden tax," the cruelest tax of all.

Now let's see what we can do about all this.

GIVING TO THE CHILDREN

Once considered the province of the very rich, tax-sheltered investments now have increasing benefit for everyone. Inflation-induced pay increases are continually forcing us into higher tax brackets, and we are now well rewarded for taking advantage of simple investments that shelter our income from the taxman.

To the uninitiated, the tax consequences of an imagined tax shelter are mysterious indeed. As one bemused investor at a recent Merrill Lynch tax shelter seminar put it, "Somehow the profits are losses and the losses highly profitable." In fact, many common tax shelters are much more simple.

Chances are that your family already benefits from some basic money-saving tax shelters. You may own a house or condominium and deduct on your tax return your real estate taxes and interest payments on your mortgage. You may own a co-op and deduct part of your maintenance payments. You may participate in a company pension, Keogh, or IRA plan and exclude some part of your income for tax purposes. Or you may invest in common stocks and generate capital gains that are taxed at a lower rate than your ordinary income.

In addition to these everyday tax shelters, one of the best techniques you can use to avoid the taxman on April 15 is a simple family tax-planning tool—*a temporary or permanent gift to your children*. This simple tax technique allows you to escape more than gift and estate taxes (you generally pay gift and/or estate taxes when you give away your property). It lets you escape *income* taxes as well.

At the time of this writing, you and your spouse can each take advantage of this federal tax loophole by giving up to $3,000 a year to each of your children. (This amount will probably be raised to $10,000 sometime shortly.) As long as each spouse gives no more than $3,000 to each of his or her children there is no federal *gift* tax due the taxman. So states the tax law. Moreover, your assets accumulate at a son or daughter's lower tax bracket once transferred. So you escape paying some income tax as well.

This type of transaction is risk-free and over the long run can be highly profitable. If you fully and continually use the annual $3,000 tax exclusion, you can transfer a substantial amount of property to the younger members of your family without gift tax costs and have this money accumulate at your children's very low income tax bracket levels. If husband and wife, for example, join in making the maximum amount of excludable gifts to three children for ten years, the donors will have transferred $180,000. In addition, the donated amounts will have accumulated during the ten-year period at a son or daughter's lower tax bracket level. To no small extent they will have escaped the inflationary effects of tax bracket creep.

You can make gifts to your children in one of two ways. The first way is to give a *permanent* gift such as stocks or your investment in a money market fund directly to your child. The second way is to set up a *short-term trust*—one that has a life of at least ten years plus one day—which receives your property and keeps it invested for your child(ren). The trust, which any lawyer should be able to set up for a small fee, receives the assets and keeps them invested. When the trust expires after ten years, you, the donor, get your assets back.

By such permanent or temporary gifts you shift some of your family income—the interest on a money market fund or capital appreciation on the Magic Assets you give —from family members in high tax brackets to those with little or no tax liability. In the usual case, your family will escape the taxman completely because as of this writing the tax laws allow each child in your family to receive "unearned" income of up to $1,000 tax-free each year.

Once you or your accountant spends some time preparing each child's tax return, you can shelter thousands, even tens of thousands of dollars from the taxman over the years. And this way, by the time your children reach their eighteenth birthday, they will probably be able to afford their own college tuition.

TAXATION WITHOUT REPRESENTATION?

Today we pay not only federal, state, local, gift, and estate taxes, but literally hundreds of other indirect, covert taxes as well. Though it sounds unbelievable, that's only because government is so skilled at camouflage. It puts on the innocent act about the total number of taxes it extracts from us. For example, when you include all the hidden taxes, there are fifty-two different taxes on a single egg and one hundred eight taxes on a loaf of bread! Producers and distributors pay the taxes first—from ad valorem to zoning taxes—then pass them along to unsuspecting consumers. All these costs of doing business are added in to calculate the final take-home price at the checkout counter.

In 1948, 24.2 cents of every dollar the average American earned went for taxes. In 1957, it was 35.5 cents per dollar. Taxes took all of 39.2 cents in 1968; followed, in 1978, by a whopping 42.0 cents of every eked-out dollar for taxes. The president, members of Congress, and other elected officials have been in the habit of eating our tax dollars as quickly as we earn them, taxing our families and businesses into economic exhaustion, crushing our ability and incentive to save, invest, and produce.

To the American people of 1789, their nation promised a new way of life: each man and woman free to live and work as he or she chose; each having the right to seek happiness. It was a new form of government in which people would be sovereign.

Thomas Jefferson and the framers of our Constitution designed the government to insure this new liberty. To do this they gave the Congress the power to "lay and collect taxes, duties, imposts and excises, to pay the debts and provide for the common defense and general welfare of the United States." They held this power to be so important that they put it at the head of the list of enumerated powers in Article I, Section 8 of the Constitution.

When our founding fathers did what they did, little did they realize how burdensome the taxing power would become or how much of the nation's economic and social independence taxes could ultimately hamper. It was impossible then to conceive that the average American taxpayer would have to work 151 days a year for the government.

Furthermore, our tax system was originally based on each person's ability to contribute to the national wellbeing. It was *not* based upon the assumption that the government itself would create accelerating inflation over a long period and thereby cause tax bracket creep that pushes us into higher tax brackets. Naturally, when we are first soaked by inflation over the long haul, then poked by inflation into artificially higher tax brackets, our remaining funds are fewer and our ability to pay taxes diminishes. As this ability to pay taxes invariably gets worse in terms of real purchasing power, where is the constitutional justification for *automatically higher* taxes?

The justification does not exist, say some constitutional lawyers. They suggest that there is no constitutional rationale or authority for automatically being prodded into higher tax brackets and that at the very least the Constitution requires the express consent of the Congress to raise taxes. Their view is that the inflation-produced bracket creep hoist in taxes means that our Congress members and senators are engaging in a devious form of national embezzlement.

TAX REVOLT

It started on the West Coast, in California, where taxpayers felt they had to fight back. The much publicized California tax revolt took the form of the Jarvis-Gann amendment to the state constitution, popularly known as Proposition 13.

For state and local governments, Proposition 13 was a

battle by middle-class homeowners against soaring tax bills and wasteful government spending. This was the way California property owners chose to resist the high cost of their own state government's bureaucracy. An historic, successful, instructive action for all of us, the California tax revolt was in a true sense a modern-day Boston Tea Party.

From all the publicity surrounding Proposition 13, it appeared to be an "overnight" success. Many think that Proposition 13 coauthor Howard Jarvis and his citizen army were simply able to steamroll their way to victory fueled by a grass-roots movement supported by hundreds of thousands of California's angry homeowners. But that's not exactly how the revolution happened. The taxpayer victory was the result of a long petition drive that culminated in a multi-million-dollar media campaign as calculating and hard fought as any political campaign in California's history.

Coauthors Howard Jarvis and Paul Gann first had to sign up the necessary number of petitioners to ensure Proposition 13's place on the statewide ballot. And not everyone was convinced to become a tax revolutionary at the start. Fearing the tax revolt would diminish state coffers, Governor Jerry Brown and the California state bureaucracy initially opposed the proposition. But as tax constituency rumbles grew louder, the governor sensed the need for tax reform.

"Quite frankly," Brown told newsmen, "I'm getting somewhat frustrated myself at the slow pace of property tax relief." At this, signatures from every county in the state poured in. One young volunteer alone gathered more than three thousand signatures in three days simply by setting up a table in front of a large department store in San Francisco. In the end, a total of 1.2 million taxpayer signatures were gathered, twice the number required to place the tax limitation measure on the ballot.

Then, with Proposition 13 officially on the ballot, a full-blown tax revolt burgeoned—buttons, posters, bumper stickers, lawn signs, and all the rest. Even Nobel prize-winning economist Milton Friedman, writing in *Newsweek*, supported the statewide revolution, urging voters to vote for economy in government and lower taxes.

On election day, that's just what California voters did, in record numbers as Proposition 13 won in a landslide.

The nation's first inflation-era Boston Tea Party had succeeded. Politicians and bureaucrats suddenly sat up straight and took notice. The people had finally put an end to skyrocketing property taxes.

The "taxquake" began in California, but the taxquake rumbles are spreading. After the approval of Proposition 13 in California, citizens' groups across the country organized and won places on ballots for various proposals to curtail government spending and taxes. Within months of the passage of Proposition 13, sixteen states and a number of local ballots carried tax and spending reform propositions. Several states, including Arizona, Oregon, Texas, Missouri, South Dakota, North Dakota, Alabama, and Michigan, approved these tax reduction proposals.

"FEDERAL PROPOSITION 13"?

As our state tax revolutions grow more vocal, many citizens are beginning to speak in terms of a "Federal Proposition 13." "He's got a pretty face but a lousy bill," said Speaker of the House Tip O'Neill about a new tax bill introduced by Jack Kemp, three-term Republican representative from Buffalo, New York, and a former Buffalo Bills quarterback. He was referring to the Kemp-Roth bill, a sort of Federal Proposition 13, cosponsored by Senator William Roth (R-Delaware), which in one fell swoop mandates the largest single tax rate reduction in the country's history.

According to one draft of the bill, personal income taxes would be cut by about a third, from the present range of about 14 percent to 70 percent to a range of 8 percent to 50 percent; the corporate tax rate would be lowered from 48 percent to 45 percent. A family of four earning $8,000 a year, for example, would have their federal tax bill cut by 90 percent. A family of four making $15,000 annually would have their federal tax bill cut by 40 percent. A family of four making $20,000 a year would pay a third less in taxes.

Despite the bill's patriotic intent, many Democrats are joining in calling the Kemp-Roth bill "outlandish," "demagogic," and "fiscally irresponsible." They feel that after a momentary fiscal "high," so to speak, the bill would ultimately increase the effects of inflation and tax bracket creep substantially.

Kemp-Roth, they say, would cost our Treasury in Washington $80 billion a year and there is simply no way that the federal budget could sustain a cutback shock of such proportions. What would happen, say the opponents, is that the government would end up flooding the economy with $80 billion in newly printed inflationary money to make up for its loss. Along with the already excessive amounts of money the government prints and spends, the additional printing would result in the largest inflation and tax bracket leap we have ever felt before.

Eventually, and for the sake of all, both the Democrats and Republicans must converge upon a common plan and the federal tax relief we need will come in the form of less inflationary printing press money *together* with a revised, more equitable federal tax system. Until then, each tax umbrella we construct and each Boston Tea Party we join will help prevent the IRS folks from getting at *our* money.

21. BRINGING IT ALL BACK HOME

While you would need considerable expertise and some luck to build a large fortune in real estate, you don't have to be an expert to build a small one. If you buy a $100,000 house, co-op, or condo today with $20,000 to $25,000 down, and inflation continues on its present course, your investment would make you considerably richer, perhaps a millionaire within twenty years. If this were your second property, which could be rented out to others, you'd be even wealthier.

Most accumulations of wealth existing in this country today have not been the result of owning *personal* property like gold, gems, or art. On the contrary, more individual fortunes, both large and small, have been made in real estate.

During almost every period of American history, realty investments have been making excellent profits for countless Americans. Today is no different. Housing in both our cities and suburbs remains the excellent lifelong, "live-in" and "rent-out" investments you can make to outdistance inflation and to profit.

Today, more than ever, housing is one of the most practical investments you can make. Since inflation influences an increase in the cost of land, construction materials, and labor, your real estate investment—whether it be your first or second home, summer cottage, ski chalet, or apartment building—will continue to rise with inflation over a period of years. As costs go up, your real estate investment becomes more valuable almost automatically.

Just how much you can profit from the simplest of real estate investments, the single-family home, is evident from the results of a study conducted by Wall Street's Salomon Brothers. According to Henry Kaufman, the study team's leader, as the average price of a new house rose from $37,000 in 1973 to nearly $65,000 in September 1978, the owner in a 30-percent marginal tax bracket saw his one-year "net benefit"—the difference between price appreciation and aftertax mortgage cost—skyrocket from $1,000 to $3,000. This, says Kaufman, implies a rise in return on the homeowner's original cash investment from 11 percent in 1974 to 21 percent in 1978, well surpassing inflation during those years.

In simpler terms, the price of a single-family house rose more than 14 percent in 1978 and more than 20 percent in 1979, and almost double the inflation rate in each of those years. As the owner of a house, co-op, or condominium, those increases would belong to you.

The main explanation for the continued long-term upward trend in real estate values is simple. The housing market has been bolstered by the long-term prospect of high housing demand from the "baby boom" generation. This pool of buyers—those in the twenty-five- to thirty-four-year-old age group—is rising. That segment of the population went from 27 million in 1972 to 33 million in 1979, and it is expected to keep rising into the early 1990s.

It is interesting to note that the preponderance of these first-time buyers today are "swingles," unmarried couples of the same or opposite sex who purchase a house as an economic alternative to apartment renting. The deluge of these new buyers, accompanied by a growing mobility in American society, have combined to force increasingly larger amounts of cash into the housing market, thrusting home prices up.

The value of real estate also increases on the assumption that there are too many users vying for too few houses, and too few co-ops in too few buildings. Monetary restrictions and high interest rates, clean air and water laws, rent control, and other inhibiting factors limit the amount of new building and force prices up.

If you're a first-time buyer there are two types of housing investments to choose from: 1) live-in investments, or

2) rent-out investments. If you don't own real estate already, a live-in investment is a good first bet.

If your landlord can raise your rent, without limit, it will probably pay in the long run to buy yourself a home to live in. You'll be building up tax-deferred cash value (you don't have to pay capital gains tax as your real estate appreciates—you pay when you sell) in a useful and practical tangible. And in most cases there are tax breaks for home sellers, so you may end up paying no capital gains tax at all.

You'll also enjoy another twofold tax break: 1) the interest you pay on the mortgage loan you use to buy your home, and 2) the real estate taxes you will pay each year, are *both* tax deductible. So in all likelihood Uncle Sam will be owing *you* at the end of the year.

Luckily, you don't have to pay for your live-in investment with all cash. Most banks or savings and loan associations will lend you 75 percent to 80 percent of the purchase price. The remainder is the "down payment."

It is interesting to note that four out of five first-time buyers make their down payment from savings and/or other sources of cash from investments. So, if you are looking forward to buying your first home, it's a good idea to start a savings and investment program now, on a regular every-payday basis.

Before we actually go through the buying process in detail, let's have a quick look at rent-out investments, otherwise known as "income-producing properties."

RENT-OUT INVESTMENTS: HOW YOU CAN PROFIT

In his book, *How You Can Become Financially Independent by Investing in Real Estate*, Albert Lowry describes the young doctor, presumably a homeowner already, who put $5,000 into an old hotel that had been converted into apartments. Within a year the doctor was making it in real estate; his rental income exceeded the expense money he had to pay out in heat, electricity, maintenance, and mortgage payments. The doctor became so fascinated with his new investment as a hobby that soon he found himself taking his profits and using them as a down payment to buy another property. Five years later he had back his original and only out-of-pocket investment of $5,000.

The doctor was so impressed with his ability to make money in an area unrelated to his field that he decided to stick with it. In the years that followed, the now middle-aged man found himself with an equity of almost $200,000 in real estate worth $1,200,000 at current market value! There was absolutely no magic involved. What the doctor did was merely to repeat his original process over and over.

The lessons to be learned by first-time investors are that: 1) the effects of inflation alone on real estate can make you wealthier over the years, and 2) whether you're a first-time real estate investor or not, it pays to learn a few simple nonmedical techniques the doctor used to become wealthier in real estate. The lessons hold true whether you have $5,000, $10,000, or $20,000 for a down payment on a one-, two-, or three-family house, condo, co-op, or even a small apartment building.

First of all, there's no magic to buying income-producing property. Just look for a property that you can rent out to someone else to live in, something you wouldn't object to living in yourself. Look for a property that will bring you in more money than it costs you each month to run.

Actually, this can be as simple as finding and buying a place for yourself, then arranging the down payment and monthly payments so that your expected rental *income* meets your monthly *costs*. For example, in figuring out whether a particular co-op or condo investment is feasible, just add up the total of the monthly maintenance and mortgage payments, then figure out whether you could cover these expenses by renting it out for more.

To determine your expected rental income, simply check the real estate rental section of a local newspaper to see what people are paying to rent similar properties. Then all you do is make your purchase as if you were buying a home for yourself but at the same time advertise it in the Houses for Rent column of the classified section of a local newspaper. Even easier, you can have a real estate broker do this for you. Call any broker listed in the real estate section of your classifieds. With the nationwide housing market growing tighter every day, you're almost guaranteed a tenant at a reasonable price in no time, especially if your home is situated in a major urban area.

But before you buy income-producing property, you must check the long-term appreciation of units in the neighborhood. Properties similar to the one you are about to buy should have appreciated by at least 10 percent per annum for a period of five years prior. This is your assurance that you'll be buying into a good neighborhood where housing has been appreciating. Now you can buy.

As inflation carries your investment's value higher over the years, you continually have the option of raising the rent or selling your investment for profit. And, of course, you always have the opportunity to reinvest some or all of your gains to repeat the process with other properties, as the doctor did.

We still haven't seen all the tricks in the doctor's real estate bag. The real trick is leverage. The doctor knew that, in general, it is best to buy income-producing property with the smallest down payment the seller or the bank would accept. In other words, you make the most money by putting down very little and by going into as much debt as possible. Usually, the greater the debt (and the smaller the down payment) the greater the *percentage* return you can realize on your investment.

It will help enormously to buy when mortgage rates are at the low point of the interest rate cycle. This way your monthly interest payments to the bank will be low. This will give you a better-leveraged situation. Your local banker can help you determine if the time is right. In fact, if interest rates are high, don't buy—*wait*.

For some people, the idea of borrowing and staying deep in debt to achieve leverage sounds troublesome. But their apprehensions fade when they realize that a giant financial institution is not only able but many times quite eager to help them manipulate their profit lever. Bankers take real estate investors under their wings, because they know the value of nearly all real estate goes up. The worst that can happen is you don't meet your mortgage payment. In this case the bank would just take over the property and sell it to someone else. It's difficult for them to lose. This is why they are usually willing to invest three or four dollars

228 MONEYSMARTS

for every one of yours. This small down payment principle means simply that you use as little as possible of your own money and as much as possible of someone else's. In other words, you use *leverage*.

How leverage works can be seen in a simplified case study. Suppose you set out to buy a $90,000 two-family duplex, and to rent each of the two units for $750 a month. This would bring you a gross income of $18,000 a year.

To achieve your cash inflow of $18,000 a year, you have two choices: 1) putting up $45,000 of your own money to buy a one-half equity in the property at the outset, or 2) investing $18,000 for a one-fifth equity. Now we have to decide which is better, which will bring you greater profits.

In Case 1, you'll get a mortgage loan from the bank of $45,000 to finance your purchase. You'd have to come up with the remaining $45,000 cash to pay the buyer out of your own pocket.

In Case 2, you'll go into debt for a whopping $72,000, and only have to pay $18,000 out of your own pocket. Let's see why going into debt for $72,000 is better.

Your first-year interest charges on the mortgage loan of $45,000 might amount to around $5,400. This assumes you have to pay 12 percent interest on the money you borrow from the bank. If you took a $72,000 loan at the same 12 percent interest rate your first year interest charges would be more: $8,640. Let's see why borrowing the larger amount from the bank (Case 2) will give you a bigger return on your money:

	Case 1 You Pay $45,000 Down	Case 2 You Pay $18,000 Down
Gross income	$18,000	$18,000
Interest on mortgage	(5,400)	(8,640)
Net income	$12,600	$ 9,360

So far, it looks as though Case 1, paying $45,000 down, wins. But wait. The most important criterion to an inflation-beating real estate investor is *yield*, or *percentage re-*

turned on capital invested. So let's have another look in a new light.

	Case 1 You Pay $45,000 Down	Case 2 You Pay $18,000 Down
Net income	$12,600	$ 9,360
Divided by down payment	÷45,000	÷18,000
Percent return on investment	28%	52%

Now, Case 2 comes out the winner, with 52 percent return on investment versus 28 percent in Case 1. The reason why: Case 2 is more highly leveraged. The rule, again: pay for your real estate with as little down as possible.

TAX SHELTER ADVANTAGES

Maybe you're conservative by nature and still like Case 1. That's the one, as we see above, with the *lower percentage* return but *larger net* return on your money invested. You might like Case 1 better, for instance, because you think you'll need all the rent dollars you can get to keep the house heated, serviced, and repaired, costs that our oversimplified example failed to take into account.

This is a keen observation, but the two buildings aren't comparable taxwise. There are tax advantages you will get on your "rent-out" property. These tax advantages will help pay your operating expenses.

The property you buy *to rent out* is a *business* property, not personal property. As a *business* property, all your operating expenses—heat, water, painting, gardening, repairs, and the like—are *business* expenses and therefore tax deductible. They provide you with a tax shelter, which means that you will pay less tax on your profits at the end of the year.

All you do is subtract your property's operating expenses—heat, water, and so on—from your gross rents when you report your income to the folks from the IRS. You also deduct your property taxes. These are some of the valued tax deductions (shelters) you get when you buy income-producing property. These tax deductions will save you tax dollars on April 15 and will go a long way to helping you pay not only the operating expenses on your rent-out property, but also the interest on your mortgage.

But the tax shelters don't stop here. There's even more you can deduct for tax purposes—your *depreciation* allowance. Depreciation is the accounting magic big investors love. It's one of the most attractive features of investing in real estate. Yet it is so misunderstood.

Depreciation on your real estate investment is simply a theoretical "using up" of your building's value. Each year, Uncle Sam allows building owners to subtract a certain proportion of their building's original cost to them, which has been *theoretically* used up over the year. It sounds ridiculous but every building theoretically loses part of its value each year because it theoretically wears out. (In point of fact, most buildings actually increase in value because of inflation.)

Since as of this writing the folks from IRS put the theoretical life of an average home at forty years, they allow you to subtract on your tax returns one-fortieth (which is equal to 2½ percent) of the *full purchase price* you paid for the building. In other words, besides subtracting all the building's yearly expenses, you can also subtract the building's theoretical loss of value, called "depreciation."

It's a great deal. Because you can subtract depreciation but don't really incur any out-of-your-pocket depreciation expenses, it is possible, for tax purposes, to show a "paper" or "fictitious" loss. You can subtract this paper loss from whatever other normal taxable income, even non-real-estate income, that you might have. This is what makes income-producing real estate one of the best investments and best tax shelters any investor—sophisticated or not—can ever own.

Now let's put all this together into a fuller picture of our rent-out investment. As before, focus on your duplex that costs $90,000. Your down payment was $18,000. Let's add our estimates for real estate taxes, utilities, and maintenance costs for a better depth of field. Now we'll really develop insight. First year income and expenses would now look like this:

Item	Yearly Amount
Rental Income	$18,000
Less: Mortgage payments	(8,640)
Real estate taxes	(2,700)
Heat and other utilities	(2,100)
Maintenance	(1,800)
Insurance	(1,000)
Net Income	$ 1,760
Less: Depreciation	(2,250)
Taxable Income (Loss)	$ (490)

Congratulations, you own a tax shelter. That negative $490 shown in the parentheses is your "fictitious" loss. Is this really a good way to use your money? Yes, it is indeed.

First of all, your *paper* loss can be subtracted from your other income at income tax time. Second, your biggest profit will come when you sell your property. It will have appreciated enormously because of inflation so you'll be able to realize a nice profit when you sell it.

FINDING THE RIGHT INVESTMENT FOR YOU

Whether you are a first-timer buying a home for yourself or a homeowner already looking for a second piece of property, you have to shop the market carefully and knowledgeably.

If it's a home for you to live in yourself, sit down with your family in a relaxed atmosphere and determine exactly what kind of property you want to buy. Take into consideration requests from the youngest to the oldest. Decide whether you want a new home with all the modern conveniences or an older, roomier one you can fix up. Decide whether a vacation home you can rent out for part of the year might be best. What style you want, how many rooms it should have, and how much land it's on are all important considerations. These decisions will take time.

A good way to determine exactly what you want is to make a list of your requirements. Your list should have two columns: "Must Haves" and "Wants." Must Haves are features your home cannot be without, such as a separate bathroom for a teen-age daughter. Stand firm on Must Haves, compromise on Wants such as a two-car garage or guest bedroom. Since you are not likely to find a home, summer cottage, ski chalet, or other investment property that meets every desire on your list, stay flexible. That's the purpose of the Want column of your list—to give you some idea of the features you might be able to live without.

Once you know what you are looking for and whether you're buying a live-in or income-producing property, take time to shop the market. Don't rush the buying process because being in a hurry puts you in a seller's market. It will probably not only cost you money, but take the fun out of the buying process as well.

For most real estate hunters, a broker is essential, since he or she knows most of the properties for sale in the area and can save you time by weeding out those that would probably be unsuitable. With your broker, your list of requirements, and notebook in hand, see as many places as possible. Go around to old and new structures in a range of prices—this will give you a good idea of the cost and quality of houses on the market.

As you shop, don't be taken in by the eye-catching frills: electric garage doors, dimmers on light switches, or mirrored walls and ceilings. Don't be overly consumed with little flaws, such as chipped tiles, that can be easily corrected. At the same time, don't assume that every problem has an easy solution. Most are correctable, but the cost of the repairs for new roofing, insulation, gutters, and a driveway, for example, may put the house out of your range.

It's a good idea to ask the owners why they are selling such a lovely home. If they don't have a reasonable answer such as "We've been transferred," or "We want something bigger," or "We need the cash," they may know of something about their home, co-op, or condo they aren't telling.

If the house looks as though it meets your requirements, check the electrical, heating, air conditioning, and water supply systems too. Check the garage, basement, and storage areas. Are they big enough for your needs? Are they suitable for tenants?

It's a good idea to use your notebook to make a checklist to compare the properties you like. After visiting each one, jot down the name, address, and phone number of the owner or builder and the selling agent. Be sure to note the asking price, required down payment, terms of monthly mortgage payments, estimated closing costs, property taxes, any deed restrictions, and past or estimated utility bills. One purpose of your broker is to help you obtain this information.

Before you decide to buy, you should have the home you have chosen inspected by an expert engineer. It's a good idea to do this even if it is a new house or co-op. New houses should be examined closely for incomplete work and missing detail. Minor flaws are to be expected and the builder should correct them or adjust the purchase price before you sign the purchase contract.

Flaws and defects especially in the roof or foundation may not be readily apparent to untrained eyes and once discovered may enable you to bargain down the price of the home. The way to do this is to have a qualified home inspector (ask your broker or lawyer to suggest one or check the Yellow Pages under "Building Inspection") assess the structural aspects of your investment. He will generally check the condition of the foundation, walls, floors, roof, electrical circuits, furnace, plumbing, and sewer system. In his written report you'll find out whether the house is well insulated and if there is evidence of damage or settlement, and whether there are termites, all of which come to bear on what you will want to pay for the property.

If you think some problems exist, you can probably negotiate a better price. Consult other specialists as well. Plumbers, electricians, and roofers can tell you whether major repairs will be needed and what they will cost.

As your final investment safeguard, you should have your broker or lawyer call in an appraiser. An appraiser's report is a valuable document if you're buying a piece of property in an area with which you are not thoroughly familiar. (If you're buying in your own home town, you probably don't need one.) Your appraiser should be able to inform you of the quality of the neighborhood, zoning regulations, population trends, property tax levels, and prospects. After you get a written report from the appraiser and your home inspector, you're ready to sign the final purchase documents.

INSURANCE

You're a real estate investor and now you'll need insurance—homeowner's insurance to protect your new investment against fire, and your belongings inside against theft and other losses.

The best advice is to insure your home for 80 percent or more of the cost of rebuilding it and keep your coverage up to date. That way you will recover 100 percent of any partial loss up to the face value of your policy. When you insure for under 80 percent, the insurance company will handle your claims differently and you may not be able to recover the current cost of replacing a loss.

As inflation increases your real estate's value, it will also increase your cost of rebuilding. Double-digit inflation in twelve months' time can make your insurance coverage obsolete. This is why the amount of homeowner's insurance you need is the cost of *rebuilding* your home, not your original purchase price. If you prefer built-in protection against inflation, there are several "inflation-guard" policies available. This will ensure that insurance coverage automatically keeps pace with inflation and that your home will be adequately protected.

If it's income-producing property you are buying, speak to any real estate insurance agent about the specific types of policies available.

REMEMBER, MORTGAGE DEBT PAYS

Many people wonder whether they should pay off their mortgage early. The answer is probably not. Quite simply, you can usually earn a better rate of return in other reasonably secure ways—gold (during accelerating inflation), stocks (during decelerating inflation), and gems, art, antiques, stamps, and coins, for example (during accelerating *or* decelerating inflation).

If your mortgage is set at an interest rate equal to or less than these investment opportunities afford—and in most cases it probably is—then paying off the mortgage is not your best choice. With the same money you would use to pay off your mortgage, you can invest in any of the Magic

Assets discussed in the first part of this book, and over the long run get a better percentage return on your money.

The dollar is sliding each year, and your mortgage—a long-term loan with a fixed-interest rate—benefits you, the borrower. As everyone living in Inflationland knows by now, a borrower pays off his loan in cheaper dollars, so his fixed payments cost him less each year in real value. (Remember, rising inflation benefits borrowers, all borrowers, mortgage borrowers included.)

If you have a "variable rate" mortgage or any other kind of mortgage that charges you higher interest with higher inflation, you are not as lucky. With these types of mortgages you don't have the same advantages as with a standard mortgage because your lender is entitled to higher interest payments as interest rates rise with inflation. Still, if you think you can earn a better return on a tangible asset, take it. Your accountant or financial advisor can help you determine what to do.

By not paying off your mortgage early you can take advantage in still another way. Because of inflation, your income, in dollar terms, will increase over the coming years. As a result bracket creep will put you in a higher income tax bracket. One of the advantages of a mortgage loan is that interest payments are deductible on your income tax return and that saves you tax dollars. As your income taxes increase, so does the value of your deduction. If you're in a 25 percent bracket, every dollar you claim as a tax deduction derived from mortgage interest saves twenty-five cents; in a 40 percent bracket, you are spared forty cents' worth of taxes on every dollar of interest paid.

So let inflation and the tax system work for you. Wait until borrowing rates are favorable. Then borrow money from a bank to buy real estate that grows in value, then pay the bank back with inflated dollars later on. You'll beat inflation and the folks from the IRS—both at the same time.

OWNING LAND

If you're not stimulated by the thought of holding and managing residential property, perhaps because of tenant aggravation or because you don't care to advertise or deal with management companies or brokers, don't despair.

Fortunately there are other investment opportunities for you in real estate.

One is unimproved land, that is, land without any buildings on it. Since there is no structure to rent out, however, an investment in unimproved land does not produce any immediate income. Instead of income you can get a handsome capital gain years down the road when you sell, *if* you have chosen carefully.

A good investment in land is one that appreciates much faster than inflation. And choosing such a piece of property isn't as hard to find as it may seem. Towns and cities grow while available land shrinks. Ocean resort areas attract more vacationers but the shorefront doesn't stretch. When you invest in unimproved property, you are betting that prime location land will become more scarce than it now is in that area.

In general, there is not so much a shortage of land as there is a shortage of prime location land. The purchase of any piece of real estate is really dependent on one thing—location. It is better for you to pay a higher price for a prime piece of real estate in the best location possible than to purchase a bargain in a poor one. Buy in the path of expansion and progress of a community. Keep away from the depreciating and deleterious effects of industrial and commercial nuisances such as noise, smoke, manufacturing odors, and fumes.

Take your time looking over the prospects. Confine yourself to nearby communities where you have some sense of the growth or decline of neighborhoods and commercial areas. Talk to the brokers and learn as much as you can. Call the telephone numbers on the "For Sale" signs in your community. Speak to owners. In short, to a large extent the value of your property may very well be dependent upon whether it has arrived as a "100 percent location" or whether it has yet to be realized as one.

Above all, be prepared to pay the taxes and mortgage loan costs of holding the property for five or ten years until the area has developed enough to carry you far ahead of inflation. And remember, your real estate taxes and mortgage payments are tax deductible.

GOING COMMERCIAL

If paying real estate taxes and mortgage interest on an unused piece of land is little help to you when Uncle Sam asks for his tribute every April 15, why not investigate a commercial property for its inflation-beating return? Owning a small building of stores or offices can really set you apart from the sluggish investor who stashes all his cash at the local bank.

Generally speaking, the economics of owning a small commercial building are the same as for residences. Instead of people living in your building, they work there. But the risk is a little higher since businesses can fail and stores can stand vacant for several months. With apartments or duplexes, there is a readier market of tenants. Along with higher risk in the commercial market, however, comes a chance for quite comfortable commercial profits.

The biggest difference between residential and commercial real estate is in the mortgage—the amount of money the bank lends you for your down payment. There are many different kinds of mortgages available for commercial property, but most are for much shorter terms and at higher rates of interest than for residences. Banks are now beginning to insist on the right to renegotiate loans on residences after three, five or ten years, but with office buildings and other commercial property they have always held that option.

Banks also like to limit the amount they lend on office buildings, even small ones, and that seems to mean a substantial down payment for you. But if you're really serious about making money, you can escape shelling out too much cash by getting a second mortgage to cover half or more of the down payment. A second mortgage, like a first mortgage, is simply a loan the bank makes you so you can buy the property.

First and second mortgages are not great mysteries. The holder of the first mortgage is first in the sense that, if you default, he has the right to sell the property and recover as much as he can of what he lent you. If there is anything left over, the holder of the second mortgage is next in line to get his. In return for his greater risk, the holder of the second mortgage charges you higher interest.

238 MONEYSMARTS

Here's a quick example of a possible investment you could make in an office building. Let's assume you buy an eighty by eighty building with six thousand square feet of usable space. That's about the size of a supermarket.

You purchase the land and building for $198,000. Your trip to the bank gets you a first mortgage loan for 60 percent of the purchase price, or $118,800. The bank agrees to lend you this money for a period of five years at 16 percent with 14 percent going to interest and the rest to pay off the principal. In addition to the loan from the bank, the previous owner of the building gives you a second mortgage loan for $39,600 at a straight 18 percent interest with no payment to principal.

You will also have to pay yearly costs to maintain your building, of course. Taxes every year will be high at approximately 7.5 percent of the full value of the building, or $7,500. Heat and utilities will be expensive at today's out-of-sight energy prices. They'll run about $6,000 annually. Those are your basic costs.

Now let's look at your revenues. A reasonable rental of $11 per square foot per year will yield you $66,000 and will cover these expenses including a contingency figure to guard against loss of rent due to the failure of a tenant's business.

Yearly revenues and expenses thus look like this:

Item	Yearly Amount
Rental income	$66,000
Less: Payments on first mortgage	(19,008)
Payments on second mortgage	(7,128)
Reserve to pay off principal of second mortgage in 5 years	(7,920)
Taxes	(14,850)
Heat and utilities	(6,000)
Maintenance	(2,000)
Contingency	(7,500)
Net income to you	$ 1,594

So far, you say, this return isn't enough to buy a vacation for two at Club Med. But don't despair. In another five years you'll have enough money for more than you've ever dreamed possible. Remember, real estate is a long-term investment.

Now it's five years later and we'll assume that inflation has pushed all costs and prices up, including the rent you charge. You go back to the bank for a new first mortgage at the same rate but on a slightly reduced principal since you have been paying back 2 percent of the principal for the past five years. The joy of real estate is that by now you no longer have to pay anything on the second mortgage because you have saved enough from the income to pay it off. That was the $7,920 figure above.

So where do we stand now? Assuming even a low inflation rate of 8 percent, your yearly income and expense figures for the second five years look like this:

Item	Yearly Amount
Rental income ($16 sq. ft.)	$96,000
Less: Payments on new first mortgage	(17,107)
Taxes	(21,681)
Heat	(8,760)
Maintenance	(2,920)
Contingency	(11,000)
Net income to you	$34,532

You're on cloud nine, earning $34,532 *annually* on your original $39,600 cash investment.

Now it's ten years later and you decide you want to cash in. The price of your property has gone up at least 8 percent a year along with inflation. You now find you can sell it for $427,467!

If you also happen to be a shopowner in your own right, you can sweeten this picture even further by renting space from yourself in your own building. Perhaps you run a flower shop, a health food stand, or have some other business idea. You could "vertically integrate" the two moneymakers by doing them together for greater return and even more protection against a shrinking dollar.

So let some real estate into your life and grow richer the old-fashioned way.

22. INFLATION-PROOFING FOR RETIREMENT

THE SCHULTZ SYNDROME

Even as inflation accelerated after her husband's death, Mattie Schultz, a ninety-one-year-old widow from San Antonio, Texas, lived on a meager $233 a month. Her income consisted of the veteran's benefits of her late husband and Social Security. The government benefits were insufficient, but Mattie Schultz was resourceful and made do with the help of a few thousand dollars she and her husband had saved over the years.

All was well, until suddenly the widow lost all but $10 of her $4,900 life savings to a swindler. Soon afterward, Mrs. Schultz found herself jailed overnight for stealing $15.04 worth of groceries from her local supermarket.

Luckily, the media picked up Mrs. Schultz's story and the publicity prompted an outpouring of sympathy *and groceries* for the woman who later said she wanted God to "close her eyes" because her plight had forced her to shoplift.

Mattie Schultz may also have been lucky for another reason. At least she was able to collect her Social Security benefits. Professor Michael Wachter, former economic advisor to President Carter, believes most people under thirty-five may not be able to collect Social Security. Incredible as it may sound the University of Pennsylvania professor believes that it's only a matter of time, about twenty years, before inflation and changing workforce patterns bankrupt the Social Security system. Even if you're close to Mattie

INFLATION-PROOFING FOR RETIREMENT

Schultz in age, you run the risk of social insecurity because the Social Security system has been tilted on its axis.

The theory goes like this: Social Security is not receiving enough fresh money and in about twenty years will not be solvent enough to pay the benefits we're entitled to. The reason for this conclusion is clear. The system is dependent in large part upon a continuous flow of new money from new workers entering the American workforce. When President Roosevelt signed the Social Security Act in the 1930s, there were ninety people in the workforce supporting each senior citizen receiving benefits. That was a system that people could rely upon. Today, however, instead of ninety workers supporting each recipient of Social Security, we have only *three*. Not enough new money is flowing into the Social Security system to support everyone who will become eligible for benefits.

The good news: Washington has finally acknowledged the problem. The bad news: Congress has not been able to figure out what to do about the problem. What Washington does from time to time, but only as a stopgap, is to increase its budget deficit, then print extra dollars to pay Social Security recipients. But the more inflationary money Washington prints, the higher prices climb, and the farther behind in purchasing power everyone falls.

Many women, in particular, will have difficulty earning their fair share of Social Security. Social Security payouts are based on the number of years you have been employed. The longer you have been in the workforce, the more Social Security benefits you receive. Raising a family may eliminate the possibility of employment for several years. A return to college, graduate, or professional school will have the same effect. And it is still an undeniable fact that women's salaries average less than men's. The result is that maximum benefits are unlikely.

Don't think that marriage will solve the problem. Although the law has been repaired to eliminate some gross inequities, it still does not recognize homemaking as an occupation with a definite economic value. The woman who happens not to be married for more than ten years to any one man simply loses out entirely unless she is also employed and is entitled to her own Social Security. She cannot collect benefits as a result of marriage and years spent managing a home.

242 MONEYSMARTS

If you intend to rely on a corporate retirement plan to bail you out, remember that corporate retirement programs will suffer as much as Social Security during an inflationary crisis. In fact, corporate retirement plans may even produce less spectacular results. The sponsors of these plans cannot print the extra money the government can to pay benefits. Just as New York City nearly went bankrupt paying pensions to city workers, so may the company you work for if it's not well capitalized now.

Even if you are not covered by a corporate pension plan, but rather by your own Individual Retirement Account (IRA) or Keogh plan, this is no guarantee you will be any better off than your friends covered by their own employer or by Uncle Sam. Just because the government has endorsed Keoghs and IRAs by granting tax benefits to those who set them up does not mean these people are automatically immune from losing retirement buying power. We will explain these plans in this chapter and illustrate that these retirement plans do serve a need, but only if you know how to use them and fund them properly. Hopefully, the tax benefits granted to these plans by the time you read the future. Remember: prices have been going up by dou- this will not be curtailed by Congress.

The one thing to remember about pension plans: who puts the money *in*—you, your employer, or the government —doesn't matter. It's what you get *back* that counts. If you'll be getting *dollars* back, they will come out of your retirement plan almost worthless. If inflation continues on its present course, prices will be so astronomical that the purchasing power of every dollar you get back will have dropped to about fifty cents by 1984, less than a quarter by 1990, and less than a dime by 2001.

DO IT NOW

A financially independent future will not come automatically. Our Constitution does not guarantee us the right to comfort during retirement. How much we enjoy our retirement years will depend in large part on how our cash-flow situation during our leisure years is structured. This in turn is dependent on the stockpile of retirement assets we have managed to accumulate during our working years.

How fruitful a cash flow you will have at your fingertips will depend upon what quantities of Magic Assets you have amassed. Your cash flow will be generated by liquidating these assets for spending money. Your other assets—bankbooks and bonds—may help a little too, but will probably have lost most of their purchasing power by the time you retire.

A large stockpile of retirement assets will not come about automatically. It requires long-range saving and planning to keep us ahead of future inflation. It requires us to concentrate on stockpiling and investing assets ahead of time. The sensible course of action is to give some serious thought to retirement now to ensure purchasing power gains from inflation rather than purchasing power losses. This way you will be fully inflation-proofed to enjoy the future.

There is no specific age to begin planning for retirement. Obviously, the sooner the better. Although it's tough enough to cope with the problems of everyday living, we must realize that time passes quickly. If you think back, you can probably remember the first day you entered school. So no matter what stage of life you are now passing through, you should begin to think now about weaving your life into a financial pattern that will pay handsomely in the future.

Planning for your golden years, in fact, is as important to the young worker as it is to those workers now in their middle years. Today's young workers will need more financial resources than a person who is retired today. They may well spend more than two decades in retirement, almost twice today's retirement span. The earlier you start planning, the easier you can amass the wealth you will need to generate the cash flow to take you through your golden years. Planning ahead will also give you greater flexibility in saving and investing your nest egg.

It's almost 2000. Doctors report a man retiring at age sixty-five can look forward to a life expectancy of another dozen years. A woman can expect to live another twenty years. So the sooner we start, the sooner we can lay the groundwork for a comfortable, independent life in the later years.

MAGIC ASSET TAX-FREE PENSIONS

As of this writing, besides stockpiling Magic Assets under the Dollar Diversification technique, you may be able to do so under a special tax-free Keogh plan. If you are self-employed, either as an individual or as a partner in an unincorporated business, you are probably eligible to establish a Keogh retirement plan. You can also set one up for your full-time employees who have been employed by you for three or more years.

Congress created the Keogh plan especially to allow self-employed individuals such as owners of small stores, consultants, doctors, lawyers, and artists to stockpile wealth for retirement and enjoy tax breaks at the same time.

Keogh plans are a device through which you can set up a tax-free retirement fund. With such a program you can build up a stockpile of assets for your retirement at a faster pace and at a smaller tax cost than you could without the tax deductions and exemptions the Keogh technique grants.

Here's how a Keogh plan works. At the time of this writing, you can set aside up to 15 percent of your earned income as your "contribution" to your Keogh plan, subject to a $1,500 limit per year. The amount you set aside each year can vary or you can forgo any contribution if you choose. In other words, you can set aside $3,000 one year, nothing the next year, and $500 the year after.

The special tax advantages of a Keogh plan are twofold. First, you can deduct the amount you contribute to your Keogh fund each year from your yearly taxable income. This can save you tax dollars every April 15. Second, all interest income and capital gains on your invested contributions accumulate tax-deferred until you withdraw from the Keogh plan and take your assets back. It is at this time that you pay tax on the amounts you have previously contributed into the Keogh fund and on the income those contributions have generated. In other words, everything is tax-free until you begin to collect the funds on retirement.

Once assets are set aside in the plan, you have to leave them until at least age fifty-nine and a half. If you withdraw them early, there are penalties, so it would not be the place

INFLATION-PROOFING FOR RETIREMENT

for your assets if you will need to convert to cash before retirement.

At the time of this writing the Keogh laws are in a state of flux. Traditionally, the best assets to buy with Keogh contributions have been, of course, the Magic Assets. Investment diamonds (Chapter 5), rare stamps (Chapter 14), and rare coins (Chapter 15) are best because of their steady uninterrupted appreciation. Gold (Chapter 2) and silver (Chapter 7) are also good; but remember, gold and silver can fluctuate violently over the short term. Hopefully, by the time you read this, Congress will not have changed the law to eliminate the tax advantages of funding your Keogh with Magic Assets.

Since you are limited to a maximum contribution of $1,500 each year, you can start with rare stamps and coins, then when your Keogh value appreciates high enough, you can replace the rare coins with diamonds. Since you can buy gold and silver in relatively small denominations, you can add these whenever you wish.

For most people, the practical way to set up a plan is to tie in with an already existing plan offered now by rare stamp and coin dealers as well as investment diamond dealers. You can call upon your banks, insurance companies, and mutual funds as well. These organizations can help you set up a plan using assets with which you feel most comfortable.

Speak with these financial consultants as well as your lawyer or accountant before choosing a specific plan because as of this writing many in Congress are talking about overhauling the Keogh law. Hear them out to be sure all tax angles are covered, then decide which plan is best for you.

A word to the young: younger people can benefit more than older people from Keogh. Their assets have a longer time to appreciate tax-free. Their problem is being able to afford setting up a plan. If this is the case, set up a plan with what you can spare—go through the motions and learn about the advantages. If you can afford to contribute in a given year, great; if not, previous contributions will accumulate in value tax-free.

THE MAGIC ASSET TAX-FREE
INDIVIDUAL RETIREMENT ACCOUNT

Like the Keogh plan, an Individual Retirement Account (IRA) allows you to shelter a small portion of your income from the IRS until you retire. The IRA law is also in the process of being overhauled. As of this writing, you are allowed to set aside, tax-free, 15 percent of your earned income up to a maximum of $1,500 each year. (If you are married, receiving compensation, and your spouse is *not* employed, you may establish separate Individual Retirement Accounts and the maximum amount of the total contribution for both accounts is raised to $1,750.) The amount you can set aside for retirement each year can vary, so you can put $300 in your IRA one year, nothing the next year, and $1,000 the next. You decide how much money you want to put in.

The tax-free angle with an IRA is the same as it is with Keogh. The money you sink into your IRA comes off the top of your earnings. That is, your contributions to your IRA are tax deductible. Moreover, all the income and capital gains that your contributed money generates accumulate tax-deferred until withdrawn from your account. You only pay these taxes when you begin to collect the funds on retirement.

You can fund your IRA with Magic Assets. As with Keoghs, investment diamonds, rare stamps, and coins are particularly excellent vehicles for your IRA. At the time of this writing, since you are limited to a maximum contribution of $1,500 (or $1,750) each year, it's a good idea to start with rare stamps or coins, then when your IRA value appreciates high enough, you can shift from rare coins to diamonds.

Rare stamp and coin dealers, investment diamond dealers, mutual funds, banks, and insurance companies all offer custom-tailored plans from which to choose. As the law is always changing, check with them as well as your lawyer or accountant to make sure you have covered all the tax angles.

You may withdraw these assets or whatever other assets you put in before retirement, but assets you withdraw for personal use prior to reaching the age of fifty-nine and a half (except in the case of complete disability) are subject to a government mandated tax penalty of 10 percent. Your IRA is a long-term investment, as the law is designed to encourage the conservation of funds put aside for retirement.

LIFE INSURANCE LIFEBOAT?

Got lots of life insurance coverage? Think your loved ones will be safe and sound in Inflationland forever? Sorry. There's nothing sacred about life insurance. During the German runaway inflation of the 1920s the postage stamp on the envelope containing a widow's insurance payment was often worth more than the enclosed check.

The benefits of life policies are as vulnerable to soaring prices and plummeting purchasing power as Bank of Inflationland passbooks, disappearing bonds, or anemic dollar retirement plans.

Under the typical life insurance policy, your insurance company promises to pay a seemingly huge sum of money to your family when you die. But don't be lulled into a false sense of security. The question to ask yourself is: *how long* will that money last?

If you bought a life insurance policy as recently as 1970, inflation has already halved its value to your beneficiaries. If prices continue to rise at their current rate, your policy's value will be quartered by 1986, then cut down to one-eighth its original value by 1992.

But rest easy. We'll now see how to keep your life insurance policies alive and pumping.

NEW IMPROVED LIFE

Because of inflation in this country, we now know that even though our present income might be sufficient to meet our family's needs today, that same income would be inadequate tomorrow. Such is also true of life insurance. An amount that is sufficient when a policy is purchased will probably prove to have lost most of its purchasing power many years later.

At long last, several life insurance companies have developed a *cost-of-living* insurance rider to solve the rising cost-of-living problem. For a small additional premium over and above the purchase of a normal life insurance policy you can buy a cost-of-living rider which helps you protect your life insurance's purchasing power from the effects of inflation.

This cost-of-living insurance rider automatically helps you protect your insurance dollars against inflation. It simply uses the cash dividends your insurance company would ordinarily pay you annually to purchase an additional amount of insurance to keep your death benefits geared to the general price level. So instead of collecting yearly dividends on your policy, you can use your would-be dividends to increase the ultimate death payoff.

The cost-of-living rider also guarantees the right to purchase a supplemental amount of insurance whenever your policy's dividends are not sufficient, so you can add enough extra insurance to keep pace with increases in the consumer price index.

Confusing as all this is, the important point to remember is that your insurance policy dividends are used to build upon the face amount of your insurance coverage to keep your "total death benefit" geared to changes in the cost of living.

In the event of runaway inflation, you are generally guaranteed the right to buy a supplemental life or endowment policy regardless of your health or occupation. Do, in fact, buy a rider that guarantees you this right.

When you invest in a cost-of-living insurance rider, be on guard against riders that help protect your life insurance from the effects of inflation for only a certain *limited* period, for example, only until you reach age sixty-five. Pay a little extra for an inflation rider that will protect your family until the policy's benefits are paid. This way, no matter the inflation rate, you will have guaranteed your family financial security for as long as possible. When the rider ends, your family will have the original face amount, the face amount of the supplemental policies still in effect, and the additional paid-up insurance bought by your dividends. You will have survived inflation.

MATTIE SCHULTZ REVISITED

Planning for Mrs. Schultz's golden years was both simple and tricky. It was simple for us because there was an easy answer to the question "How much should she put aside

INFLATION-PROOFING FOR RETIREMENT

and invest for retirement?" The answer was, "As much as Mrs. Schultz possibly could." But it was tricky because there was no simple formula to follow. Mrs. Schultz could have cut her preretirement expenses to the bone in order to fund a handsome retirement income. Or she could have decided that it was more important to live well while she was young. Children present other questions. If she had wanted to leave an inheritance, she would have had to decide how much and include that goal in her plans.

To ensure a high degree of comfort during later life, start out by making a list of your retirement needs now. Include the usual necessities. Add in taxes, transportation, vacations, and any large one-time expenses that may extend into your retirement years. With delayed marriages and childrearing becoming more common, perhaps college loans for your children will still be a factor. Or you may want to plan for one last grand tour of a foreign country or a trip around the world.

Make all your calculations in current dollars, then correct for inflation by adding about 10 percent per year into the future. Remember: prices have been going up by double-digit levels for the past few years. And even if they slow down temporarily because of a tough new national anti-inflation policy, they are bound to steamroll ahead again eventually.

You will have to choose a retirement age to figure out this calculation. The new laws on forced retirement allow you to work until age seventy without fear of being pushed out the door. But you may want to choose an earlier date. Early retirement means you will have to work harder to counter inflation. If you meet your goals and then decide to retire at a later age, you will have additional income.

Your calculation of yearly retirement expenses indicates the amount of money you need for retirement income. To allow for contingencies, add 10 percent to the expenses to be on the safe side.

Now to make sure you have an adequate income when your rainbow years arrive, add up your expected yearly cash inflow. We have already seen that Social Security is a question mark, but don't rule it out completely. Too many people rely on Social Security for the government to abandon it or allow its benefits to be eaten away *entirely* by inflation. And since pegging Social Security benefits to inflation is now the government's common practice, you should receive at least a small amount.

So let's start with Social Security. We have seen that Social Security, at best, will only be a small supplement to other retirement income, such as pensions, which may also be only modestly supplemental, and income from the sale of your Magic Assets. To figure your Social Security, a pamphlet called "Estimating Your Social Security Retirement Check" will help, and it's available from your local Social Security office. But since it doesn't explicitly cover anyone retiring after 1984, you will have to be ingenious in adapting it. A calculator and crystal ball would certainly help. Next, add in your expected pension income per year. Now let's put this analysis to work.

Pretend that you are retiring in 2001 and let's suppose that you receive $10,000 in Social Security benefits and $10,000 in pension income. Subtract the total of these amounts, which we will assume is $20,000, from your estimated retirement yearly income, which we'll assume is $80,000. (You'll need the $80,000 because with 10 percent inflation prices will double about every seven years!) The difference between our assumed $80,000 you'll need and $20,000 you'll get is $60,000. That is the income you will need from your own sources.

Besides income from the sale of Magic Assets, a typical way of meeting this need is to purchase an *annuity* from an insurance company. An annuity is a right to receive a fixed payment from your insurance company every year during your retirement. The cost of the annuity will depend on your intended retirement age, the income desired, and the insurance company's best guess about your longevity and the investment outlook over the expected life of the annuity. It is important to note, however, that over the last decade annuities have provided less return per dollar invested than the Magic Assets.

You could call your insurance agent and ask for the current purchase price of an annuity that fits your requirements. But by retirement you may have become so confident of your investment skills that you will want to live off sales of your Magic Assets. The safer middle course is to purchase a small annuity for an assured income while continuing to use your Magic Assets as the real retirement protection.

You know yourself best. The most rewarding course of action is to carefully analyze your circumstances. Be cautiously low in estimating your Social Security and other pension benefits. Plan on self-reliance—on providing most of your retirement income yourself. In this book we've covered many ways to do it. At your convenience concentrate on the investment strategies discussed throughout the book to build a comfortable and secure retirement.

23. THE MONEY SAGES

If your new financial awareness is beginning to make you feel that your personal affairs might benefit from some honest, expert money advice, you're in good company. Increasing numbers of us, slightly baffled by today's inflationary spiral, are looking for professional guidance with our money plans, especially in putting them into action.

Today, professional guidance can be as near as a telephone. Financial consultants now come in all shapes and sizes to fit your every money need. You can easily reach any of a number of these astute "personal financial planners" to help with your investments, taxes, insurance, real estate, or retirement plans. Some of them are independent practitioners. Others are attached to financial consulting organizations, accounting firms, banks, insurance companies, or brokerage houses. Some serve only the rich, but most have more modest aims.

Rich and not-so-rich alike in increasing numbers are buying into the minds of the money sages, not only because the money sages' fees are tax deductible, but because with inflation salaried families have more paper dollars to defend, protect, and multiply than they ever dreamed possible.

Before you engage a money sage, however, you have to understand how to buy his or her services and what it will cost. You must decide what advice you should buy and what you can supply yourself. So take the broadest view possible. Map out your life needs and goals and build a money plan around them.

Perhaps you anticipate a career change or a return to the job market after managing a home. You will need education or retraining and must plan for the expense. Perhaps one of your life goals is to own a house or condominium that is a showplace for entertaining. Or travel could be the experience that makes the difference for you.

Certainly these goals are attainable along with the routine needs of food, clothing, and shelter. List all the important ones. Attach a time frame. When do you want to achieve each? Now you're ready to speak to an advisor.

First, you have to realize that financial advisors come in two varieties—generalists and specialists. If you have substantial money to invest or large assets to manage and are uncertain about how to divide your money among different investments, a financial *generalist* is best. He or she can suggest relative amounts for investment to maximize returns without raising risks to a level that makes you uncomfortable. A generalist can warn you of tax consequences and suggest insurance policies to fit your life budget.

On the other hand, you may feel confident about the way you are allocating your resources and only want advice on the stock market, precious metals, or taxes. A *specialist* is best in this situation.

No matter the path you choose, never forget that you are your best decision maker. Learn enough about the areas of investment to understand and act on the advice you receive. Letting someone else do it all is a prescription for failure because it will be impossible for your advisor to keep up with your special needs and goals as they change. You have to work together to stay on top of your personal situation as well as the general economy.

The range of advisory services and products is exceptionally wide. Let's have a look at the field.

BROKERAGE HOUSES

Many stockbrokerage firms are now as bullish on financial planning for individuals and families as they are on stocks. Some of these firms offer their services for "free," hoping you will purchase your investments through them. Others offer their services for a fee which may be refunded if you place orders.

Fortunately, these days you do not have to worry that brokerage firms are biased only toward stocks. The range of financial products offered—stocks, precious metals, money market funds, tax shelters—will probably be broad enough to satisfy most of your needs.

Brokerage firms today are making an effort to provide financial planning and diversify their product line. Stocks, they know, are not right for all seasons.

You may be surprised, in fact, to know that E. F. Hutton now has a financial planning department, as does Merrill Lynch. The feeling on Wall Street these days is that if you have a coordinated investment plan, you will be more comfortable and confident managing your wealth. This is why even more firms than ever are going into the financial planning area.

Merrill Lynch, for example, already offers a financial analysis and fairly detailed plans for individuals at rates running from $600 and up. For an individual or couple without a house, condo, or co-op or much in the way of assets, the $600 will buy investment advice on insurance, corporate fringe benefits, and real estate. While their $600 fee may not sound cheap, especially for those with modest assets, it may make sense for the young professional or those expecting to inherit.

If you go to a brokerage house for financial advice, don't let them bury you in data printouts or overwhelm you with unusable recommendations. Before you put your money on the line, request a sample report. In reviewing it, try to determine how such a financial report and recommendations would help you. Watch out for pages of boiler plate, especially if it wallows in business school jargon such as "reposition your assets," which is often used in conjunction with the need to take advantage of "changing economic conditions." While these principles are right, the tipoff to whether you will get your money's worth from the information and recommendations is whether the jargon is usable, not how impressive it looks on paper. The value of the advice is directly proportionate to how quickly and efficiently you can put it into action. And, of course, how well it works to raise your comfort level.

INDEPENDENT FINANCIAL PLANNING COMPANIES

You may be able to benefit from one of the many financial planning companies through your present employer. Many of the Fortune 500 companies now hire financial planning specialists for their employees. As these financial planning firms are not in the stock, shelter, or insurance business per se, their advice is usually objective and their research generally thorough.

Sometimes you have to be at management level in your place of employment to qualify for the service. But if you do not qualify, you can usually buy the service if you're willing to pay the price. It can cost anywhere from a few hundred to a few thousand dollars, depending on what you need.

One of these larger planning organizations, The Ayco Corporation for example, charges a first year fee of $5,000 and a retainer of $2,000 each year thereafter. For this fee you receive royal treatment, from tax shelters to insurance, from investments to estate planning.

If such a royal smorgasbord is out of your range, less extravagant work is also available. Kanaly Trust Company, based in Houston, Texas, offers a "fee-for-service" planning for individuals. The trust company's fees start at about $1,000 for a basic financial analysis and plan of action.

If you do not want to pay a sum total outright, still other independent financial planners sometimes work on commissions. This way you might not have to pay a lump sum for financial work. For example, one counseling and financial service company, Financial Management Resources in the Washington, D.C. area, sells insurance, mutual funds, money funds, public real estate partnerships, and private natural gas partnerships that its own people operate directly. You can invest in one, two, or more vehicles and obtain an analysis of your assets, net worth, and investment objectives.

Most planning companies are willing to supply the names of some of their clients so you can contact these clients to find out if their services seem right for you. These clients can tell you whether or not they are satisfied with what they paid for. But do not be put off by not being given a long list of names, endorsements, or other people's financial statements. With most people, money is a private matter.

INSURANCE COMPANIES

For some time, and for your sake and theirs, major insurance companies have been expanding their product lines. In addition to buying insurance you can now buy money advice and financial vehicles as well. Even some small insurance companies now have a whole spread of financial products to sell besides insurance.

When dealing with the insurance people, try to remember that while their estate planning tends to be good, it's more difficult for them to keep as abreast as others on investments. But do not ignore this source, since not too many stockbrokers know their way around tax shelters or estate planning.

ACCOUNTANTS AND LAWYERS

An experienced accountant or tax lawyer who is investment oriented can be an excellent source for personal financial advice. These experts sell their time, not any particular product, so they're especially unbiased as to what to do with your assets. This is not to say that all are expert financial advisors. It's necessary to appraise the level of their expertise. As with the independent planning companies, you should know their reputation by knowing of their work personally or obtaining references.

NEWSLETTERS

You can subscribe to literally scores of newsletters written by money advisors who analyze the economy and give specific investment advice. This way you can draw your own conclusions about what's best for you. Some newsletters deal with individual investment vehicles such as stocks, gold, silver, diamonds, colored gemstones, art, antiques, real estate, while some deal with a number or all of these topics. Check the financial sections of newspapers and magazines for trial subscription application forms (which are usually reasonably priced).

Another good source is *Investment Information and Advice: A Handbook and Directory* published by Fir Publishing Company. R. R. Bowker, a subsidiary of Xerox, publishes the *Bibliography of Investment Methods,* which should prove useful. And Gale Research Company of Cincinnati publishes *Investment Information Sources.* For more specialized directories, see the Banking and Investments section of the *Guide to American Directories* from B. Klein Publications. You should also look through Chapter 24 of this book.

IT'S YOUR MONEY

Whatever advisor you end up with, if any at all, remember that the range of services varies and that the first thing you have to do is understand what financial product or products the advisor is selling. Then, before you put yourself in the hands of a perfect stranger, ask yourself these questions:

1. Is this the right advisor for you?
    a. Does he or she regularly handle clients like yourself?
    b. Is he or she organized to help a person with your income or assets?
    c. What is this advisor's general reputation in your community?
2. What is your advisor's track record?
    a. Could you have used this kind of advice in the past?
    b. If you had followed your advisor's past advice, would you be better off today using his or her smarts?

Even when you get perfectly good answers to these questions, you may still wonder if any particular advisor is the right one for you. If you continue to have doubts about the whole idea, here is an exercise you can try with different sorts of advisors.

Set up an imaginary portfolio similar in size to the one you chose in Chapter 10, "Magic Portfolios." Pick the past year or longer, and assume you invested this imaginary money according to your proposed advisor's past advice to his or her clients. Check with the advisor and some of his or her clients as to what the advisor's general recommendations were during that period. Use your best judgment along the way just as you would have if you had actually been following his or her advice. Now go to the library and review the actual performance of these investments.

Stocks, bonds, and precious metals have recognized markets with published prices in the newspapers. Real estate information is more difficult to get, but in most communities the actual sale price of houses is a matter of public record. The information may be three to six months old, but it will be there somewhere in the town hall records. Even easier, check with local brokers who truly know the real estate market.

Check the prices at least every three months, and keep your advisor's recommendations in front of you. Every time you make an imaginary transaction, remember to subtract a commission for the broker or agent. You may think, "Why am I doing all this when checking up on investments is actually my advisor's role?" This is an excellent exercise. You'll actually be taking a mini-course in portfolio analysis designed just for you.

Now total up the results. If you haven't had a yearly return of at least 4 percent or 5 percent over the inflation rate for the same period, you can probably do better by yourself.

Above all, realize that the risks and rewards in putting your money where your advisor's mouth is are yours completely. The more you know and care for your own financial affairs, the greater control you will have over your own destiny and the more self-satisfaction you will receive. That's moneysmarts.

24. MONEYSMARTS BOOSTERS

Now, here's some specific help in putting your money plans into action. I have listed by topic everything from books and publications to clubs and other helpful services.

First skim this chapter as a quick review of the book. Most of the magazines and newspapers I mention are available at your newsstand. If they're not, use the addresses and telephone numbers provided for sample copies and subscriptions. Subscription prices quoted are per year. You'll nearly always get a price break for longer subscriptions. Most of the publications mentioned can also be borrowed from your library for free.

Next, read this chapter again as you begin to think through the Dollar Diversified portfolio and inflation-beating lifestyle which is most comfortable for you.

DOLLAR DIVERSIFICATION

Here's what you can review to get a feel for the general economic circumstances and the investments we've talked about in this book:

MAGAZINES:

Money (at your newsstand with subscription form inside)

NEWSPAPERS:

Barron's (at your newsstand with subscription form inside)

NEWSLETTERS:

Harry Browne Special Reports
207 Jefferson Square
Austin, TX 78731
(512) 453-7313
$225 per year

The International Harry Schultz Letter
P.O. Box 2523
Lausanne 1002, Switzerland
Phone 392918
$258 per year

GOLD, SILVER, AND STRATEGICS

BOOKS:

War on Gold, Antony Sutton, '76 Press, Seal Beach, CA 90740, $9.95

NEWSLETTERS:

James Sinclair & Company
90 Broad Street
New York, NY 10004
$150 per year

GOLD AND SILVER DEALERS: The names of major gold and silver dealers appear in the business sections of your local newspapers. Here are some popular names:

Deak-Perera
29 Broadway
New York, NY 10006
(212) 635-0515

MONEYSMARTS BOOSTERS

Monex
4910 Birch Street
Newport Beach, CA 92660
(714) 752-1400 in California
(800) 854-3361

Manfra, Tordella & Brookes
One World Trade Center, Suite 3331
New York, NY 10048
(212) 775-1440 in New York
(800) 223-0998

Republic National Bank of New York
Fifth Avenue at 40th Street
New York, NY 10016
(212) 930-6000 in New York
(800) 223-0840

James Sinclair & Company (also a strategic metals broker)
90 Broad Street
New York, NY 10004
(212) 425-2360 in New York
(800) 221-4120

Bache Halsey Stuart (also a strategic metals broker)
100 Gold Street
New York, NY 10038
(212) 791-3549

GOLD CERTIFICATES:

Dreyfus Gold Deposits
600 Madison Avenue
New York, NY 10022
(212) 935-6666 in New York
(800) 223-7750

BOOKS ON GOLD PROSPECTING:

Gold Hunter's Fieldbook, Jay Ellis Ransom, Harper & Row, $4.95

Principal Gold-Producing Districts of the U.S., A. H. Koschman, U.S. Geological Survey Professional Paper no. 610. Write to: U.S. Geological Survey, 109 National Center, Reston, VA 22092

GOLD PROSPECTING EQUIPMENT SUPPLIERS:
(write for catalogs):

Keene Engineering
9330 Corbin Avenue
Northridge, CA 91324

Relco (detecting equipment)
P.O. Box 10839
Houston, TX 77018

STOCKS AND BONDS

BOOKS:

How to Buy Stocks, Louis Engel, Bantam, $3.25

The Battle for Investment Survival, Gerald Loeb, Simon & Schuster, $4.95

NEWSPAPERS:

The *Wall Street Journal* (at your newsstand)
Call (800) 628-9290 for a subscription; in New York call (212) 285-5000

MAGAZINES:

Business Week (at your newsstand with subscription form inside)

ADVISORY NEWSLETTERS:

Dow Theory Letters
P.O. Box 1759
La Jolla, CA 92038
$150 for 36 letters a year

Value Line Investment Survey
Arnold Bernhard & Co., Inc.
711 Third Avenue
New York, NY 10017
(800) 331-1750
$33 for a 10-week trial; $330 per year

ART AND ANTIQUES

BOOKS:

The Official Sotheby Parke Bernet Price Guide to Antiques and Decorative Arts, edited by Charles Cott, Simon & Schuster, $9.95

American Antique Toys, Barenholtz and McClintock, Harry N. Abrams, Inc., $45

Antique Toys and Dolls, Constance E. King, Rizzoli, $35

The Collector's Encyclopedia of Dolls, Evelyn J. Coleman, Crown, $27.50

Collecting Americana, Matthew J. Bowyer, A. S. Barnes, $20

Photograph Collector's Guide, Witkin and London, New York Geographic Society, $32.50

Photography in America, William Welling, T. Y. Crowell, $29.95

Book Collecting, Seumas Stewart, Elsevier-Dutton, $14.95

The Lyle Official Arts Review, Lyle Publications, $16.95

MAGAZINES AND NEWSPAPERS:

Antique Monthly
Boone, Inc.
P.O. Drawer 2
Tuscaloosa, AL 35402
$14 per year

The Antique Trader Weekly
P.O. Box 1050
Dubuque, IA 52001
$19 per year

The Magazine ANTIQUES
Straight Enterprises, Inc.
551 Fifth Avenue
New York, NY 10017
$33 per year

Antiques World
Subscription Service
P.O. Box 990
Farmingdale, NY 11737
$18 per year

The Antiques Journal
P.O. Box 1046
Dubuque, IA 52001
$11 per year

The Collector Investor
740 Rush Street
Chicago, IL 60611
$20 per year

Art and Auction
The Auction Guild
250 West 57th Street
New York, NY 10019
$25 per year

Art in America
542 Pacific Avenue
Marion, OH 43302
$29.95 per year

Arts Magazine
23 East 26th Street
New York, NY 10160
$32 per year

Artforum
P.O. Box 980
Farmingdale, NY 11737
$30 per year

ARTnews
Subscription Service
P.O. Box 969
Farmingdale, NY 11737
$20 per year

Black Art
259 W. Radcliffe Drive
Claremont, CA 91711
$12 per year

Portfolio
Subscription Service Bureau
P.O. Box 2714
Boulder, CO 80321
$15 per year

DIAMONDS AND COLORED GEMSTONES

BOOKS:

Encyclopedia of Gemstones, Dr. Joel Arem, Van Nostrand Reinhold, $35
Gems and Jewelry, Dr. Joel Arem, Bantam, $2.25

MAGAZINES:

Lapidary Journal
3564 Kettner Boulevard
P.O. Box 80937
San Diego, CA 92138

Mineralogical Record
P.O. Box 783
Bowie, MD 20715

Diamond World Review
P.O. Box 1381
Tel Aviv, Israel

NEWSLETTERS:

The Gemstone Price Report
Suite 1318
250 West 57th Street
New York, NY 10019
(212) 582-5633
$180 per year

MUSEUM COLLECTIONS:

American Museum of Natural History
Central Park West
New York, NY

Smithsonian Institution
Washington, DC

FOR CERTIFICATES OF AUTHENTICITY, GEM IDENTIFICATION, AND HOME STUDY COURSES:

Gemological Institute of America, Inc. (three branches)
580 Fifth Avenue
New York, NY 10036
(212) 221-5858

606 South Olive Street
Los Angeles, CA 90014
(213) 629-5435

1660 Stewart Street
Santa Monica, CA 90404
(213) 829-2991

TO CHECK WHETHER A GEM DEALER IS REGISTERED IN NEW YORK:

New York State Attorney General Securities Bureau
2 World Trade Center
New York, NY 10047
(212) 488-3357

WHOLESALE DEALERS (be careful here):

Reliance Diamonds
1900 Olympic Boulevard
Walnut Creek, CA 95696
(800) 227-1590
Collect: (415) 938-6510 in California, Alaska, Hawaii, Canada

Gemstone Trading Corporation
30 Rockefeller Plaza
New York, NY 10020
(212) 975-0777 in New York
(800) 223-0490

Kohinoor International Ltd.
One Lincoln Plaza
New York, NY 10023
(212) 595-6282 in New York
(800) 223-0175

MONEYSMARTS BOOSTERS

BARTER

NATIONAL BARTER NEWSPAPER:

Barter Communique
Full Circle Corp.
5200 Midnight Pass Road
Sarasota, FL 33681
$20 for a 2-year subscription

ENERGY SMARTS

BOOKS:

Energy Future, Stobaugh and Yergin,
Random House, $12.95

ELECTRIC CAR COMPANIES:

Electric Vehicle Associates
9100 Bank Street
Valley View, OH 44125
(216) 524-5992

U.S. Electricar Corp.
250 South Main Street
Athol, MA 01331
(617) 249-2177

Electric Passenger Cars and Vans, Inc.
5127 Galt Way
San Diego, CA 92117
(714) 272-8288

Jet Industries, Inc.
P.O. Box 17184
Austin, TX 78760
(512) 385-0660

Marathon Vehicles, Inc.
9120 Christopher Street
Fairfax, VA 22031
(703) 280-1717

UTILITY COMPANIES: Utility companies can suggest energy-saving investments. Ask your own utility company what it recommends; its telephone number is probably on your monthly bill.

SOLAR INSTALLERS:

The National Solar Heating and Cooling
Information Center
Toll-free (800) 523-2929
Toll-free in Pennsylvania (800) 462-4983
Toll-free in Alaska and Hawaii (800) 523-4700

BASEBALL CARD COLLECTING

BOOKS:

A Baseball Album (mail $15.00 to *Baseball Digest*, P.O. Box 270, Evanston, IL 60204)

Sport Americana Baseball Card Price Guide no. 2, Beckett & Eckes, Edgewater, $7.95

NEWSPAPERS:

Baseball Hobby News
P.O. Box 128K
Glen Cove, NY 11542
$13.95 per year

The Trader Speaks
3 Pleasant Drive
Lake Ronkonkoma, NY 11779
$12 per year

The Sporting News
100 Stadium Drive
Marion, OH 43302
$27.50 per year

MAGAZINES:

Baseball Digest
P.O. Box 5031
Des Moines, IA 50340
$9.95 per year

DEALERS:

Renata Galasso, Inc.
Dept. BD3
1170 75th Street
Brooklyn, NY 11228
(212) 748-7222

G.S. Gallery
Dept. B4
P.O. Box 4
Coopersburg, PA 18036

Superstar Cards, Inc.
P.O. Box 25732
Los Angeles, CA 90025
(213) 475-4764

CIGAR-BOX LABEL COLLECTING

DEALERS:

Gregorie Galleries
3479 Fairmount Boulevard
Cleveland, OH 44118
(216) 321-4200

Smolin's Prints & Posters
1215 Lexington Avenue
New York, NY 10028
(212) 876-1464

WORTHLESS STOCK CERTIFICATE COLLECTING

NEWSLETTERS:

Friends of Financial History
R. M. Smythe & Co.
170 Broadway
New York, NY 10038
$25 per year

FIRMS THAT CAN TELL YOU WHAT WORTHLESS CERTIFICATES ARE WORTH:

R. M. Smythe & Co.
170 Broadway
New York, NY 10038
(212) 349-1116
$40 per company

Tracers
39 Broadway
New York, NY 10006
(212) 558-6550
$50 per company

BOOKS:

The Questioned Stock Manual, Subtitled "A Guide to Determining the True Worth of Old and Collectible Securities," McGraw-Hill, $14.95. (The book is a useful "how to" manual for finding out if your old certificates have value. One chapter is devoted to securities as collectibles.)

HOBBY IDEAS

MAGAZINES:

Americana
475 Park Avenue South
New York, NY 10016
$11.90 per year

STAMPS

NEWSPAPERS AND MAGAZINES:

Linn's Stamp News
911 Vandermark Road
Box 29
Sidney, OH 45365
$8.50 per year

Stamps (a weekly magazine)
H. L. Lindquist Publications
153 Waverly Place
New York, NY 10014
$11.50 per year

STAMP CLUBS:

American Philatelic Society
State College, PA 16801
(814) 237-3803

Society of Philatelic Americans
P.O. Box SPA
Darby, PA 19023
(215) 534-0760

American Topical Association
3306 North 50th Street
Milwaukee, WI 53216
(414) 873-8280

PRICE CATALOGUES:

Scott Stamp Catalogue, Pocket Books, $2.50

STAMP VERIFICATION:

American Philatelic Society
State College, PA 16801
(814) 237-3803

COINS

COIN MAGAZINES AND NEWSPAPERS:

Coin World
P.O. Box 150
911 South Vandermark Road
Sidney, OH 45367
$18 per year

COINage
17337 Ventura Boulevard
Encino, CA 91316
$12 per year

Numismatic News
Iola, WI 54990
$11.50 per year

Coins Magazine
Iola, WI 54990
$11 per year

NEWSLETTERS:

The Coin Dealer Newsletter
P.O. Box 2308
Hollywood, CA 90028

The Fortune Teller
Carson City Assoc.
P.O. Box 36
Midland Park, NJ 07432

Coin Investment Reporter
Littleton Rare Coins
253 Union Street
Littleton, NH 03561
(800) 250-4645

CLUBS:

American Numismatic Association
818 North Cascade Avenue
Colorado Springs, CO 80903
(303) 473-9142

COIN PRICE CATALOGUES:

Coin Prices (6 issues per year)
700 East State Street
Iola, WI 54990

A Guide Book of United States Coins (The Redbook),
R. S. Yoeman, Western Publishing, $3.95

COIN VERIFICATION:

American Numismatic Association
818 North Cascade Avenue
Colorado Springs, CO 80903

International Numismatic Society
P.O. Box 19386
Washington, DC 20036

DEALERS:

Manfra, Tordella & Brookes
59 West 49th Street
New York, NY 10112
(212) 974-3455

Littleton Rare Coins
253 Union Street
Littleton, NH 03561
(800) 250-4645

Investment Rarities
1 Appletree Square
Minneapolis, MN 55420
(800) 328-1860

FUTURES

To check whether complaints have been filed against a commodities firm call the Commodity Futures Trading Commission (CFTC) hotline in Washington, D.C., (202) 254-3067.

UPPING YOUR SALARY—WINNING THE JOB-CHANGING GAME

BOOKS:

The Professional Job Changing System, Robert Jameson Gerberg, Performance Dynamics, $9.95

What Color Is Your Parachute?, Richard Nelson Bolles, Ten Speed Press, $6.95

Woman's Work Book, Abarbanel and Siegel, Warner Books, $2.50

WEEKLY LISTING OF JOB OPENINGS:

National Business Employment Weekly (on major newsstands)
$2.50 per issue

RECRUITMENT COMPANIES:

Performance Dynamics International (PDI)
400 Lanidex Plaza
Parsippany, NJ 07054
(201) 887-8800
(call Information for an office near you)

BEING YOUR OWN BEST CASH CAPTAIN: MONEY MARKET FUNDS

BOOKS:

Complete Money Market Guide, William E. Donoghue, Harper & Row, $12.95

MONEY FUND REPORTS:

Donoghue's Money Letter
770 Washington
Holliston, MA 01746
(617) 429-5930
$87 per year

MONEY MARKET FUNDS:

Cash Reserve Management
Any office of E. F. Hutton

Daily Cash Accumulation
P.O. Box 300
Denver, CO 80201
(800) 525-9310

Dreyfus Liquid Assets
767 Fifth Avenue
New York, NY 10022
(212) 935-6621 in New York
(800) 223-5525

Fidelity Daily Income
82 Devonshire Street
Boston, MA 02109
(800) 225-6190

InterCapital Liquid Assets
Any office of Dean Witter

Merrill Lynch Ready Assets
Any office of Merrill Lynch

Moneymart Assets
Any office of Bache Halsey Stuart

Paine Webber Cash Fund
Any office of Paine Webber

Reserve Fund
810 Seventh Avenue
New York, NY 10019
(212) 977-9880 in New York
(800) 223-5547

Shearson Daily Dividend
Any office of Shearson

SAVING ON TAXES

BOOKS:

The Complete List of IRS Tax Deductions, Rosalie and Howard Minkow, Playboy Paperbacks, $2.50

REAL ESTATE

BOOKS:

How You Can Become Financially Independent by Investing in Real Estate, Albert J. Lowry, Simon & Schuster, $10.00

How to Successfully Manage Real Estate in Your Spare Time, Albert Lowry, Capital Printing, $19.95

How I Turned $1,000 into Five Million in Real Estate, William Nickerson, Simon & Schuster, $14.95

REAL ESTATE INVESTMENT TRAINING:

Lowry-Nickerson Educational Advancement Institute
50 Washington Street
Reno, NV
(800) 648-5955

INDEX

Aaron, Hank, 161-62
ABD Securities, 31
Accountants, advice from, 256
Adams, Ansel, 56-57
ADRs (American Depository Receipts), 34
Alexandrites, 87-88
American Depository Receipts (ADRs), 34
American Express Co., 168
American Museum of Natural History, 94, 265
American Numismatic Association, 181-83, 189, 272, 273
American Philatelic Society (APS), 172, 177, 271
American Stock Exchange, 34
American Topical Association (ATA), 173, 271
Amethysts, 87
Antimony, 111, 114
Antique galleries, 58
Antiques
 technical definition of, 53
 See also Art and antiques
Aquamarines, 85, 87
Art and antiques, 49-66, 125
 auctions of, 51-52, 61-65
 bibliography on, 263-65
 exotic, 160-61
 inflation and, 51-52, 128-29
 presale estimates on, 64
 rule for buying, 58, 63
 speculation in, 58-61
Art experts, 52-53
Art galleries, 58
Assay charge on gold, 31
Auctions
 of art and antiques, 51-52, 61-65
 of coins, 188
Australia, 87
Autographs on stock certificates, 168-69
Ayco Corp., 255

Bache Halsey Stuart, 261, 275
Banks
 IRA plans and, 246
 savings in, 206-9, 211, 212
 stocks of, 46
Bargaining, 141-43
Barning, Vivian, 162
Barron's, 83, 93
Barter, 137-41
 diamonds for, 71
Barter Communique, 140, 267
Barth, John Simmons, 60
Baseball Hobby News, 161, 163, 268
Baseball memorabilia, 161-65, 268-69
"Bear" markets, 39
Belgium, storing gold in, 31

277

Bench, Johnny, 165
Berra, Yogi, 164
Beryllium, 111-12, 114
Beta stocks, 44-46
Bibliographies, 256-57, 259-76
Boiler rooms, futures, 190-91
Bolivia, 111
Bond and Share Society, 169
Bonds, 119-23, 131-32
  gold-mine stock as substitutes for, 35
  inflation and, 22, 120-21
Books, collecting, 60
Borrowing, 143-44
Brady, Mathew, 57
Brasher doubloon, 179-80
Brazil, 87, 88, 89, 112
Brown, Jerry, 220
Bruxelles Lambert Bank, 31
Budget, balancing, 130
"Bull" markets, 39
Burdette, Lew, 164
Bureaucracy, government, costliness of, 14-15
Burma, 86, 89
Business Week, 130, 262
Buttersworth, James, 55
Buying, hints on, 141-43
Buying power, rapid loss of, 13-14

California, 158
  gold fever in, 36
  Proposition 13 in, 219-21
Cambodia, 86, 87
Cameron, Julia Margaret, 57
Canada, 88, 112
  gold-mining companies of, 34, 35
Capote, Truman, 60
Carat weight of diamonds, 72
Career as investment, 199-205, 274
Carnelian, 86
Carroll, Lewis, 57
Carter, Jimmy, 22, 25

Cash
  paying, 142
  quick conversion into, 125
Cash Reserve Management, 210, 275
Casilear, John William, 55
Cat's-eyes, 87-88
China, 69, 111, 186
Chinese porcelain, 50
Christie's, 61, 64
Chromium, 108, 109, 112, 114
Chrysoberyls, 87-88
Cigar-box labels, 165-67, 269
Clarke, John, 59
Cleveland (Ohio), 166
Clocks, antique, 50
Clothing, vintage, 54
Coal, 146
Cobalt, 108, 109-10, 114
Cobb, Ty, 163
Coca-Cola caps, 164
Coin Dealer Newsletter, 185, 272
Coin Investment Reporter, 184, 272
Coin Prices, 181, 273
Coin World, 181, 272
Coins
  collecting of, 179-89
  funds for investment in, 189
  gold, 29-30, 185-86
  investment-grade, 184
  for retirement plans, 245, 246
  silver, 100-1, 103-4, 186-87
Colavito, Rocky, 164
Cole, Thomas, 55
Collectibles, *see* Art and antiques
Colman, Samuel, 55
Colombia, 87
Colorado, gold fever in, 36
Colored gemstones, 85-94, 125
  carat weight of, 90
  certification of, 91
  clarity of (flaws), 90-91
  color of, 90
  cut of, 91

INDEX 279

inflation and, 128-29
selling, 92-93
source materials on, 265-66
where to buy, 91-92
Columbium, 109, 112, 114
Commodity futures, *see*
    Futures market
Commodity Futures Trading
    Commission (CFTC),
    191, 273
Commodity pools, 193
Comparison shopping, 141-42
Conservation, productive, 151
Consumer credit, 196-98
Consumer price index (CPI),
    130
  acceleration of, 28
  decline of, 42
  See also Inflation
Copper, 106
Corporate profits
  accelerating inflation and,
    40
  stock prices and, 39
Corporate recruitment, 204-5
Coupon rate, definition of,
    122
CPI, *see* Consumer price index
Cripple Creek (Colo.), 35-36

Daguerreotypes, 57
Dali, Salvador, 51
Davidson, Joseph A., 165
Deak-Perera, 30, 260
De Beers syndicate, 68-69
Demantoids, 88
Depreciation
  accelerating inflation and,
    40-41
  on real estate, 230
Diamonds, 27, 67-84, 125
  carat weight of, 72
  certification of, 77-80
  clarity of (flaws), 73-75
  color of, 72-73
  cut of, 75-77
  inflation and, 67-69, 73, 75,
    82, 128-29

investment-grade, 67, 71-72,
    132
in retirement plans, 71, 245,
    246
selling, 82-84
source materials on, 265-66
special factors of, 68-70
syndicates of holders of,
    133
where to buy, 80-82
DiMaggio, Joe, 163
Dividends from gold stocks,
    32-33
Dodd, David, 39
Dollar Diversification, 17, 21-
    24
  bibliography on, 259-60
  gold and, 29, 44
  See also Magic Assets;
    Magic portfolios
Dollars
  Euro- and petro-, 42
  gold held in preference to,
    26, 28
Dolls, antique, 53-54
Doughty, Thomas, 55
Dow Jones industrial average
    (1929), 38
Dresner Bank, 31
Drexel Burnham Lambert, 31
Dreyfus firms, 210, 261, 275
Durand, Asher, 55

Economic uncertainty
  diamonds and, 70
  stock prices and, 39, 41-42
Egypt, ancient, 27, 28, 86
Electric cars, 147-49, 267
Emeralds, 85, 86-87
Energy, 145-59
  money and, 14
  source materials on, 267-68
Energy Future, 156
Energy Policy and Conserva-
    tion Act, 151
Equal time method of
    bartering, 139-40

Estate sales, buying diamonds from, 81-82
Estes, Richard, 59
Eurodollar market, 42

Fabergé, 65
Fair market value method of bartering, 139
Fargo, William, 168
Farouk, King, 179
Farrell, James T., 60
Federal deposit insurance, 211
Fidelity Daily Income, 210, 275
Financial company stocks, 46-48
Financial consultants, 252-58
Financial Management Resources, 255
Financial planning companies, 254-55
Flaws
  in colored gemstones, 90-91
  in diamonds, 73-75
Floating exchange rates, 42
Forbes magazine, 130
Ford, Gerald, 22
Ford, Henry, 149
Ford Motor Co., 152-53
Foreign competition, accelerating inflation and, 41
Fortune Teller, The, 185, 272
Friedman, Milton, 220
Friends of Financial History, 169, 270
Fringe benefits, 200
Furniture, antique, 50
Futures market, 190-95
  sharks in, 190-93
  silver in, 105, 107
  strategies for, 193-95

Gann, Paul, 219, 220
Garnets, 88
Gasohol, 149-50
Gasoline, *see* Oil; OPEC
Gem brokers, 92, 93
Gem clubs, 93
Gemological Institute of America (GIA), 73, 74, 77-80, 81, 82, 91, 269
  study courses of, 94
Gemstones, *see* Diamonds; Colored gemstones
Germanium, 108, 112-13, 114
Germany, storing gold in, 31
Getty, John Paul, 169
GIA, *see* Gemological Institute of America
Gifts
  antiques as, 54
  diamonds as, 70
  tax-free, to children, 212, 216-18
Gold, 25-37
  buying, 29-31
  coins of, 29-30, 185-86
  in Keogh plan, 245
  prospecting for, 35-37
  short-term fluctuations in, 28
  silver compared to, 95, 102
  source materials on, 260-62
  when to hold, 25-26, 28-29, 40-41, 44, 127-31
  why it is valuable, 26-28
Gold certificates, 32
Gold stocks, 32-35
  penny, 35
Graham, Benjamin, 39
Greene, Graham, 60
Gregorie Galleries, 166
Groat, Dick, 164
Grossularites, 88
Guide to American Directories, 257
Guns, antique, 50

Harvard Business School, 156
Higbee's department stores, 166-67
Hildesley, Hugh, 66
Hobbies, inflation-beating, 160-69, 270
Hostage agreement with Iran 28

Housing, see Real estate
Hudson River school, 55
Hunt, Nelson Bunker, 101, 102
Hutton, E. F., 254
Hydro energy, 146

IBM building in Michigan, 154
India, 69, 87
   silver of, 101
Individual Retirement Accounts, see IRA
Inflation, 13-14, 21-24
   accelerating, 25, 28, 40-41, 127-31
   art and antiques as hedge against, 51-52, 128-29
   bank savings and, 206-9, 212
   bonds and, 22, 120-21
   built into U.S. economy, 16-17
   colored gemstones and, 85
   consumer credit and, 196-98
   current rate of, 22, 209
   decelerating, 26, 42, 44, 127-31
   diamonds and, 67-69, 73, 75, 82, 128-29
   gold and, 25-26, 28
   hobbies for beating, 160-69, 270
   real estate and, 224, 226, 227, 234, 239
   salaries and, 200
   stock prices and, 22, 39-41, 46, 127-29, 131
   taxes and, 213-16
Insulation of houses, 154-55
Insurance
   homeowners', inflation and, 234
   life, 247-48, 250
Insurance companies as financial consultants, 256
InterCapital Liquid Assets, 210, 275

Interest rates
   bond prices and, 120-21, 122-23
   on savings, 206, 208
   short-term, 42, 46-47
   stock prices and, 39, 41, 42, 46-48
International Numismatic Association, 189, 273
Intuitive method of bartering, 140
Inventory windfalls, 40
Investment Information and Advice, 256
Investment Information Sources, 257
Investment Rarities, 184, 173
Investments
   eight levels of, 126-27
   loss of value of, 14
   See also Tangible investments
IRA (Individual Retirement Accounts), 71, 216, 242, 246-47
Iran, 28, 145-46
Isabella Gold Mining Co., 168

Jackson, Reggie, 165
Jacobsen, Antonio, 55
Jade, 88
Jadeite, 88
Jarvis, Howard, 219-20
Jefferson, Thomas, 218
Jet Industries, 148-49, 267
Job changing, 199-205, 274
Johnson, David, 55

Kanaly Trust Company, 255
Kashmir, 87
Kaufman, Henry, 224
Kemp-Roth bill, 221-22
Kenya, 86, 88, 89
Keogh plans, 216, 242, 244-45
   tangible assets in, 71, 245
Kestner, J. D., 53
Keynes, John Maynard, 206

282 MONEYSMARTS

Kilogram, ounce equivalent of, 31
Klein, Eugene, 170
Koufax, Sandy, 164
Krugerrand, 29-30

Lajoie, Napoleon, 162
Lapidary Journal, 83, 93, 265
Lapis lazuli, 86
Lead, 106
Leake, Henry, 38
Leverage
  of gold stocks, 32-34
  in real estate, 227-29
  of silver stocks, 105
Levine, Marilyn, 59
Linn's Stamp News, 172, 271
Lithium, 113, 114
Lithographs, 51
Littleton Rare Coins, 184, 273
London (England), 29, 116
Loupe, definition of, 73
Lowry, Albert, 225

Magic Assets
  definition of, 23-24
  See also Magic portfolios; Tangible assets
Magic portfolios, 124-33
  accelerating or decelerating, 127-31
Magnesium, 113, 114
Manfra, Tordella & Brookes, 30, 180, 184, 261, 273
Manganese, 109, 111, 114
Mann, Percy McGraw, 170
Mantle, Mickey, 163, 165
Marathon Vehicles, 149, 267
Massachusetts Institute of Technology, 64
Mays, Willie, 164
Mekeel's Weekly Stamp News, 170
Mendenhall, Jack, 59
Merrill Lynch, 210, 216, 254, 275
Metals, 108-18
  how to buy, 115-17
  silver as by-product of, 106-7
  source materials on, 260-61
  summary of (chart), 114
  when to buy, 111, 132
  when to sell, 117-18, 132
  from whom to buy, 111
Mexico, 89
Mileage, gas, 151-53
Miró, Joan, 51, 54-55, 56, 60
Mission Development Company, 169
Moller, Adrian H., and Son, – 38
Monex, 30, 261
Money, function of, 23
Money crisis, nature of, 13-16
Money Market mutual funds, 206-7, 209-12, 274-75
Moneymart Assets, 210, 275
Mortgages, 227, 234-35, 237
Mucha, Alphonse, 60
Mutual funds, 246
  money market, 206-7, 209-12, 274-75
  no-load, 46, 47

National Bureau of Economic Research, 43
National Solar Heating and Cooling Information Center, 157, 268
Natural gas, 146
Nephrite, 88
New England Rare Coin Management, 189
New York and Harlem Railroad Co., 169
New York City, 30, 59, 153, 167
New York State Attorney General, 81, 266
Nin, Anaïs, 60
Nixon, Richard M., 22
No-load mutual funds, 46, 47
Norway, 89
Nuclear energy, 14, 88, 146

INDEX

Oak Ridge National Laboratory, 154
Oil (gasoline), 145-47
  conservation of, 151-53
  See also Gasohol; OPEC
O'Neill, Tip, 221
Ontario Hydro, 154
Opals, 88-89
OPEC (Organization of Petroleum Exporting Countries), 14, 146, 147, 156
  gold bought by, 26, 28, 42
Oriental rugs, 50
Over-the-Counter Securities Markets, 34

Paintings, 50-51, 54-56
  speculation in, 58-61
Pakistan, 88
Parke Bernet, *see* Sotheby Parke Bernet Galleries
Pawn shops, buying diamonds from, 81-82
Penny gold and silver stocks, 35
Performance Dynamics International (PDI), 205, 274
Peridots, 89
Perry, William, 110
Perschke, Walter, 179
Personal marketing firms, 204-5
Petrodollar market, 42
Phantom bidders, 65
Philatelic Foundation, 177
Photographica, 56-57
Picasso, Pablo, 54, 56, 60
Pierce-Arrow Motor Car Co., 167
Plank, Eddie, 162
Platinum, 109
Plato, 69
Presale exhibitions, 62-64
Primitive art, 56
Prints, 59-60
Proof sets, 187-88
Proposition 13, 219-22
Prospecting for gold, 35-37

Reader's Digest, 213
Reagan, Ronald, 22, 110, **115**
Real estate, 223-39
  buying a home, 231-35
  information sources for, 258, 276
  as tax shelters, 229-31
Real estate investment trusts, 48
Recessions
  buying metals during, 111, 132
  fear of, 41
  1950–75 (chart), 43
  stock prices and, 42-44
Redbook, The (for coins), 181, 273
Rembrandt, 55
Republic National Bank, 30, 261
Reserve Fund, 210, 275
Resumes, 200-1
Retirement plans, 240-51
  corporate, 242
  inflation and, 22, 216
  Social Security, 240-41, 249-51
  tangible assets in, 71, 245, 246
Retrofit, 154
Rhodesia, 87
Rhodium, 108, 113, 114
Ringling Brothers and Barnum & Bailey, 168
Robbins, David E., 81
Robey, W. T., 170-71
Roth, William, 221
Rothko, Mark, 56
Rotterdam (Holland), 116
Rubens, Peter Paul, 55
Rubies, 85, 86
Russia, 88, 89, 109-13

Salary, increasing your, 199-205, 274
Sales tax on gold, 30

284 MONEYSMARTS

Salmon, Robert, 55
Salomon Brothers, 25, 171, 179, 224
Sapphires, 87
Saroyan, William, 60
Saudi Arabia, 146
Savings and loan associations, 48
Scott Stamp Catalogue, 174, 175, 271
Scripophily, definition of, 168
Self-reliance, 196-98
Silicon, 108, 113, 114
Silver, 95-107
  antique, 50
  coins of, 103-4, 186-87
  coming shortage of, 100-1
  compared to gold, 95, 102
  Indian, 101
  industrial demand for, 96, 98-100
  inflation and, 128-29
  in Keogh plan, 245
  source materials on, 260-61
  U.S. policy toward, 97-98
  what to buy, 103-7
  when to buy, 101-2
Silver stocks, 35, 105-7
Sinclair, James, & Co., 261
Smithsonian Institution, 68, 94
Smolin's Prints, 167
Smythe, R. M., and Co., 169, 270
Social Security, 240-41, 249-51
Society of Philatelic Americans, 172, 271
Solar energy, 155-58, 268
Sotheby Parke Bernet Galleries, 51, 53, 61, 66, 263
South Africa, 88, 110-13
  gold mines of, 34-35
  Krugerrand of, 29-30
Spahn, Warren, 164
Sporting News, The, 163, 268
Sri Lanka, 86, 88, 89

Stamp collecting, 170-78
  for retirement plans, 245, 246
  source materials for, 271
Stamps (magazine), 172, 271
Standard & Poor's average, 43
Standard Oil of California, 154
Steady income, portfolio for, 125
Steichen, Edward, 57
Stieglitz, Alfred, 57
Stockbrokers, 253-54
Stocks, 38-48
  bibliography on, 262
  "bull" vs. "bear" markets in, 39
  gold, 32-35
  growth, 46
  high-beta, 44-46
  inflation and, 22, 39, 41, 46, 127-29, 131
  interest-rate sensitive, 46-48
  1929 crash of, 38-39
  silver, 35, 105-7
  strategic-metal, 111
  when to buy, 42-44, 130, 131
  when to sell, 40-42, 48, 131
  worthless, 167-69, 270
Strategic metals, *see* Metals
Strong, Margaret Woodbury, 160-61
"Submarines," 82-83, 93
Swapping, *see* Barter
Swiss banks, 31

Tangible investments
  inflation's effects offset by, 23
  See also Art and antiques; Coins; Diamonds; Futures market; Gold; Hobbies; Magic Assets; Metals; Real estate; Silver; Stamp collecting
Tantalite, 114
Tantalum, 113-14

Tanzania, 86, 88, 89
Tanzanites, 89-90
Tax lawyers, 256
Tax shelters, 213-18, 229-31
Taxes
  book on, 276
  diamonds and, 71
  inflation and, 213-16
  insatiable rate of, 14-15, 218-19
  money market funds and, 212
  solar savings on, 157-58
  See also Keogh plans; IRA
Texas Instruments, 169
Thailand, 86
Thomson, John, 57
Three Mile Island incident (1979), 14
Tiffany & Co., 89
Titanium, 108, 114
Topazes, 89
Toronto stock exchange, 35
Toulouse-Lautrec, Henri de, 60
Tourmalines, 89
Toys, antique, 53-54
Tracers (company), 169, 270
Trader Speaks, The, 163, 268
Treasury bills, 206, 211
Trusts, short-term, 217
Tungsten, 114-15
Turquoise, 86

Uncertainty, *see* Economic uncertainty
United States
  gems produced by, 87, 88, 89
  military spending by, 131
  silver policy of, 97-98
  stockpiling by, 111-12, 114
  See also Inflation
United States Geological Survey, 36

Vanadium, 109, 114, 115
Vanadium grossularites, 88
Vancouver stock exchange, 35
Vonnegut, Kurt, 60

Wachter, Michael, 240
Wagner, Honus, 163
Wall Street Journal, 83, 93, 101, 104, 130, 262
Washington Natural Gas Co., 155
Wells, Henry, 168
Wholesale price of diamonds, 80-81, 83
Wholesale price index (WPI), 130
Williams, Ted, 163
WIN (Whip Inflation Now), 22
Wolfe, Thomas, 60
Worthless stock certificate collecting, 167-69, 270
WPI (wholesale price index), 130

Yamani, Ahmed Zaki, 146
York, William, 55

Zaire, 109
Zambia, 87, 88, 110
Zimbabwe, 110
Zinc, 106
Zirconium, 114, 115
Zoisites, 89-90

ABOUT THE AUTHOR

Michael Assael, a lawyer and certified public accountant, has had a fascination with money, the stock market, and tangible forms of wealth since childhood. At age seven, he began trading and flipping baseball cards with his friends. Shortly after, he sold floor wax from door to door and invested the money he earned in silver dollars, old coins, and proof sets. During his high school years, he purchased his first shares of stock.

Michael Assael majored in economics, finance, and accounting. He earned his B.A. at George Washington University and his M.B.A. at Columbia University Graduate School of Business. He graduated from St. John's Law School in 1977, and has worked for Price Waterhouse & Company's New York and Tokyo offices. He currently resides and practices in New York City.

WE HOPE YOU ENJOYED THIS BOOK
IF YOU'D LIKE A FREE LIST
OF OTHER BOOKS AVAILABLE FROM
PLAYBOY PAPERBACKS,
JUST SEND YOUR REQUEST TO:
PLAYBOY PAPERBACKS
BOOK MAILING SERVICE
P.O. BOX 690
ROCKVILLE CENTRE, NEW YORK 11571